Java Programming for Beginners

Learn the fundamentals of programming with Java

Mark Lassoff

BIRMINGHAM - MUMBAI

Java Programming for Beginners

First published: October 2017

Production reference: 1301017

Published by Packt Publishing Ltd.
Livery Place
35 Livery Street
Birmingham
B3 2PB, UK.

ISBN 978-1-78829-629-8

www.packtpub.com

Credits

Author
Mark Lassoff

Acquisition Editor
Dominic Shakeshaft

Content Development Editor
Venugopal Commuri

Technical Editor
Nidhisha Shetty

Copy Editor
Gladson Monteiro

Project Editor
Suzanne Coutinho

Proofreader
Safis Editing

Indexer
Pratik Shirodkar

Graphics
Tania Dutta

Production Coordinator
Arvindkumar Gupta

About the Author

Mark Lassoff, according to his parents' frequent claim, was born to be a programmer. In the mid-eighties, when the neighborhood kids were outside playing kickball and throwing snowballs, Mark was hard at work on his Commodore 64, writing games in the BASIC programming language. Computers and programming continued to be his strong interest in college, where Mark majored in communications and computer science. After completing his college career, Mark worked in the software and web development departments at several large corporations. In 2001, on a whim, while his contemporaries were conquering the dot com world, Mark accepted a position training programmers in a technical training center in Austin, Texas. It was there that Mark fell in love with teaching programming, which has been his passion ever since. Today Mark is a top technical trainer, traveling the country providing training for software and web developers. Mark's training clients include the Department of Defense, Lockheed Martin, Discover Card Services, and Kaiser Permanente. He has consulted for companies such as Dell, Target, and Lockheed Martin, and government agencies including the US House of Representatives. In addition to traditional classroom training and consulting, Mark releases video tutorial training for aspiring programmers on his websites. He lives in coastal Connecticut near the Connecticut River, where he is in the process of redecorating his house.

www.PacktPub.com

For support files and downloads related to your book, please visit www.PacktPub.com.

Did you know that Packt offers eBook versions of every book published, with PDF and ePub files available? You can upgrade to the eBook version at www.PacktPub.com and as a print book customer, you are entitled to a discount on the eBook copy. Get in touch with us at service@packtpub.com for more details.

At www.PacktPub.com, you can also read a collection of free technical articles, sign up for a range of free newsletters and receive exclusive discounts and offers on Packt books and eBooks.

https://www.packtpub.com/mapt

Get the most in-demand software skills with Mapt. Mapt gives you full access to all Packt books and video courses, as well as industry-leading tools to help you plan your personal development and advance your career.

Why subscribe?

- Fully searchable across every book published by Packt
- Copy and paste, print, and bookmark content
- On demand and accessible via a web browser

Customer Feedback

Thanks for purchasing this Packt book. At Packt, quality is at the heart of our editorial process. To help us improve, please leave us an honest review on this book's Amazon page at `https://www.amazon.com/dp/178829629X`.

If you'd like to join our team of regular reviewers, you can email us at `customerreviews@packtpub.com`. We award our regular reviewers with free eBooks and videos in exchange for their valuable feedback. Help us be relentless in improving our products!

Table of Contents

Preface

Whether this is your first foray into high-level object-oriented programming languages such as Java, or if you've been programming for some time and you're just looking to add Java to your repertoire, or even if you've never touched a line of code in your life, this book is designed to accommodate you. We'll move quickly and we'll not shy away from heavy subjects, but we'll begin this book from the very ground up and learn the concepts behind object-oriented programming as we go. I will consider the book to be successful if it helps you understand what Java programming is about, why it is important, and how you can start developing Java applications in NetBeans. I will be equally happy if Java becomes your favorite programming language!

What this book covers

Chapter 1, *Getting Started with Java*, teaches you what Java is and shows its features. We will see the vastness of Java's application by looking at various fields it is used in. We will walk through the steps to install the Java Development Kit. We will then set up a development environment called NetBeans for writing Java programs, and execute these programs. We'll also see how to use NetBeans and write our first Java program in it. You'll also learn to use NetBeans to detect errors and rectify them.

Chapter 2, *Understanding Typed Variables*, shows what variables are and how they are important for creating better programs. We'll look at some of the primitive data types of Java, `int`, `long`, `float`, `char`, and `double`, in detail. You'll also learn about the `String` class and two of its manipulation methods.

Chapter 3, *Branching*, basically portrays how to work with conditional `if...else` statements, running through complex conditionals using functions such as `contains`, `complex`, and `boolean`. We will go through the intricacies of switch, case, and break with the help of programs; we'll also deep dive into using loop functionality with `while`, `do...while`, and `for` loops.

Chapter 4, *Data Structures*, discusses arrays and presents an example that prints the English alphabet using an array. Then, we'll take a look at multidimensional arrays and write a program that creates a two-dimensional chess board. We'll walk through what ArrayList is and how it enhances the functionality of arrays. We'll write a program using ArrayList with functionality that would have been quite difficult to implement using an array. Finally, you'll learn about Maps and implement an example to understand them better.

Chapter 5, *Functions*, helps you to start with some of the basic Java functions, such as methods, and then move on to understanding you advanced Java functions. As you become a more experienced programmer, you'll begin to internalize concepts like these and you won't have to really think about them explicitly when you're writing day-to-day code. For now though, there are some logical shortcuts that we can use to keep from getting too tripped up.

Chapter 6, *Modeling with Object-Oriented Java*, teaches how to create classes and objects in Java. We will also walk through creating custom classes, member variables, and member functions. We will also look into a very special member assigned to our custom classes, the constructor, and types of constructor.

Chapter 7, *More Object-Oriented Java*, reveals some intricacies of object-oriented programming, precisely, those using the concept of Inheritance, by creating something called as superclass and subclass, and establishing an *is-a* relationship between them. You'll learn how to use key aspects such as overriding subclass and super class, data structures, and the Protected method. We also get to know how an abstract method works, in detail.

Chapter 8, *Useful Java Classes*, presents the Calendar class, which is used to work with dates and times. You will learn about the String class in detail. We'll also see what exceptions are and how to handle them to make our programs more robust. Then, we will walk through the Object class and some of its methods. Finally, we will take a look at primitive classes in Java.

Chapter 9, *File Input and Output*, walks you through the concept of writing and reading data files, where we'll see the usage of the FileWriter and FileReader classes and learn to free up resources using the close () method. You'll also learn to catch an exception and handle it. Then, we'll see how to use the BufferedWriter and BufferedReader classes to wrap the FileWriter and FileReader classes, respectively. Lastly, we will talk about one more aspect of I/O, the Serializable class. We will analyze what serialization is and its use with respect to serializing and deserializing objects.

Chapter 10, *Basic GUI Development*, shows the basic functions of the GUI in NetBeans. We will learn how to create an application window with the jFrame class by setting its size, adding labels to it, and closing our application. Then we'll talk about the working of palette and components available in it. Lastly, we'll learn about triggering events by adding a button and adding functionality to it.

Chapter 11, *XML*, explains the Java code to read an XML file into a Document object. You'll also learn how to parse XML data using Java. Finally, you'll learn how to write and modify XML data in Java.

What you need for this book

For this book, you'll need a **Java Development Kit** (**JDK**) and NetBeans

Who this book is for

This book is for anyone wanting to begin learning the Java language, whether you're a student, casual learner, or existing programmer looking to add a new language to your skillset. No previous experience of Java or programming in general is required.

Conventions

In this book, you will find a number of text styles that distinguish between different kinds of information. Here are some examples of these styles and an explanation of their meaning.

Code words in text, database table names, folder names, filenames, file extensions, path names, dummy URLs, user input, and Twitter handles are shown as follows: "The Source Packages file is where we'll be writing our code."

A block of code is set as follows:

```
public class HelloWorld {
    public static void main(String[] args) {
        System.out.println("Hello World!");
    }
}
```

When we wish to draw your attention to a particular part of a code block, the relevant lines or items are set in bold:

```java
public class HelloWorld {
    public static void main(String[] args) {
        System.out.println("Hello World!");
    }
}
```

Any command-line input or output is written as follows:

```
java -jar WritingToFiles.jar
```

New terms and important words are shown in bold. Words that you see on the screen, for example, in menus or dialog boxes, appear in the text like this: "Choose the **Download** button below the **Java SE** column."

> Warnings or important notes appear in a box like this.

> Tips and tricks appear like this.

Reader feedback

Feedback from our readers is always welcome. Let us know what you think about this book—what you liked or may have disliked. Reader feedback is important for us to develop titles that you really get the most out of.

To send us general feedback, simply send an email to feedback@packtpub.com, and mention the book title via the subject of your message.

If there is a topic that you have expertise in and you are interested in either writing or contributing to a book, see our author guide on www.packtpub.com/authors.

Customer support

Now that you are the proud owner of a Packt book, we have a number of things to help you to get the most from your purchase.

Downloading the example code

You can download the example code files from your account at `http://www.packtpub.com` for all the Packt Publishing books you have purchased. If you purchased this book elsewhere, you can visit `http://www.packtpub.com/support` and register to have the files emailed directly to you. You can download the code files by following these steps:

1. Log in or register to our website using your email address and password.
2. Hover the mouse pointer on the **SUPPORT** tab at the top.
3. Click on **Code Downloads & Errata**.
4. Enter the name of the book in the **Search** box.
5. Select the book for which you're looking to download the code files.
6. Choose from the drop-down menu where you purchased this book from.
7. Click on **Code Download**.

Once the file is downloaded, please make sure that you unzip or extract the folder using the latest version of:

- WinRAR / 7-Zip for Windows
- Zipeg / iZip / UnRarX for Mac
- 7-Zip / PeaZip for Linux

The code bundle for the book is also hosted on GitHub at `https://github.com/PacktPublishing/Java-Programming-for-Beginners`. We also have other code bundles from our rich catalog of books and videos available at `https://github.com/PacktPublishing/`. Check them out!

Downloading the color images of this book

We also provide you with a PDF file that has color images of the screenshots/diagrams used in this book. The color images will help you better understand the changes in the output. You can download this file from `https://www.packtpub.com/sites/default/files/downloads/JavaProgrammingforBeginners_ColorImages.pdf`.

Errata

Although we have taken every care to ensure the accuracy of our content, mistakes do happen. If you find a mistake in one of our books—maybe a mistake in the text or the code—we would be grateful if you could report this to us. By doing so, you can save other readers from frustration and help us improve subsequent versions of this book. If you find any errata, please report them by visiting http://www.packtpub.com/submit-errata, selecting your book, clicking on the **Errata Submission Form** link, and entering the details of your errata. Once your errata are verified, your submission will be accepted and the errata will be uploaded to our website or added to any list of existing errata under the Errata section of that title.

To view the previously submitted errata, go to https://www.packtpub.com/books/content/support and enter the name of the book in the search field. The required information will appear under the **Errata** section.

Piracy

Piracy of copyright material on the Internet is an ongoing problem across all media. At Packt, we take the protection of our copyright and licenses very seriously. If you come across any illegal copies of our works, in any form, on the internet, please provide us with the location address or website name immediately so that we can pursue a remedy.

Please contact us at copyright@packtpub.com with a link to the suspected pirated material.

We appreciate your help in protecting our authors, and our ability to bring you valuable content.

Questions

You can contact us at questions@packtpub.com if you are having a problem with any aspect of the book, and we will do our best to address it.

1
Getting Started with Java

Whether this is your first foray into high-level object-oriented programming languages, such as Java, or if you've been programming for some time and you're just looking to add Java to your repertoire, or even if you've never touched a line of code in your life, this book is designed to accommodate you. We're going to move quickly, and we're not going to shy away from heavy subjects; however, we're going to begin this book from the very ground up and learn about the concepts behind object-oriented programming as we go.

In this chapter, we'll understand what Java is and also look at its features. We'll then follow a step-by-step process to set up a development environment to enable us to write and execute Java programs. Once we accomplish this, we'll write our very first Java program and run it. Lastly, we'll look at what to do when we get an error.

Specifically, we'll cover the following topics:

- What is Java
- Features and applications of Java
- Installing JDK
- Installing the NetBeans IDE
- Writing `HelloWorld.java`
- NetBeans' error detection capabilities

What is Java?

Java was developed by Sun Microsystems in 1995, but it has stood the test of time and remains highly relevant and widely used to this day. So what exactly is Java? Java is a high-level, general-purpose object-oriented programming language.

Features of Java

The following are Java's main features:

- **High level and general purpose**: Rather than being created to accomplish one very specific task, Java allows us to write computer-readable instructions in an open-ended environment. Because it's not really feasible, or even desirable, for every computer system to have its own specialized programming language, the vast majority of the code is written in high-level, general-purpose languages such as Java.

- **Object-oriented**: Java is also what we call an object-oriented language. While we won't get into the specifics of objects and classes until a bit later in this book, know for now that objects allow us to define modular entities within our program that make them much more human-readable and much more manageable to create large-scale software projects. A firm grasp of object-oriented concepts is absolutely essential for any modern software developer.

- **Platform-independent**: Lastly, Java was designed with the intention that it be a write once, run anywhere language. This means if you and I both have systems with Java installed and even if our systems are not normally identical--for example, I'm on a Windows machine and you're on a Mac--a Java program on my machine that I give to you will still run essentially the same on your machine without the need for it to be recompiled.

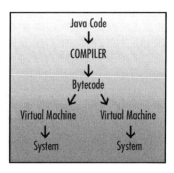

Compiling a programming language such as Java is the act of taking the human-readable code that we've written and converting it into an interpreted machine-friendly code. Unfortunately, it's usually not very friendly for humans to read or write. To do this, we use a program called the compiler that takes in our code as text and converts it into machine code.

Traditionally, we would have to recompile a program for every system that it was going to run on because all systems have a different idea of what their machine code should look like. Java circumvents this issue by compiling all Java programs to the same type of interpreted code called bytecode.

A compiled Java program in bytecode can be run by any system in which Java is installed. This is because when we install Java on your system, we also install a Java virtual machine with it that's specific to that system. It is this machine's responsibility to convert the bytecode into the final instructions that head to the processor in that system.

By making it the system's responsibility to do this final conversion, Java has created a write once, run anywhere language where I can hand you a Java program and you can run it on your machine while being fairly certain that it's going to run in the same manner that it did on mine. This impressive level of cross-platform support on a language as powerful as Java has made it one of the software developing world's go-to tools for quite some time.

Java applications

In today's modern times, Java is used to develop desktop applications, web servers, and client-side web applications. It's the native language of the Android operating system, which operates on Android phones and tablets.

Java has been used to write video games and is sometimes even ported to smaller devices without a traditional operating system. It remains a huge player in today's technical world, and I'm looking forward to learning it with you.

Setting up your development environment

In this section, we're going to write our first Java program, but before we start coding away, we need to set up an environment that is Java-development friendly.

Installing JDK

To start off this process, let's download a **Java Development Kit** (**JDK**) or a Java SDK. This kit contains libraries and executables that allow us to do lots of different things with Java code. Most importantly, with our SDK installed, we'll be able to compile Java code and then run completed Java programs.

You may already have Java installed on your machine; however, unless you've done this explicitly, you probably haven't installed a Java SDK. The version of Java an average user has installed on their machine is called the **Java Runtime Environment** (**JRE**). This allows the execution of Java programs, and Java programs won't run on environments without the JRE installed. But the JRE doesn't contain any real development tools, which we're going to need. The good news is that a Java JRE and a Java SDK can exist harmoniously. A Java JRE is really just a subset of the SDK, so if we only have the Java Development Kit installed, which we're about to download, we're going to be fine.

If you have downloaded the Java Development Kit in the past, when you actually go to install this kit, Java will let you know that it's already installed and you can skip that portion of the section. For everyone else, check out how to download a development kit:

1. To begin with, navigate to
   `www.oracle.com/technetwork/java/javase/downloads/index.html` through
   your browser.

2. We're going to be using the Java SE, or Standard Edition, Development Kit maintained by Oracle. To acquire this kit, simply go to the **Downloads** tab, and express that we would like the **JDK** by selecting that option:

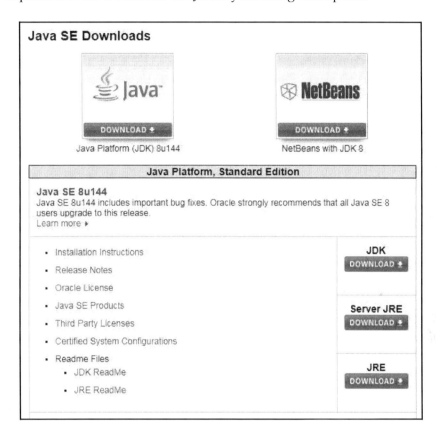

Scroll down, check out the license agreement, accept the license agreement, and then download the version of the SDK that's appropriate for your operating system. For me, that's `jdk-8u144-windows-x64.exe`, listed at the end:

Java SE Development Kit 8u144 Demos and Samples Downloads

You must accept the Oracle BSD License. to download this software.
Thank you for accepting the Oracle BSD License.; you may now download this software.

Product / File Description	File Size	Download
Linux ARM 32 Hard Float ABI	9.95 MB	jdk-8u144-linux-arm32-vfp-hflt-demos.tar.gz
Linux ARM 64 Hard Float ABI	9.94 MB	jdk-8u144-linux-arm64-vfp-hflt-demos.tar.gz
Linux x86	52.66 MB	jdk-8u144-linux-i586-demos.rpm
Linux x86	52.52 MB	jdk-8u144-linux-i586-demos.tar.gz
Linux x64	52.72 MB	jdk-8u144-linux-x64-demos.rpm
Linux x64	52.54 MB	jdk-8u144-linux-x64-demos.tar.gz
Mac OS X	53.09 MB	jdk-8u144-macosx-x86_64-demos.zip
Solaris x64	13.52 MB	jdk-8u144-solaris-x64-demos.tar.Z
Solaris x64	9.31 MB	jdk-8u144-solaris-x64-demos.tar.gz
Solaris SPARC 64-bit	13.58 MB	jdk-8u144-solaris-sparcv9-demos.tar.Z
Solaris SPARC 64-bit	9.34 MB	jdk-8u144-solaris-sparcv9-demos.tar.gz
Windows x86	53.8 MB	jdk-8u144-windows-i586-demos.zip
Windows x64	53.82 MB	jdk-8u144-windows-x64-demos.zip

3. Once your download is complete, install it as we would any other program. Choose the default options when appropriate and make sure to take note of the directory to which we will install our development kit.

Installing the NetBeans IDE

With our Java Development Kit installed, we technically have all the tools we need to start writing Java programs. However, we'd have to compile them through a command line, which can look a little different on different operating systems.

So to keep everything simple, let's start learning Java by writing our Java code in an **Integrated Development Environment** (**IDE**). This is a software program of its own that helps us write, compile, and run Java programs. We're going to use the NetBeans IDE, which is awesome because it is free, open source, and it's going to operate just about the same on Windows, Mac, and Linux environments.

To acquire this IDE, head to `netbeans.org/downloads/`.

You'll see the following page:

Because we've downloaded the Java Standard Edition Development Kit, Java SE is the version of NetBeans that we're going to download here. Choose the **Download** button below the **Java SE** column. NetBeans should start our download automatically, but if it doesn't, click on the link shown in the following image:

Once again, we're going to install NetBeans as we would any other program, choosing the default options when appropriate. Most likely, NetBeans will locate the Java Development Kit on our machine. If it doesn't, it will prompt us for the directory in which we installed the Java Development Kit.

Writing our first Java program

Hopefully, you have gotten NetBeans installed and have booted it up without any hassle. NetBeans will manage the file structure of our programs, but first, we need to tell NetBeans that we're ready to begin a new project.

Creating a new project

To create a new project, click on **File**, then **New Project**, and choose **Java Application**:

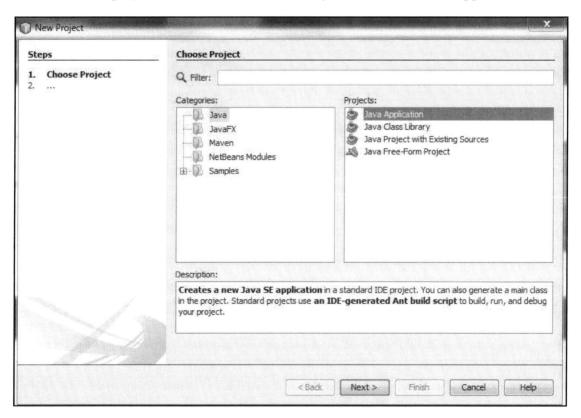

We're going to need to give our project a distinctive name; let's call this one `HelloWorld`. Then, we can choose a location to put the file. Because this is our very first Java program, we should probably start from as close to scratch as possible. So let's uncheck the **Create Main Class** option so that NetBeans would give us pretty much a blank project. Then, click on **Finish**:

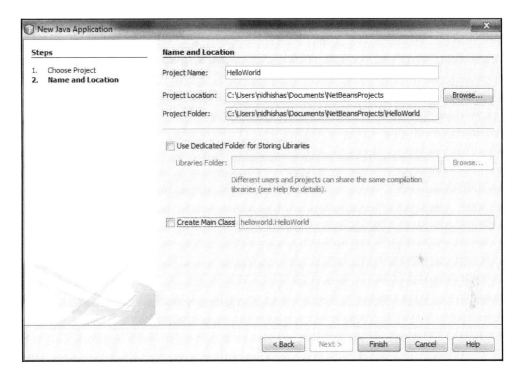

NetBeans will set up a filesystem for us. We can navigate this filesystem just like we were in a standard filesystem explorer:

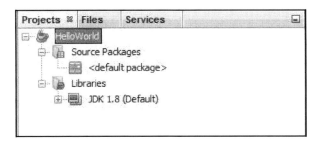

The `Source Packages` file is where we'll be writing our code. You'll notice under the `Libraries` file that the JDK is linked, allowing us to access all of its many library resources:

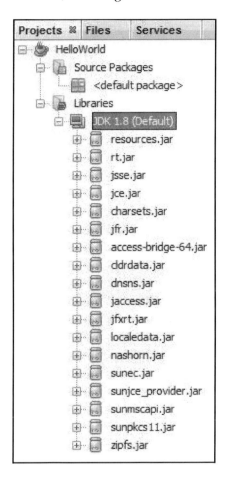

Creating a Java class

Once we have created a new project, we should see the **Projects**, **Files**, and **Services** tabs like I have in the following image. Let's look at the **Files** tab. Whereas the **Projects** tab is a bit of an abstraction, the **Files** tab shows us what's actually contained within the filesystem where our `HelloWorld` project lives:

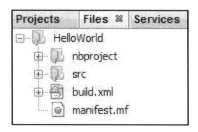

Most importantly, you'll see that the `src` file here has no files in it. That's because there's no source code associated with our project, so right now it won't do anything. To remedy this, right-click on `src`, choose **New**, and then **Java Class...**:

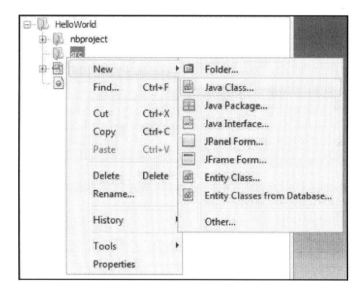

We're going to name our Java Class `HelloWorld`, just like the name of the project because it is our main class where the program should be entered and start from. Everything else is going to work just fine here for now, so click on **Finish** and NetBeans will create `HelloWorld.java` for us. A `.java` file is essentially a text file, but it should only contain Java code and comments:

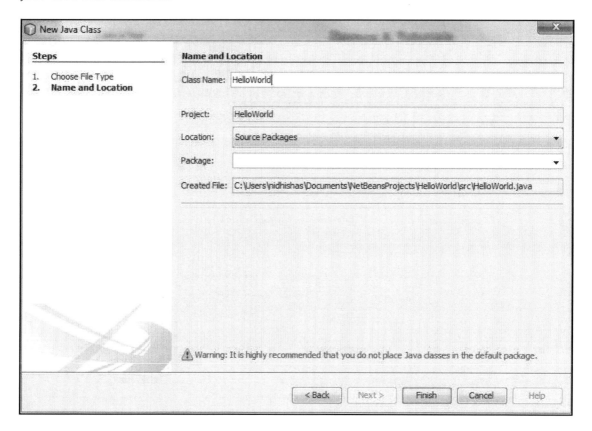

Writing the code

When we told NetBeans to make the `HelloWorld.java` file, it took some liberties and added some code for us already as shown in the following screenshot:

Java comments

You'll notice that some of the contents of this document are completely human-readable; these are what we call comments. Any text that appears in a Java file between the `/*` and `*/` symbols will be completely ignored by the compiler. We can write whatever we would like in here and it will not affect how our program would operate. For now, let's just delete these comments so that we can deal purely with our Java code.

The main() function

Java code, like the English language, is read top down and left to right. Even if our project contains many files and many classes, we still need to start reading and executing our code at a specific point. We named this file and class `HelloWorld`, the same name as our project, because we would like it to be special and contain the `public static void main(String[] args)` method where the execution of our code will begin. That's quite a mouthful of jargon. For now, just type it out and know that this is the area of our code from where our Java program will begin reading and executing. Once again, this will become much clearer as we begin to learn Java; just know this is the starting point of our Java program. The `main()` function's code is enclosed in curly brackets:

```
public class HelloWorld {
  public static void main(String[] args) {
  }
}
```

One of the great things about working in an IDE is that it will highlight which brackets correspond to each other. The brackets allow us to place code within other areas of code. For example, our `main()` method is contained within the `HelloWorld` class, and the Java code which we're about to write and execute is going to be contained in our `main()` method. Line 4, which currently contains nothing, is where our program will look to start reading and executing the Java code.

Printing a string

Our goal with this `HelloWorld` program is pretty modest. When it runs, we'd like it to print some text to this output box at the bottom of our screen.

When we downloaded the Java SDK, we acquired a library of useful functions, one of which will do just this. This is the `println()`, or print line, function. When our Java code executes over this function, which it will do right away because it's the first function in our `main()` method's entry point, the Java code will print some words to our output box. Function names are followed by open and close parentheses. Inside these parentheses, we put information that the functions need to complete their task. The `println()` method, of course, needs to know what we would like it to print. In Java, a line of text is contained by two double quotation marks and we call it a **string**. Let's have our program print `"Hello World!"`:

```
public class HelloWorld {
    public static void main(String[] args) {
        println("Hello World!")
    }
}
```

Java syntax

You might have noticed that NetBeans has been yelling at us for a little bit. There's a light bulb and a red dot on the left and some red jittering under our text, a lot like if we had made a spelling error in some text editors. And that's really what we've done. We've made a syntax mistake. There's something clearly wrong with our Java code and NetBeans knows it.

There are two things wrong here. The first is that our code doesn't end with a semicolon. Java doesn't do a good job of reading spaces and carriage returns, so we need to put semicolons at the end of every functional line of code for the same reason that a Morse code operator would send the message "stop" at the end of every line. Let's add a semicolon at the end of our `println()` statement:

NetBeans has become a little more satisfied; the jittering has decreased, but there's still something wrong as shown in the preceding screenshot.

The issue is that functions in a programming language, just like files on a computer, have a location where they exist. NetBeans isn't sure where to find the `println()` function that we've attempted to use. So we simply need to tell NetBeans where this function exists. The full path to the `println()` function starts from the `System` package, which includes the `out` class, which has the definition of the `println()` function. We write that in Java as `System.out.println("Hello World!");` as shown in the following code block.

Let's get rid of the extra spaces I created at lines 5, 6, and 7, not because they would affect the way our program runs, but because it doesn't make it look quite as nice. Now we've written our `HelloWorld` program:

```
public class HelloWorld {
    public static void main(String[] args) {
        System.out.println("Hello World!");
    }
}
```

Executing our program

So what do we do with this? Well, as we know, our computer can't read this Java code directly. It must convert it into a computer-readable language. So executing this code becomes a two-step process:

1. **Compiling our program**: First, we're going to ask NetBeans to build our project. This means that all of the code within our project will be compiled and converted into computer-readable code in a, essentially, computer-readable project:

When we press the Build Project button, we'll see a bunch of text in our output box at the bottom of the screen--hopefully the nice BUILD SUCCESSFUL message, followed by the time it took to build the project:

2. **Running our program**: Once we've built our project, we can press the Run Project button to execute our code and our `println` statement:

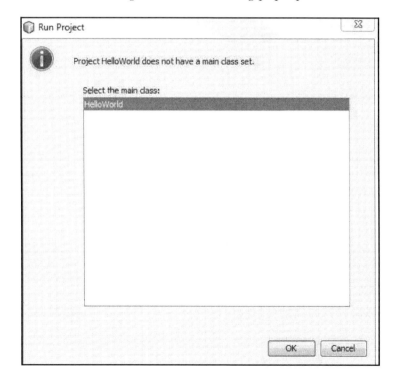

NetBeans will then give us the following pop-up box:

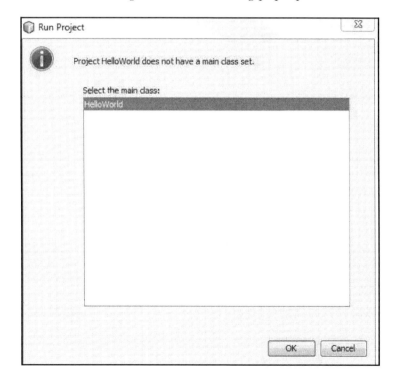

When we execute a program outside of an IDE, we execute it by launching one of its executable files. Because we're in an integrated development environment right now, NetBeans wants to be sure which of our files we would like to be the entry point of our program. We only have one option here because we've only written one Java class. So let's confirm to NetBeans that HelloWorld is our main class and the main() function in the HelloWorld program will, therefore, be where we start executing our Java program. Then, when we hit **OK**, our output box will tell us the program has begun to run and our program then prints "Hello World!" to the output box as we intended:

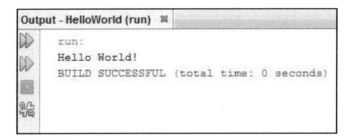

There we have it! Now we're Java programmers. Of course, there's more than a little bit left to learn. In fact, HelloWorld in Java is probably the simplest program you'll ever write. Java is extremely powerful, and the reality is we simply can't hope to appreciate all of its intricacies while writing our first program. The really good news is that from this point on, we need to take far fewer leaps of faith and we can begin to build a very solid understanding of Java by taking a step-by-step approach.

How to interpret errors detected by NetBeans?

As we write more and more complicated Java programs, we're inevitably going to make some mistakes. Some of these mistakes will be significant logic errors or misunderstandings on our part that we might have to further educate ourselves before we can solve them. But, especially while we're starting our programming, we're going to make a lot of small silly errors that are really easy to fix as long as we know where to look.

Fortunately, Java compilers are designed to point errors out to us when they come across them. To see this in action, let's simply make our `HelloWorld` program incorrect by removing the semicolon from the end of the `println` statement:

```
public class HelloWorld {
    public static void main(String[] args) {
        System.out.println("Hello World!")
    }
}
```

Now NetBeans red-jitters the line to let us know that it's pretty sure something's wrong, but we can ask our compiler to take a shot at it anyway. If we attempt to build this project, we don't get the `COMPILATION SUCCESSFUL` message we otherwise would; instead, we get an error message:

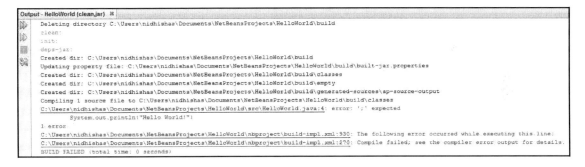

This error is '; ' expected, which is a pretty handy and self-explanatory error message. Of equal importance is the number after the colon in this message, which is 4. This lets us know on what line the compiler came across this error. In NetBeans, if we click on an error message, the IDE will highlight that line of code:

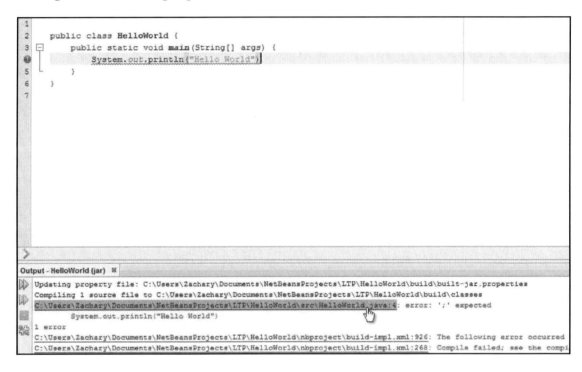

If we add in our semicolon, then our program builds successfully as shown in the following screenshot:

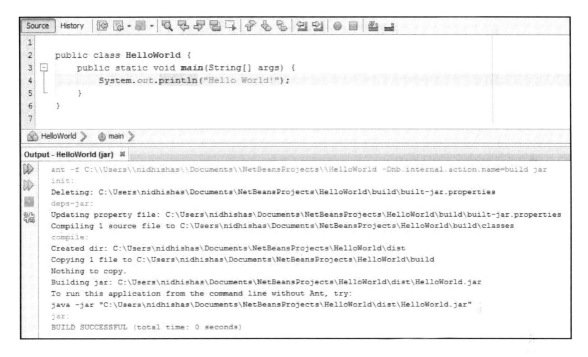

That's all there is to it.

Of course, not all error messages are quite that self-explanatory. For the sake of argument, let's create a slightly more complicated error. What would have happened if we had forgotten to insert one of our parentheses in this program? This is illustrated in the following code:

When we press Build Project, we get not one but two errors, even though we really only made one mistake:

```
Compiling 1 source file to C:\Users\nidhishas\Documents\NetBeansProjects\HelloWorld\build\classes
C:\Users\nidhishas\Documents\NetBeansProjects\HelloWorld\src\HelloWorld.java:4: error: not a statement
        System.out.println"Hello World!");
C:\Users\nidhishas\Documents\NetBeansProjects\HelloWorld\src\HelloWorld.java:4: error: ';' expected
        System.out.println"Hello World!");
2 errors
C:\Users\nidhishas\Documents\NetBeansProjects\HelloWorld\nbproject\build-impl.xml:930: The following error occurred while executing this line:
C:\Users\nidhishas\Documents\NetBeansProjects\HelloWorld\nbproject\build-impl.xml:270: Compile failed; see the compiler error output for details.
BUILD FAILED (total time: 0 seconds)
```

Our first error is `not a statement`, then it lets us know the line that it doesn't understand. If we look at the first error for a little bit, we'll probably notice that we're missing a pair of parentheses, so we will be able to fix this error; however, what about the second error? We got `';'` `expected` again even though in this case we really do have a semicolon.

Well, once one error has occurred in the program, the compiler's ability to understand the lines of the code gets shattered very quickly. When we're debugging our code, the general rule of thumb is to address only the top error on our list; that's the first error that the compiler came across in our code. We might be able to glean some helpful information from errors further down, but more often than not, they're simply going to be errors generated by the first syntax mistake we made. Nothing too mind-blowing here, but I wanted to point this out to you because being able to track compiler errors can save us a lot of headaches while we're learning to program.

The code completion feature

While we're talking about NetBeans, let's quickly go over one other IDE feature. Let's say I wanted to write a new line of code and I'm going to use something from the `System` library:

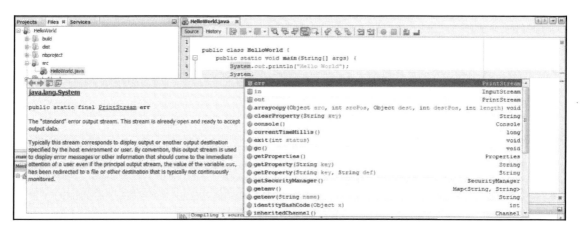

Once I've typed `System.`, NetBeans can suggest valid responses for me. Only one of these, of course, is going to be what I'm looking for. The NetBeans compiler has a lot of helpful features such as these. If you're the kind of person who thinks code completion is awesome, go ahead and leave these tools on. We can do this by going to **Tools** | **Options** | **Code Completion** and checking the features that we'd like:

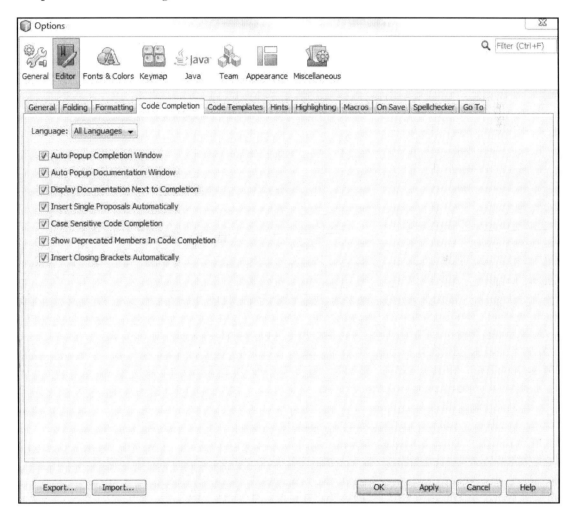

If you'd rather NetBeans behave a little more like a text editor, go ahead and uncheck all the features.

There we go, lots of housecleaning in this section, but hopefully quick and not too painful.

Summary

In this chapter, you learned what Java is and saw its features. We saw the expanse of Java's application by looking at the various fields it is used in.

We walked through the steps to install a Java Development Kit. We then set up a development environment called **NetBeans** for writing Java programs and executing them. We saw how to use NetBeans and wrote our first Java program in it. Next, we saw how to use NetBeans' ability to detect errors for rectifying them.

In the next chapter, we'll look at the various Java data types and how to work with variables.

2
Understanding Typed Variables

To create even modest Java programs, we're going to need a way to store and manipulate information. Our chief resource, when doing this, is the variable, and that's what we're going to take a look at in this chapter. We'll look at the different data types in Java and how to use them in our programs. We'll also see the Math class library and one of its functions.

Specifically, we'll walk through the following topics:

- Introduction to variables and why they're needed
- Integer variables
- Floating-point variables
- The Math class library and its pow() function
- Character variables
- The String class and its methods

Integer variables

To begin, let's create a new project in NetBeans. I'm going to call mine `Variables`, and this time we'll allow NetBeans to create the main class for us so that we can get to coding as quickly as possible. We need to delete all the comments that are created automatically by NetBeans when we create our new project, just to keep everything as readable as possible, then we'll be good to go:

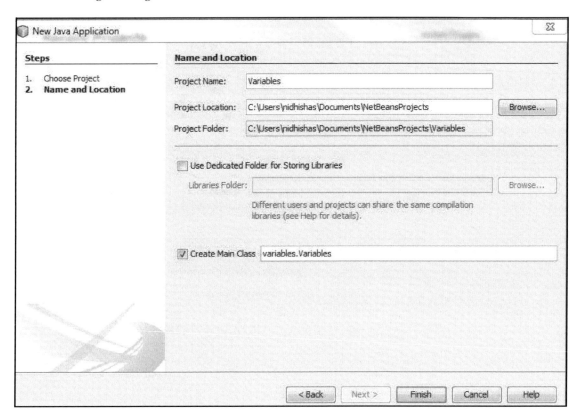

The first computers were little more than calculators, and Java, of course, retains this functionality. For example, Java can evaluate 1+1, which will evaluate to 2, of course. However, Java is pretty complicated and designed to do a lot of different things, so we need to provide context to our commands. Here, we tell Java that we'd like it to print the result of 1+1:

```
package variables;

public class Variables {

    public static void main(String[] args) {
        System.out.println(1+1);
    }
}
```

Our preceding program will run as expected:

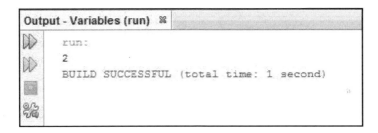

In addition to some others, Java can perform all the basic arithmetic operations. It can do addition, subtraction, multiplication (for which we use *, not X on our keyboard), and division. If we run the following program with the input of 2 and 3, we'll see four `println()` commands, all of which will give the proper result of the calculations. We can, of course, change these numbers to be any combination of numbers we see fit:

```
package variables;

public class Variables {

    public static void main(String[] args) {
        System.out.println(2+3);
        System.out.println(2-3);
        System.out.println(2*3);
        System.out.println(2/3);
    }
}
```

The following is the output of the preceding code:

```
Output - Variables (run)  ✕
⏩    run:
⏩    5
     -1
     6
     0
     BUILD SUCCESSFUL (total time: 0 seconds)
```

Changing these lines manually is kind of a pain and quickly becomes infeasible if we're writing very complicated programs or dynamic programs that take user input.

The solution of variables

Fortunately, programming gives us a way of storing and retrieving data; this is called the **variable**. To declare a variable in Java, we first have to specify what kind of variable we're going to be using. Variables come in a number of different types. In this instance, we're content with using whole numbers, that is, numbers that do not have a specified decimal place and aren't fractions. Also, in this case, it's appropriate to use one of Java's primitive types. These are essentially as base level as we can get with information in the Java programming language; just about everything else we work with in Java is built of the primitive types.

To declare a variable of the integer primitive type, that is, whole numbers, we use the `int` keyword, all lowercase. Once we do this, we need to give our variable a name. This is a unique identifier that we'll use to access this piece of information in future. Each variable in our local program should have its own name. Let's call our first variable x and our second variable y:

```
package variables;

public class Variables {

    public static void main(String[] args) {
        int x;
        int y;
        System.out.println(2+3);
        System.out.println(2-3);
        System.out.println(2*3);
        System.out.println(2/3);
    }
}
```

We've just written two perfectly legitimate lines of Java code. If we run our program now, we'll see the same output we did before:

However, behind the scenes, Java will also be setting aside memory space for our x and y variables. This allocation doesn't affect our `println` commands because the variables are not referenced in them yet.

So let's store some information in our variables. We can reference a variable once we've created it simply by the variable's name. It's important that we do not reference our variable by typing `int x` again because this is the command for Java to create a brand new variable x, not access the existing variable x:

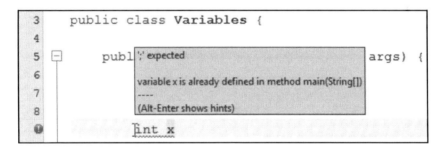

Once we've referenced our variable, we can change its value using the equal sign. So let's set x to 4 and y to 3. Our `println` commands currently operate with two explicitly declared integers: the numbers 2 and 3. Since x and y are also integers, it stands to reason that we can simply replace the existing numbers with the variables x and y:

```
package variables;

public class Variables {

    public static void main(String[] args) {
        int x;
        int y;
        x = 4;
```

```
            y = 3;
            System.out.println(x+y);
            System.out.println(x-y);
            System.out.println(x*y);
            System.out.println(x/y);
        }
    }
```

The following is the output of the preceding code:

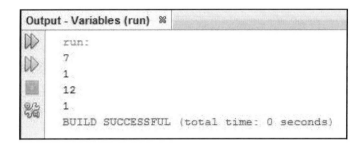

When our Java code comes to the variables x and y, it will look to see what integer value they have currently been given. It will find the numbers 4 and 3. So if we run our program, we should expect the first `println` statement, x+y, to evaluate to 4+3, which then evaluates to 7. This is exactly what occurs.

So here's something interesting. The last line of our program, in which we divide x by y, isn't evaluating as we might mathematically expect it to. In this line of code, x has the value 4, and y has the value 3, Now 4 divided by 3 equals 1.3, but our program is simply outputting 1. That's because 1.3 is not a valid integer value. Integers are only whole numbers and never fractions or decimal numbers. So, to keep us working with integers, Java simply rounds down any calculations that have fractional portions to their nearest whole number. If we want to work in an environment where we could have fractional results, we would need to use a primitive type other than an integer.

Anyway, now that we've set up our `println` commands to take integer variable input instead of explicit numbers, we can modify the behavior of all four lines of the calculation by simply changing the values of these integer variables. For example, if we wanted our program to run on the input values -10 and 5 (integers can be negative; they just can't have fractional components), all we would need to do is change the values we give to our variables x and y:

```
package variables;

public class Variables {
```

```
public static void main(String[] args) {
    int x;
    int y;
    x = -10;
    y = 5;
    System.out.println(x+y);
    System.out.println(x-y);
    System.out.println(x*y);
    System.out.println(x/y);
}
}
```

If we run the preceding code quickly, we will see the expected results:

```
Output - Variables (run)  %
 ▷▷    run:
 ▷▷    -5
        -15
 ▣      -50
 ❄      -2
        BUILD SUCCESSFUL (total time: 0 seconds)
```

Awesome! You've just learned the very basics of working with both integers and variables in Java.

Memory allocation for integer variables

Let's go over an edge case and learn a little bit more about how Java thinks. You might remember from earlier, I spoke about how Java sets aside memory when we declare new variables. This is one of the huge advantages of working in a high-level programming language, such as Java. Java abstracts away or automatically takes care of most of the memory management for us. Quite often, this makes writing programs simpler, and we can write shorter, cleaner, and more easily readable code. Of course, it is important that we appreciate what's happening behind the scenes, lest we run into issues.

For example, whenever Java sets aside memory for an integer variable, it also sets aside the same amount of memory for all integer variables. This means there's a maximum and minimum value that Java could ever conceivably store in an integer variable. The maximum integer value is 2147483647 and the minimum integer value is 2147483648.

So let's do an experiment. What happens if we attempt to store and print out an integer variable that is one larger than the maximum value? To start with, let's simplify our program. We're simply going to assign a value, one higher than possible, to the variable x:

```
3    public class Variables {
4
5        public static void main(String[] args) {
         integer number too large: 2147483648
6            int....
7            (Alt-Enter shows hints)
8            x =  2147483648;
9
10           //2147483647
11           //-2147483648
12
13           System.out.println(x);
14       }
15   }
```

When we attempt to do this, NetBeans yells at us. It's got some logic built in that attempts to stop us from making this very basic and common mistake. If we were to attempt to compile this program, we would also get an error.

However, we want to make this mistake in the name of science, so we're going to trick NetBeans. We're going to set the value of our variable x to the largest possible integer value, and then in the next line of our code, we're going to set the value of x to be one higher than what x is currently, that is, x=x+1. Actually, there's a nifty little shorthand we can use for this: x=x+1 is equivalent to x++. OK, so when we run this program, which will sneak by the compiler and NetBeans, and do our addition at runtime, we attempt to print out an integer value that is one plus the highest integer value that Java can store in a memory location:

```
package variables;

public class Variables {

    public static void main(String[] args) {
        int x;
        x = 2147483647;
        x++;
        System.out.println(x);
    }
}
```

When we run the preceding program, we get the following negative number:

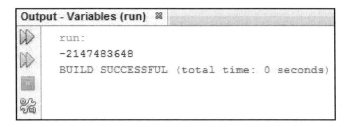

This number happens to be the smallest number that we could ever store in an integer. This makes some sort of visual sense. We've gone so far positive, or to the right, on our integer number line, that we've arrived at the leftmost or the most negative point. Of course, in a mathematical sense, this could get pretty confusing pretty quickly.

It's unlikely that we're ever going to write programs that will need integer numbers higher than this value. However, if we do, we certainly need to be aware of this issue and circumvent it, using a variable type that can handle larger values. The `long` variable type is just like an integer but we need to allocate more memory for it:

```
package variables;

public class Variables {

    public static void main(String[] args) {
        long x;
        x = 2147483647;
        x++;
        System.out.println(x);
    }
}
```

When we run the preceding program, we will get a mathematically accurate result:

Output - Variables (run)
run:
2147483648
BUILD SUCCESSFUL (total time: 0 seconds)

Floating point variables

When we're simply counting and manipulating whole objects, integers are fantastic. However, sometimes we need to deal with numbers in a more mathematical sense, and we need a data type that will allow us to express ideas that are not entirely whole numbers. Floating-point numbers, or floats, are a Java primitive type that allow us to express numbers that have decimal points and fractions. In this section, we'll modify some float and integer variables side by side to see how they are similar and different.

Let's create a new Java project (you know the drill by now) and call it `FloatingPointNumbers`. Let's start by declaring two variables: one integer (`iNumber`) and one float (`fNumber`). As we know, once we've declared these variables, we're free to modify and assign values to them in our Java program later. This time, let me show you that we can also modify and assign to these variables in the same line that they're declared. So where I have declared my `iNumber` integer variable, I'm free to immediately give it the value of 5:

```
package floatingpointnumbers;

public class FloatingPointNumbers {
    public static void main(String[] args) {
        int iNumber = 5;
        float fNumber;
    }
}
```

Notice that if we try and do something very similar with our float variable, NetBeans will yell at us, by displaying a light bulb and red dot on the left-hand side:

In fact, if we attempt to compile our program, we'll get a legitimate compiler error message:

Let's analyze why this happens. When we use an explicit number in Java, that is, typing out the digits rather than working with a variable, that explicit number is still given a type by Java. So when we type out a number without any decimal places, the type that the number is assumed to be is an integer. So our assignment works just great. However, a number with decimal places is assumed to be of this type and is called `double`; it's a sister type of the `float` data type, but it's not quite the same. We'll talk about `double` a little later. Right now, what we need to do is tell Java to treat `5.5` as a `float` type number instead of `double`. To do this, all we need to do is put `f` after the digits, as follows:

```
float fNumber = 5.5f;
```

You'll see that the bulb and red dot have disappeared. To make sure we get the syntax right, let's give our program some super basic functionality. Let's use `System.out.println()` to print our integer number and then our floating-point number variable in sequence:

```
System.out.println(iNumber);
System.out.println(fNumber);
```

When we build this program, our compiler error goes away, and when we run it, we see the two assigned values as expected. Nothing too exciting there:

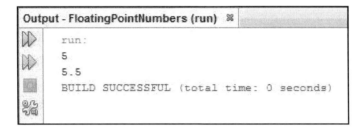

Behavior difference between integer and float data types

Now, rather than assigning explicit values to our variables, let's do some basic arithmetic so we can see how integer and floats, when modified in Java, behave differently. In Java, both `float` and `int` are primitive types, the logical building blocks of the programming language. This means we can compare and modify them using mathematical operators, such as division.

We know that if we attempt to divide one integer by another, we'll always get a whole number as a result, even if the rules of standard mathematics don't make that the expected result. If we divide a floating-point number by another floating-point number, however, we'll get a more mathematically accurate result:

```
package floatingpointnumbers;

public class FloatingPointNumbers {

    public static void main(String[] args) {
        int iNumber = 5/4;
        float fNumber = 5.0f/4.0f;
        System.out.println(iNumber);
        System.out.println(fNumber);
    }
}
```

The following is the output of the preceding code:

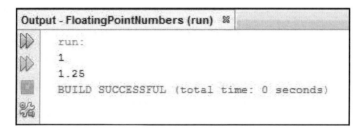

Sometimes, Java will let us do things that might not be such a good idea. For example, Java lets us set the value of our floating-point variable `fNumber` to one integer divided by another instead of one floating-point number divided by another:

```
int iNumber = 5/4;
float fNumber = 5/4;
```

Because the computation on the right-hand side of our equals sign occurs before the value of our floating-point variable fNumber changes, we're going to see the same output in both the calculations of 5/4. This is because both the 5's and 4's are integer variables. So when we run our program, even though fNumber remains a floating-point number (as we can tell because it prints out with the decimal place), its value is still set to the rounded down whole number of 5/4:

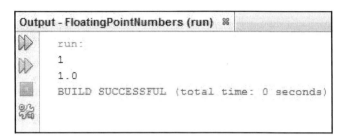

Solving this problem is pretty straightforward; we simply need to change one of our integer values to be a floating-point number by appending f to it:

```
int iNumber = 5/4;
float fNumber = 5/4.0f;
```

Now the computation will know how to proceed with a decimal place division:

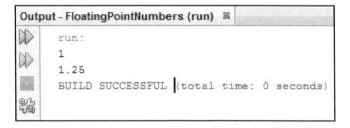

This becomes a little trickier and more important to navigate properly when we stop working with explicitly declared numbers and begin working with variables.

Let's declare two integer variables now. I'll just call them iNumber1 and iNumber2. Now, rather than attempting to set the value of fNumber to one explicitly declared number divided by another, we'll set its value to iNumber1/iNumber2, and we'll just print out the results stored in fNumber:

```
package floatingpointnumbers;

public class FloatingPointNumbers {
    public static void main(String[] args) {
        int iNumber1 = 5;
        int iNumber2 = 6;
        float fNumber = iNumber1/iNumber2;

        System.out.println(fNumber);
    }
}
```

When we run this program, because once again we're dividing one integer by another, we're going to see the rounding down phenomenon. The value being stored in our floating-point variable is 0.0, the rounded down result of 5/6:

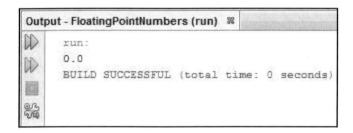

If we were working with explicitly declared numbers, we would solve this problem by changing one of the two integer numbers to be treated as a floating-point number by simply putting a decimal place and f after it. In this context, using iNumber2f is not an option because rather than thinking that we're asking it to treat iNumber2 as a floating-point number, Java now believes it's looking for a variable called iNumber2f, which certainly doesn't exist within this context.

Type casting

We can achieve a similar result though, using what's called a **cast**. This is a command in which we ask Java to treat a variable of one type like it is another one. Here we're circumventing Java's natural inclination to treat iNumber1 and iNumber2 as integers. We're stepping in and saying, "You know what Java, treat this number here as a float," and we're assuming some responsibility when we do this. Java will attempt to do what we ask, but if we choose poorly and attempt to cast one object to an object that it cannot, our program will crash.

Fortunately, we're working with primitives here, and primitive types know how to act like another type. So, we can cast the variable iNumber1 to temporarily operate like a floating-point number by prefacing it with (float):

```
float fNumber = (float)iNumber1/iNumber2;
```

Now if we run our program, we'll see the expected result of 5/6:

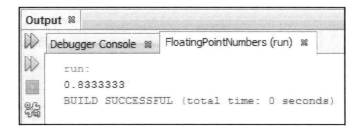

That's a pretty solid introduction to working with floating-point numbers, which we're going to use just about any time we want to work with numbers in their mathematical sense rather than as integers for counting whole objects.

The double data type

Let's quickly talk about the double data type. It is a sister type of float. It provides a greater resolution: double numbers can have even more decimal places. But they take up a little more memory. At this point in time, using double or float is almost always a style or personal preference decision. Unless you're working with complicated software that must run at peak memory efficiency, the extra memory space taken up by a double is not very significant.

To illustrate how `double` works, let's change the two integer numbers in our `FloatingPointNumbers.java` program to a `double` data type. When we only change the names of the variables, the logic of our program doesn't change at all. But when we change the declaration of these variables from declaring integers to doubles, the logic does change. Anyway, when we explicitly declare a number with decimal places, it defaults to being `double`:

```
7    double dNumber1 = 5.7;
8    double dNumber2 = 6.85431;
9    float fNumber = dNumber1/dNumber2;
```

Now we need to fix the error. The error occurs because dividing a `double` data type by another one is going to return a `double` result. We can solve this issue in two ways:

1. First, we could cast `dNumber1` and `dNumber2` to floating-point numbers and then divide them:

```
float fNumber = (float) dNumber1/ (float) dNumber2;
```

2. However, dividing our two double numbers by each other is a perfectly legitimate operation. So why not allow this to occur naturally and then cast the resulting double to a floating-point number, thereby preserving a greater amount of resolution. Just like in algebra, we can break up conceptual blocks of our program that we would like to occur before another block using parentheses:

```
float fNumber = (float) (dNumber1/dNumber2);
```

Now if we run this program, we get the expected result:

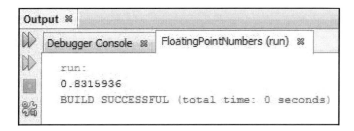

The Math class library

A good portion of our time on any software development project is going to be spent teaching our program to solve the types of problems it would comes across on a regular basis. As programmers, we too will run into certain problems time and time again. Sometimes, we'll need to code our own solutions to these problems and hopefully save them for later use. However, more often than not, someone has run into these problems before, and if they've made their solution publicly available, one of our options is to leverage their solution for our own gain.

In this section, we'll use the `Math` class library, which is bundled with the JDK to solve some math problems for us. To start this section, create a brand new NetBeans project (I'm going to name it `TheMathLib`) and enter the `main()` function. We're going to write a very simple program. Let's declare a floating-point number variable and give it a value (don't forget the `f` alphabet at the end of our explicit number to let Java know that we've declared a floating-point number), then use `System.out.println()` to print this value to the screen:

```
package themathlib;

public class TheMathLib {
    public static void main(String[] args) {
        float number = 4.321f;
        System.out.println(number);
    }
}
```

OK, there we go:

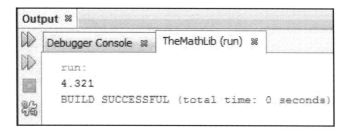

Now, with this program, we'd like to make it really easy to raise our floating-point number to various powers. So, if we simply want to square this number, I guess we could just print out the value of `number*number`. If we want to cube it, we could print out `number*number*number`. And, if we want to raise it to the power of six, we could multiply it six times by itself. Of course, this gets unwieldy pretty quickly, and there's certainly a better way.

Let's leverage the Java `Math` class library to help us raise numbers to varying exponential powers. Now, I've just told you that the functionality we're looking for lives in the `Math` class library. This is the kind of push in the right direction you should expect to get from a Google search, or if you're an experienced software developer, you can implement a specific API. Unfortunately, that's not quite enough information for us to start using the functionality of this class library. We don't know the specifics of how it works or even exactly what functionality it offers us.

To find this out, we're going to have to look at its documentation. Here's the documentation web page managed by Oracle for the libraries found in our Java Development Kit: `docs.oracle.com/javase/7/docs/api/`. Among the libraries that show up on the page is `java.lang`. When we select it, we'll find the `Math` class that we've been looking for under **Class Summary**. Once we navigate to the `Math` class library page, we get two things. First we get some human-friendly text write-up about the library, its history, what its intended uses are, very meta-level stuff. If we scroll down, we see the functionality and methods implemented by the library. This is the nitty-gritty of where we'd like to be:

Methods

Modifier and Type	Method and Description
static double	`abs(double a)` Returns the absolute value of a double value.
static float	`abs(float a)` Returns the absolute value of a float value.
static int	`abs(int a)` Returns the absolute value of an int value.
static long	`abs(long a)` Returns the absolute value of a long value.
static double	`acos(double a)` Returns the arc cosine of a value; the returned angle is in the range 0.0 through *pi*.
static double	`asin(double a)` Returns the arc sine of a value; the returned angle is in the range *-pi*/2 through *pi*/2.
static double	`atan(double a)` Returns the arc tangent of a value; the returned angle is in the range *-pi*/2 through *pi*/2.
static double	`atan2(double y, double x)` Returns the angle *theta* from the conversion of rectangular coordinates (x, y) to polar coordinates (r, *theta*).

Using the pow() function

One of these functions should stick out for us, which is `pow()`, or the power function. It returns the value of the first argument (`double a`) raised to the power of the second argument (`double b`). In short, it will allow us to raise numbers to an arbitrary power:

static double	`pow(double a, double b)` Returns the value of the first argument raised to the power of the second argument.

Let's get back to coding. Alright, let's employ this `pow()` function to modify the value of our variable `number` after we've declared it. We're going to do something along the lines of `number = pow`, but we need a little more information:

```
float number = 4.321f;
number = pow;
```

How exactly do we employ this `pow()` function? Well, if we click on our documentation, we'll see that when the `pow()` function is declared, in addition to its name, there's also, between parentheses, two arguments specified. These arguments, `double a` and `double b`, are the two pieces of information the function is requesting before it can operate as expected.

Our job, in order to use this function, is to replace the requests `double a` and `double b` with actual variables or explicit values so that the `pow()` function can do its thing. Our documentation tells us that `double a` should be replaced with the variable or value that we'd like to raise to the power of `double b`.

So let's replace the first type argument with our variable `number`, which is what we want to raise to an arbitrary power. On that note, `number` is `float` not `double`, and that's going to give us some trouble unless we simply change it to `double`. So let's do that. For the second argument, we don't have a precreated variable to replace `double b` with, so let's just use an explicit value, such as `4.0`:

```
double number = 4.321;
number = pow(number, 4.0);
```

Notice that I get rid of the `double` specifier when I call the `pow()` function. This specifier only exists to let us know what type Java is expecting.

In theory, the `pow()` function now has all the information it needs to go ahead and run and raise the value of our number variable to the power of 4. However, NetBeans is still giving us our red warning sign. Right now, that's because NetBeans, and Java by extension, doesn't know where to find this `pow` keyword. For the same reasons that we need to specify a full path to `System.out.println()`, we need to specify a full path in which it can find the `pow()` function for Java. This is the same path we followed to get to the `pow()` function in our documentation. So let's specify `java.lang.Math.pow()` as it's path in our code:

```
package themathlib;

public class TheMathLib {
    public static void main(String[] args) {
        double number = 4.321;
        number = java.lang.Math.pow(number, 4.0);
        System.out.println(number);
    }
}
```

Now we're pretty much good to go. Let's utilize the `number` variable once in our `println` statement, then we should be able to run our program:

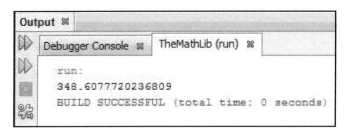

We can plug it into our calculator if we want, but I'm pretty confident that our program has outputted the value of 4.321 raised to the power of 4.

So this is great! We've just employed external code to not only make our program easier to write, but also to keep it very human-readable. It required much fewer lines of code than it would have otherwise.

Importing class libraries

One thing that's not super human-readable about our program is the long paths to functions such as `pow()` and `println()`. Is there a way we could shorten them? There certainly is. If the makers of Java had wanted to, they could have allowed us to call this function by simply typing `Math.pow()` in all instances. This unfortunately would have some unintended side effects. For example, if there were two libraries linked up to Java and they both declared a `Math.pow()` function, Java would not know which one to use. Hence, by default, we're expected to link to libraries directly and explicitly.

So, if we'd like to just be able to type out something like `Math.pow()`, we can import a library into the local space that we're working in. We just need to do an `import` command above our class and the `main()` function declaration. All the import command takes as input is the path that we'd like Java to look for when it comes across a keyword, such as `pow()`, that it doesn't immediately recognize. In order to allow us to employ the easier syntax `Math.pow()` in our program, we simply need to type `import java.lang.Math`:

```
package themathlib;

import java.lang.Math;

public class TheMathLib {
    public static void main(String[] args) {
        double number = 4.321;
        number = java.lang.Math.pow(number, 4.0);
        System.out.println(number);
    }
}
```

There is some special syntax for imports. Let's say we wanted to import all the class libraries in `java.lang`. To do this, we could replace `.Math` with `.*` and make it `java.lang.*` which translates to "import every library from the `java.lang` package." I should probably inform you that for those of us working in NetBeans, this import is done by default. However, in this case, we're going to do it explicitly because you may have to do this while working in other Java environments as well.

Char variables

Programs that manipulate numbers are all well and good, but quite often, we want to be able to work with text and words as well. To help us do this, Java defines the character, or `char`, the primitive type. Characters are the smallest entity of text that you can work with on a computer. We can think of them to start off with as single letters.

Let's create a new project; we'll call it `Characters.java`. We'll start our program by simply defining a single character. We'll call it `character1` and we'll assign to it the value of uppercase `H`:

```
package characters;

public class Characters {
    public static void main(String[] args) {
        char character1 = 'H';
    }
}
```

Just as we have to use some extra syntax when defining a floating-point number explicitly, we need some extra syntax when defining a character. To tell Java that we're explicitly declaring a character value here, we surround the letter we would like to assign to our variable with two single quotation marks. The single quotation marks, as opposed to double quotation marks, let Java know that we're working with a character or a single letter, as opposed to trying to use an entire string. Characters can only have single entity values. If we attempt to assign the value of `Hi` to `character1`, NetBeans and Java would both let us know that that's not a valid option:

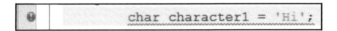

Now, let's move on and write a somewhat convoluted program that will nonetheless work pretty well for our example purposes. Let's define five characters. We'll call them `character1` through `character5`. We'll assign each one of them with one of the five letters of the word "Hello," in that order. When these characters are printed together, our output will show `Hello`. In the second portion of our program, let's use `System.out.print()` to display these letters on the screen. The `System.out.print()` code works just the same as `System.out.println()`, except that it doesn't add a carriage return at the end of our line. Let's have the last command as `println` so that our output is separated from all of the additional text presented in our console:

```
package characters;

public class Characters {

    public static void main(String[] args) {
        char character1 = 'H';
        char character2 = 'e';
        char character3 = 'l';
        char character4 = 'l';
        char character5 = 'o';
```

```
        System.out.print(character1);
        System.out.print(character2);
        System.out.print(character3);
        System.out.print(character4);
        System.out.println(character5);
    }
}
```

If we run this program, it greets us. It says `Hello` and then there is some additional text:

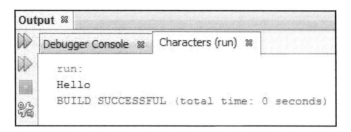

That's pretty straightforward.

Now let me show you something that will give us a little insight into how our computer thinks about characters. It turns out that we can set the value of `character1` not only by explicitly declaring the capital letter `H` between two single quotation marks, but also by giving it an integer value. Each possible character value has a corresponding number that we can use in lieu of it. If we replace `H` with the value of `72`, we're still going to print out `Hello`. If we were to use the value `73`, one greater than `72`, instead of the capital `H`, we'll now get the capital letter `I`, as I is the letter that follows H.

We have to make sure we don't put `72` between single quotation marks. The best case scenario is that Java recognizes that `72` is not a valid character and that it looks more like two characters, then our program won't compile. If we use a single digit number surrounded by single quotation marks, our program would compile just fine, but we would get the completely unexpected output of `7ello`.

So how do we figure out the numeric value of characters? Well, there's a universal lookup table, the **ASCII** table, which maps characters to their numeric values:

Dec	Hx	Oct	Char		Dec	Hx	Oct	Html	Chr	Dec	Hx	Oct	Html	Chr	Dec	Hx	Oct	Html	Chr
0	0	000	NUL	(null)	32	20	040	&#32;	Space	64	40	100	&#64;	@	96	60	140	&#96;	`
1	1	001	SOH	(start of heading)	33	21	041	&#33;	!	65	41	101	&#65;	A	97	61	141	&#97;	a
2	2	002	STX	(start of text)	34	22	042	"	"	66	42	102	&#66;	B	98	62	142	&#98;	b
3	3	003	ETX	(end of text)	35	23	043	&#35;	#	67	43	103	&#67;	C	99	63	143	&#99;	c
4	4	004	EOT	(end of transmission)	36	24	044	&#36;	$	68	44	104	&#68;	D	100	64	144	&#100;	d
5	5	005	ENQ	(enquiry)	37	25	045	&#37;	%	69	45	105	&#69;	E	101	65	145	&#101;	e
6	6	006	ACK	(acknowledge)	38	26	046	&	&	70	46	106	&#70;	F	102	66	146	&#102;	f
7	7	007	BEL	(bell)	39	27	047	'	'	71	47	107	&#71;	G	103	67	147	&#103;	g
8	8	010	BS	(backspace)	40	28	050	&#40;	(	72	48	110	&#72;	H	104	68	150	&#104;	h
9	9	011	TAB	(horizontal tab)	41	29	051	&#41;	)	73	49	111	&#73;	I	105	69	151	&#105;	i
10	A	012	LF	(NL line feed, new line)	42	2A	052	&#42;	*	74	4A	112	&#74;	J	106	6A	152	&#106;	j
11	B	013	VT	(vertical tab)	43	2B	053	&#43;	+	75	4B	113	&#75;	K	107	6B	153	&#107;	k
12	C	014	FF	(NP form feed, new page)	44	2C	054	&#44;	,	76	4C	114	&#76;	L	108	6C	154	&#108;	l
13	D	015	CR	(carriage return)	45	2D	055	&#45;	-	77	4D	115	&#77;	M	109	6D	155	&#109;	m
14	E	016	SO	(shift out)	46	2E	056	&#46;	.	78	4E	116	&#78;	N	110	6E	156	&#110;	n
15	F	017	SI	(shift in)	47	2F	057	&#47;	/	79	4F	117	&#79;	O	111	6F	157	&#111;	o
16	10	020	DLE	(data link escape)	48	30	060	&#48;	0	80	50	120	&#80;	P	112	70	160	&#112;	p
17	11	021	DC1	(device control 1)	49	31	061	&#49;	1	81	51	121	&#81;	Q	113	71	161	&#113;	q
18	12	022	DC2	(device control 2)	50	32	062	&#50;	2	82	52	122	&#82;	R	114	72	162	&#114;	r
19	13	023	DC3	(device control 3)	51	33	063	&#51;	3	83	53	123	&#83;	S	115	73	163	&#115;	s
20	14	024	DC4	(device control 4)	52	34	064	&#52;	4	84	54	124	&#84;	T	116	74	164	&#116;	t
21	15	025	NAK	(negative acknowledge)	53	35	065	&#53;	5	85	55	125	&#85;	U	117	75	165	&#117;	u
22	16	026	SYN	(synchronous idle)	54	36	066	&#54;	6	86	56	126	&#86;	V	118	76	166	&#118;	v
23	17	027	ETB	(end of trans. block)	55	37	067	&#55;	7	87	57	127	&#87;	W	119	77	167	&#119;	w
24	18	030	CAN	(cancel)	56	38	070	&#56;	8	88	58	130	&#88;	X	120	78	170	&#120;	x
25	19	031	EM	(end of medium)	57	39	071	&#57;	9	89	59	131	&#89;	Y	121	79	171	&#121;	y
26	1A	032	SUB	(substitute)	58	3A	072	&#58;	:	90	5A	132	&#90;	Z	122	7A	172	&#122;	z
27	1B	033	ESC	(escape)	59	3B	073	&#59;	;	91	5B	133	&#91;	[	123	7B	173	&#123;	{
28	1C	034	FS	(file separator)	60	3C	074	&#60;	<	92	5C	134	&#92;	\	124	7C	174	&#124;		
29	1D	035	GS	(group separator)	61	3D	075	&#61;	=	93	5D	135	&#93;	]	125	7D	175	&#125;	}
30	1E	036	RS	(record separator)	62	3E	076	&#62;	>	94	5E	136	&#94;	^	126	7E	176	&#126;	~
31	1F	037	US	(unit separator)	63	3F	077	&#63;	?	95	5F	137	&#95;	_	127	7F	177	&#127;	DEL

In this section, we've been dealing with columns 1 (**Dec**) and columns 5 (**Chr**), which have the decimal number and the character that they are mapped to. You'll notice that while many of these characters are letters, some are keyboard symbols, numbers, and other things, such as tabs. As far as programming languages are concerned, new lines, tabs, and back spaces are all character elements.

To see this in action, let's try replacing some of the characters in our program with the decimal value 9, which should correspond to a tab character. If we replace the middle three letters of our word with tabs, as output, we should expect H, three tabs, and o:

```
package characters;

public class Characters {

    public static void main(String[] args) {
        char character1 = 'H';
```

```
        char character2 = 9;
        char character3 = 9;
        char character4 = 9;
        char character5 = 'o';
        System.out.print(character1);
        System.out.print(character2);
        System.out.print(character3);
        System.out.print(character4);
        System.out.println(character5);
    }
```

The following is the output of the preceding code:

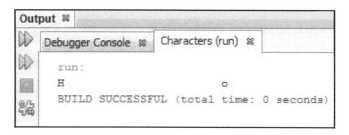

Strings

Let's talk about strings in Java. To begin, create a new NetBeans project, name it StringsInJava, and enter the main() function. Then, declare two variables: a character called c and String called s. Right away, it becomes clear to us that String is a little different. You'll notice that NetBeans did not choose to color code our String keyword with blue, as it would have done if we were declaring a variable of a primitive type:

```
package stringsinjava;

public class StringsInJava {
    public static void main(String[] args) {
        char c = 'c';
        String s = "string";
    }
}
```

This is because `String`, unlike `char`, is not a primitive type. `String` is what we call a class. Classes are the backbone of object-oriented programming. Just as we can declare variables of a primitive type, we can also declare variables of a class, which are called instances. In our program, the variable `s` is an instance of the `String` class. Unlike variables of primitive types, instances of a class can contain their own special methodologies and functions declared by the class of which they are an instance. In this section, we'll use some of these string-specific methods and functions to manipulate text.

But first, let's take a look at what makes the `String` class so special. As we know, we can pretty much use our character variables and our character literals interchangeably, as we can with just about any other primitive type. The `String` class also maps interchangeably with the string literal, which is like a character literal but uses double quotation marks and can contain many or no characters at all. Most Java classes do not map to any sort of literal, and our ability to manipulate string literals through the `String` class is what makes it so valuable.

The concatenation operator

Another thing strings can do, which most Java classes cannot, is make use of the addition sign (+) operator. If we declare three strings (say, s1, s2, and s3), we can set the value of our third string to be one string plus another string. We can even add a string literal into the mix. Then, we print s3:

```
package stringsinjava;

public class StringsInJava {
    public static void main(String[] args) {
        char c = 'c';
        String s1 = "stringone";
        String s2 = "stringtwo";
        String s3 = s1+s2+"LIT";
        System.out.println(s3);
    }
}
```

When we run this program, we'll see these three strings added together in much the manner that we would expect:

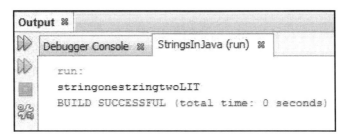

The toUpperCase() function

So I promised you that strings had the functionality not seen in a simple primitive type. To employ this, let's navigate to the `String` class in our Java documentation at `docs.oracle.com/javase/7/docs/api/`. Select **java.lang** shown under **Packages**, then scroll down and select **String** from **ClassSummary**. As with the documentation for all Java classes, the String documentation contains **Method Summary**, which will tell us about all the functions we can call on an existing `String` object. If we scroll down in **Method Summary**, we'll come to the `toUpperCase()` function that converts all the characters in a string into uppercase letters:

String	toUpperCase()
	Converts all of the characters in this String to upper case using the rules of the default locale.

Let's employ this function now. Back in NetBeans, we now need to determine the best place in our program to employ our `toUpperCase()` function:

```
package stringsinjava;
public class StringsInJava {
    public static void main(String[] args) {
        char c = 'c';
        String s1 = "stringone";
        String s2 = "stringtwo";
        String s3 = s1 + s2 + "LIT";
        System.out.println(s3);
    }
}
```

We know we need to employ the `toUpperCase()` function on the s3 string after finalizing the value of s3 in our `StringsInJava.java` program. We could do either of these two things:

- Employ the function on the line immediately after finalizing the value of s3 (by simply typing `s3.toUpperCase();`).
- Call the function as part of the line where we would print out the value of s3. Instead of printing out the value of s3, we could simply print out the value of `s3.toUpperCase()`, as shown in the following code block:

```
package stringsinjava;

public class StringsInJava {
    public static void main(String[] args) {
        char c = 'c';
        String s1 = "stringone";
        String s2 = "stringtwo";
        String s3 = s1+s2+"LIT";
        System.out.println(s3.toUpperCase());
    }
}
```

If you remember from our documentation, the `toUpperCase()` function requires no arguments. It knows that it's being called by s3, and that's all the knowledge it needs, but we still provide the double empty parentheses so that Java knows we are in fact making a function call. If we run this program now, we'll get the uppercased version of the string, as expected:

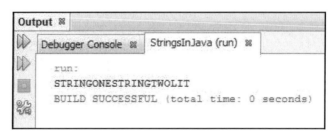

If you remember from our documentation, the `toUpperCase()` function requires no

But, it's important we understand what's going on behind the scenes here. The `System.out.println(s3.toUpperCase());` code line is not modifying the value of `s3` and then printing out that value. Rather, our `println` statement evaluates `s3.toUpperCase()` and then prints out the string returned by that function. To see that the actual value of `s3` is not modified by this function call, we can print the value of `s3` again:

```
System.out.println(s3.toUpperCase());
System.out.println(s3);
```

We can see that `s3` keeps its lowercase components:

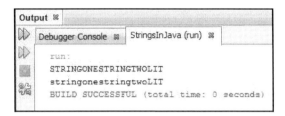

If we want to permanently modify the value of `s3`, we could do that on the previous line, and we could set the value of `s3` to the function's result:

```
package stringsinjava;

public class StringsInJava {
    public static void main(String[] args) {
        char c = 'c';
        String s1 = "stringone";
        String s2 = "stringtwo";
        String s3 = s1 + s2 + "LIT";

        s3 = s3.toUpperCase();
        System.out.println(s3);
        System.out.println(s3);
    }
}
```

The following is the output of the preceding code:

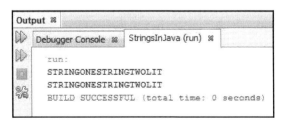

The replace() function

To confirm that we're all on the same page, let's employ one more method from the `String` class. If we head back to our documentation and scroll up, we can find the String's `replace()` method:

String	replace(char oldChar, char newChar)
	Returns a new string resulting from replacing all occurrences of oldChar in this string with newChar.

Unlike our `toUpperCase()` method, which took no arguments, `replace()` takes two characters as arguments. The function will return a new string where all the instances of the first character (`oldChar`) we give as an argument are replaced with the second character (`newChar`) we gave as an argument.

Let's utilize this function on our first `println()` line in `StringsInJava.java`. We'll type `s3.replace()` and give our function two characters as arguments. Let's replace the character g with the character o:

```
package stringsinjava;

public class StringsInJava {
    public static void main(String[] args) {
        char c = 'c';
        String s1 = "stringone";
        String s2 = "stringtwo";
        String s3 = s1 + s2 + "LIT";

        s3 = s3.toUpperCase();
        System.out.println(s3.replace('g', 'o'));
        System.out.println(s3);
    }
}
```

If we run our program, of course, nothing happens. This is because by the time we reach the print statement, there are no lowercase g characters, and there are no lowercase g characters left in s3; there are only uppercase G characters. So let's try and replace the uppercase G characters:

```
System.out.println(s3.replace('G', 'o'));
System.out.println(s3);
```

Now if we run our program, we see the replacement happen on the first instance of `println`, not on the second instance. This is because we haven't actually changed the value of `s3`:

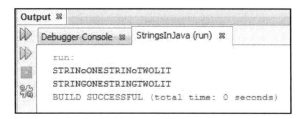

Excellent! You are now well-equipped, as long as you have the Java documentation handy, to call all sorts of `String` methods.

Escape sequences

If you spend a lot of time working with strings though, I anticipate that you're going to run into a common problem. Let's take a look at it quickly. I'm just going to write a brand new program here. I'm going to declare a string, then I'm going to have our program print the string to the screen. But the value I'm going to assign to this string is going to be a little tricky. I'd like our program to print out `The program says: "Hello World"` (I'd like `Hello World` to be surrounded by double quotation marks):

```
 4  □     public static void main(String[] args) {
 5            /*char c = 'c';
 6            String s1 = "stringone";
 7            String s2 = "stringtwo";
 8            String s3 = s1 + s2 + "LIT";
 9
10            s3 = s3.toUpperCase();
11                                            ';' expected
12            System.out.println( s3.replace  ';' expected
13            System.out.println( s3 );*/     ----
14                                            (Alt-Enter shows hints)
 ⬤        String s = "The program says: ["Hello World"";
16            System.out.println(s);
17     }
```

The problem here is that putting double quotation marks inside a string literal confuses Java as shown in the preceding screenshot. When it reads through our program, the first full string it sees is `"The program says: "` that tells Java that we've ended our string. This is, of course, not what we want.

Fortunately, there's a system in place for us to tell Java that we'd like a character to be treated as a character literal instead of the special functionality that it might otherwise have. To do this, we put a backslash in front of the character. This is known as an escape sequence:

```
String s= "The program says: \"Hello World\"";
System.out.println(s);
```

Now, when Java reads through this string, it will read `The program says:` and then see the backslash and know how to treat our double quotation marks as double quotation marks, the character, instead of the double quotation marks that surround a string. When we run our program, we will not see backslashes; they themselves are special characters:

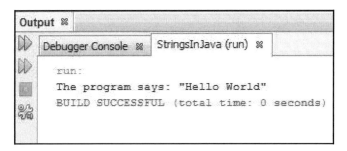

If we do want to see a backslash in our string, we need to preface it by a backslash of its own:

```
String s= "The program says: \\ \"Hello World\"";
System.out.println(s);
```

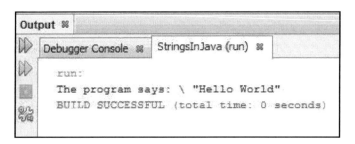

That's strings 101!

Summary

In this chapter, we explained what variables are and how important they are for creating better programs. We looked at some of the primitive data types of Java, namely `int`, `long`, `float`, `char`, and `double`, in detail. We also saw the `String` class and two of its manipulation methods.

In the next chapter, we'll look at branching statements in Java.

3
Branching

Programs that perform the same action every time they run are all well and good, but the most interesting computer programs do something a little different each time they run, whether it's because they have differing input or even because a user is actively interacting with them. With this, let's kick-start this chapter by understanding conditional statements, then we will further explore how Java handles complicated conditional statements, modify the control flow of our program, and study loops functionality.

Specifically, we'll cover the following topics in this chapter:

- Understanding `if` statements
- Complex conditionals
- The `switch`, `case`, and `break` statements
- The `while` and `do...while` loops
- The `for` loop

Understanding if statements

Today, we're going to explore the very basic `if` and `else` conditional statements. To understand this further, refer to the following bullet list:

1. Let's create a new Java project in NetBeans. I'm going to call mine `ConditionalStatements`, and I will allow NetBeans to create the `main` class for me; refer to the following screenshot:

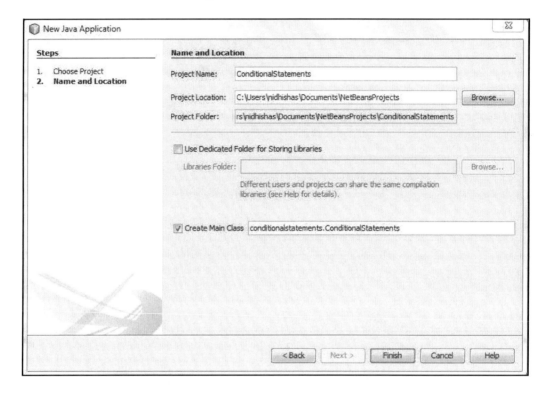

To keep things clean, we can get rid of all our comments; now we're good to go. To allow us to write more interesting programs, we're going to quickly learn how to do some basic user input in Java. At this point in time, you don't have the knowledge base to fully grasp the intricacies of what we're about to do, but you may have a basic understanding of what's going on and you can certainly repeat the process on your own in future.

While writing to this **InputStream/Console** window is kind of a simple fire-and-forget process, reading input in Java can be a little more complicated:

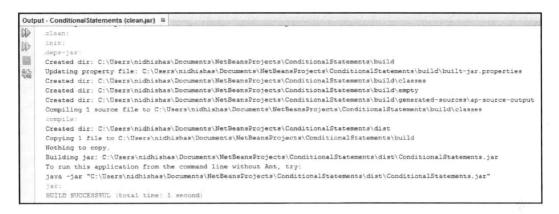

```
Output - ConditionalStatements (clean,jar)
  clean:
  init:
  deps-jar:
  Created dir: C:\Users\nidhishas\Documents\NetBeansProjects\ConditionalStatements\build
  Updating property file: C:\Users\nidhishas\Documents\NetBeansProjects\ConditionalStatements\build\built-jar.properties
  Created dir: C:\Users\nidhishas\Documents\NetBeansProjects\ConditionalStatements\build\classes
  Created dir: C:\Users\nidhishas\Documents\NetBeansProjects\ConditionalStatements\build\empty
  Created dir: C:\Users\nidhishas\Documents\NetBeansProjects\ConditionalStatements\build\generated-sources\ap-source-output
  Compiling 1 source file to C:\Users\nidhishas\Documents\NetBeansProjects\ConditionalStatements\build\classes
  compile:
  Created dir: C:\Users\nidhishas\Documents\NetBeansProjects\ConditionalStatements\dist
  Copying 1 file to C:\Users\nidhishas\Documents\NetBeansProjects\ConditionalStatements\build
  Nothing to copy.
  Building jar: C:\Users\nidhishas\Documents\NetBeansProjects\ConditionalStatements\dist\ConditionalStatements.jar
  To run this application from the command line without Ant, try:
  java -jar "C:\Users\nidhishas\Documents\NetBeansProjects\ConditionalStatements\dist\ConditionalStatements.jar"
  jar:
  BUILD SUCCESSFUL (total time: 1 second)
```

2. User input is put into a buffer that our program accesses when it's prompted to; therefore, we need to declare a variable that will allow us to access this buffer when we need to get some new user input. For this, we're going to use the `Scanner` class. Let's call our new instance `reader`. NetBeans yells at us because `Scanner` lives in the `java.util` package, which we need to access explicitly. We can always import the `java.util` package:

```
package conditionalstatements;

public class ConditionalStatements {

    public static void main(String[] args) {
        java.util.Scanner reader;
    }
}
```

3. Here's the part where you kind of have to take a leap of faith and jump a little bit ahead of what you're really ready to completely and totally understand. We need to assign a value to this `reader` variable of the `Scanner` type so that it links with the InputStream window, where our user will be entering their input. To do this, we're going to set its value to the value of a brand new `Scanner()` object, but this Scanner object is going to be created with a type argument, that is, `(System.in)`, which happens to be the link to the InputStream our users will be using:

```
package conditionalstatements;

import java.util.*;

public class ConditionalStatements {
```

```
        public static void main(String[] args) {
            Scanner reader = new Scanner(System.in);
        }
    }
```

The following is the output of the preceding code:

4. Like I said, this is some heavy hitting stuff and you certainly shouldn't expect to understand how this works at a lower level right now. For now, know that `reader` is connected with our InputStream window, and our `Scanner` object has the `next()` function that allows us to access the input that the user has just entered into the stream. Like most functions, this function simply returns this input, so we're going to have to create a string to store this input.

5. Once we've done this, we can use our `System.out.println()` function to print the `input` value back to the console:

```
        package conditionalstatements;

        import java.util.*;

        public class ConditionalStatements {

            public static void main(String[] args) {
                Scanner reader = new Scanner(System.in);
                String input = reader.next();
                System.out.println(input);
            }
        }
```

6. When we run our program, nothing appears to happen, but in actuality, our console here is waiting for some user input. Now, when we type our input into this console and hit *Enter* key, it will echo right back at us:

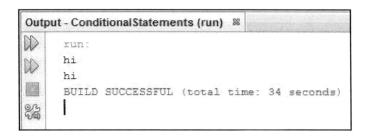

7. We can make this a little nicer to use by having our program prompt the user for the input rather than simply waiting quietly:

```
public static void main(String[] args) {
    Scanner reader = new Scanner(System.in);
    System.out.println("Input now: ");
    String input = reader.next();
    System.out.println(input);
}
```

Conditional statements

At the beginning of this chapter, I promised you'd learn about conditional statements, and we're about to do that now. But first, let's make a quick modification to the user input portion of our program. Rather than acquiring a string, it's going to be a lot easier if we learn conditional statements working with a user-provided integer value. So let's change the value or the type of our `input` variable to an `int` datatype; the `reader.next()` function returns a string, but there's a similar function called `nextInt()` that will return an integer:

```
int input = reader.nextInt();
```

We're certainly not going to bother putting any error-handling mechanism in our very simple program.

 Know that if we accidentally provide this Java program with anything besides an integer, the program will crash.

So what are conditional statements exactly? Well, conditional statements allow us to send our program down different paths, executing different lines of code depending on whether or not something is true or not. In this chapter, we'll use conditional statements to print different responses to our user depending on the value of the input they give us. Specifically, we'll let them know whether the value they've given us is less than, greater than, or equal to the number 10. To start this process off, let's set up our output cases.

If our user provides us with input that is greater than 10, we print out MORE. If the user provides us with input that happens to be less than 10, we print out LESS. Of course, if we run this program right now, it will simply print out MORE or LESS, both the lines. What we need to do is use conditional statements to make sure that only one of these two lines executes in any program run, and that the proper line executes of course. You may have noticed that the default project NetBeans created for us divides our code into segments that have curly brackets around them.

We can further divide our code into segments using brackets of our own. Convention dictates that once we've created a new set of brackets, a new segment of code, we need to then add a tab before everything between the brackets to make our program more readable.

Using if statements

Once we've sectioned off our two `system.out.println` statements, we're now ready to provide cases that must be true if these statements are to run. To do this, we preface our new sections with the Java `if` statement, where `if` is a Java keyword and it's followed by two parentheses between which we put the statement to be evaluated. If Java determines that the statement we write between the parentheses is true, the code in the following brackets will execute. If Java determines that the statement is false, the code in the brackets will be completely skipped. Essentially, we're going to give this `if` statement two pieces of input. We're going to give it the variable `input`, which if you remember contains the integer value that we got from the user, and we're going to give it the explicit value `10`, which is what we're comparing it to. Java understands the greater than (>) and the less than (<) comparison operators. So, if we make this `if` statement `if(input > 10)`, then the `System.out.println` command (as seen in the following screenshot) will only run if the user has provided a value that's greater than 10:

```
if(input > 10)
    {
        System.out.println("MORE!");
    }
    {
        System.out.println("LESS!");
    }
```

Now, we need to provide an `if` statement to make sure that our program doesn't always print out LESS anyway.

We could use the less than operator to ask our program to print out LESS whenever the user provides input that is less than 10. This would be good in almost all cases, but if our user provides the input value 10, our program would print out nothing. To fix this, we can use the less than or equal to operator to ensure that our program always responds to the user input:

```
package conditionalstatements;

import java.util.*;

public class ConditionalStatements {

    public static void main(String[] args) {
        Scanner reader = new Scanner(System.in);
        System.out.println("Input now: ");
        int input =  reader.nextInt();
        if(input > 10)
        {
            System.out.println("MORE!");
        }
        if(input <= 10)
        {
            System.out.println("LESS");
        }
    }
}
```

Now, let's quickly run our program to make sure that it works.

There's a prompt for input in the InputStream window. Let's start by giving it a value that is greater than 10 and pressing the *Enter* key. We get the MORE response and not the LESS response; this is what we expected:

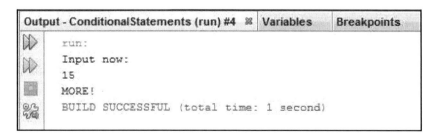

Our program doesn't loop, so we're going to have to run it again to test the LESS output, and this time let's give it the value 10, which should trigger our less than or equal to operator. Tada!

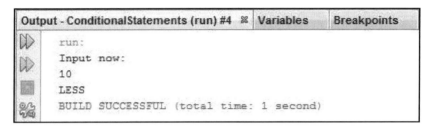

Using else statements

It turns out that there's a slightly easier way to write the preceding program. When we write a conditional statement or rather a pair of conditional statements in which we're always going to execute one of the two code blocks, it's probably a good time to make use of the else keyword. The else keyword must follow a bracketed if block, then it's followed by brackets of its own. The else statement will evaluate to true and execute the code between its brackets only if the code between the previous if brackets was not executed:

```
import java.util.*;

public class ConditionalStatements {

    public static void main(String[] args) {
        Scanner reader = new Scanner(System.in);
        System.out.println("Input now: ");
        int input =  reader.nextInt();
        if(input > 10)
        {
            System.out.println("MORE!");
        }
        else
        {
            System.out.println("LESS");
        }
    }
}
```

If we run this program, we will get the same results as we did before with one less bit of logic code to write:

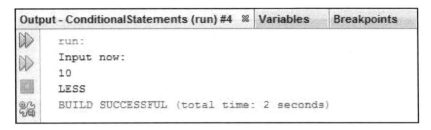

Let's end this topic with a brief run-through of what other operators we can use in our `if` statements, then we'll take a look at what to do if we need to compare items that are not primitives. In addition to the greater than and less than operators, we can also make use of the equality operator (==), which is true if the items on both the sides have the same value. Make sure when you use the equality operator, do not accidently use the assignment operator (=) instead:

```
if(input == 10)
```

In some instances, your program won't compile, but at other times it will compile and you'll get very weird results. If you'd like to use the opposite of the equality operator, you can use not equals (!=), which returns true if the two items do not have the same value:

```
if(input != 10)
```

 It's important that we do not attempt to use these equality operators when comparing instances of a class. We should only use them when we're working with primitives.

To show this, let's modify our program so that we could take `String` as user input. We'll see whether `String` is equivalent to the secret password code:

```
10          System.out.println("Input now: ");
11          String input = reader.next();
12
            if(input == "password")
```

If it is, it will print out YES; if not, it will print out NO. Now, NetBeans gives us a warning (as shown in the preceding screenshot); in fact, if we attempt to compare strings with some different operators, NetBeans would let us know that our program is probably not even going to compile. That's because Java does not expect us to compare instances of a class with these operators. Instead, classes should expose functions that allow us to compare them logically. Almost every object in Java has a few functions for this purpose. One of the most common ones is the equals() function that takes an object of the same type and lets us know whether they're equivalent. This function returns what's called a **Boolean type**, which is a primitive type of its own that can have a value of either true or false. Our if statement understands how to evaluate this Boolean type:

```
import java.util.*;

public class ConditionalStatements {

    public static void main(String[] args) {
        Scanner reader = new Scanner(System.in);
        System.out.println("Input now: ");
        String input =  reader.next();
        if(input.equals("password"))
        {
            System.out.println("YES");
        }
        else
        {
            System.out.println("NO");
        }
    }
}
```

Let's run our program quickly and start by inputting a bad string, then let's input password to see our program work:

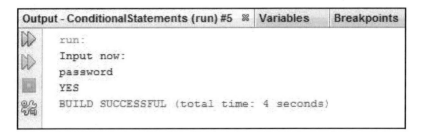

That's the basics of `if-else` statements. I would encourage you now to play with some of the comparison operators that we looked at and try nesting `if...else` statements within each other.

 As a very last note, you may sometimes see `if` statements without their following brackets. This is a valid syntax and is basically the equivalent of putting the entire statement on one line.

Complex conditionals

To begin with, let's write a very simple Java program. We'll start by importing `java.util` so that we can get some user input via a `Scanner` object, and we'll link this `Scanner` object with the `System.in` input string so we can use it in the console window.

Once we've done this, we're going to need to get some input from the user and store it, so let's create a new string and assign its value to whatever the user gives us. To keep things interesting, let's give ourselves two more String variables to work with. We'll call them sOne and sTwo; we'll assign the value of our first string variable to abc and the value of our second string variable to just z:

```
package complexconditionals;

import java.util.*;

public class ComplexConditionals {
    public static void main(String[] args) {
        Scanner reader = new Scanner (System.in);
        String input = reader.next();
        String sOne = "abc";
        String sTwo = "z";
    }
}
```

Because this topic is about conditional statements, we're probably going to need one of those, so let's create an `if...else` block. This is where we'll evaluate our conditional statement. We'll set ourselves up some output so we can see what's going on. If our conditional statement evaluates to true and we enter the following portion of the block, we'll simply print out TRUE:

```
if()
{
    System.out.println("TRUE");
```

```
    }
    else
    {
    }
```

If the conditional statement evaluates to false and we skip the previous `if` portion of the block and instead enter the `else` portion, we'll print out `FALSE`:

```
if()
{
    System.out.println("TRUE");
}
else
{
    System.out.println("FALSE");
}
```

The contains function

Now it's probably time to write our conditional statement. Let me introduce you to a new string function called the `contains` function:

```
if(input.contains())
```

The `contains` function takes as input a sequence of characters of which a string qualifies. As output, it gives us a Boolean value, which means it will either output `TRUE` or `FALSE`. So our `if` statement should understand the result of this function and evaluate to the same. To test our program, let's start by simply going through the following process.

We'll provide our `contains` function with the value stored in the `sOne` string which is `abc`:

```
package complexconditionals;

import java.util.*;

public class ComplexConditionals {
    public static void main(String[] args) {
        Scanner reader = new Scanner (System.in);
        String input = reader.next();
        String sOne = "abc";
        String sTwo = "z";
        if(input.contains(sOne))
        {
            System.out.println("TRUE");
        }
        else
```

```
        {
            System.out.println("FALSE");
        }
    }
}
```

So, if we run our program and provide it with `abcdefg` which contains within it the `abc` string, we get the `TRUE` result. This is because `input.contains` evaluates to true and we enter the `if` portion of our `if...else` block:

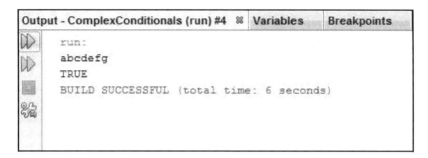

If we were to run and provide some gibberish that does not contain the `abc` string, we could instead enter the `else` statement of the block and return `FALSE`:

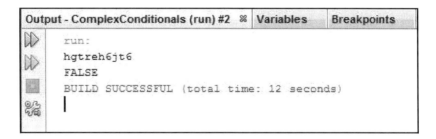

Nothing too crazy there. But, let's say we want to make our program a little more complicated. Let's look at this in the next section.

Complex conditional statements

What if we want to check and see whether our input string contains both the strings, namely sOne and sTwo? There's a couple of ways to do this, and we'll take a look at some others. But probably, the simplest way for our purposes is to use a **complex** conditional on the if(input.contains(sOne)) line. Java allows us to evaluate multiple true or false statements, or Boolean objects, at once using the && or the | conditional operator. The && operator gives us a true result when all conditionals compared with the && operator have evaluated to true. The | operator gives us a true result when any of the conditionals compared with the | operator evaluate to true. In our case, we want to know whether our input string contains both the contents of sOne and sTwo, so we're going to use the && operator. This operator works by simply providing two conditional statements on either side of it. So, we're going to run our input.contains function on both sOne and sTwo. If both these functions on either side of the && operator, which is expressed as (if(input.contains (sOne) && input.contains (sTwo)), evaluate to true, our conditional statement will be true as well:

```
package complexconditionals;

import java.util.*;

public class ComplexConditionals {
    public static void main(String[] args) {
        Scanner reader = new Scanner (System.in);
        String input = reader.next();
        String sOne = "abc";
        String sTwo = "z";
        if(input.contains(sOne))
        {
            System.out.println("TRUE");
        }
        else
        {
            System.out.println("FALSE");
        }
    }
}
```

Let's run our program. The `abcz` string should evaluate to true in both cases, and when we press *Enter* key, we see that this is in fact the case:

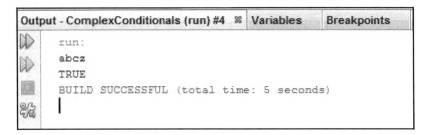

If we were to provide only the valid string `z`, we would get a false result because our `&&` operator would evaluate false and true, which evaluates to false. If we were to use the `|` operator, this would be the string:

```
if(input.contains(sOne) || input.contains(sTwo))
```

The following is the output of the preceding code:

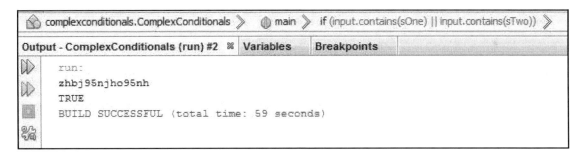

This would in fact give us a true result because we only need one of these functions to return true now. Boolean logic can get pretty crazy pretty quick. For example, we can put the `&& false` statement at the end of our Boolean condition, namely `if(input.contains(sOne) || input.contains(sTwo) && false)`. The `true` and `false` code terms in Java are keywords; in fact, they're explicit values, just like a number or a single character would be. The `true` keyword evaluates to true and the `false` keyword evaluates to false.

Any single conditional statement that ends with `false` will always evaluate as a whole to false:

```
if(input.contains(sOne) && false)
```

Curiously though, if we return to our previous original statement and run the following program providing it with the most valid possible input, we're going to get the true result:

```java
package complexconditionals;
import java.util.*;
public class ComplexConditionals {
    public static void main(String[] args) {
        Scanner reader = new Scanner(System.in);
        String input = reader.next();
        String sOne = "abc";
        String sTwo = "z";
        if(input.contains(sOne) || input.contains(sTwo) && false)
        {
            System.out.println("TRUE");
        }
        else
        {
            System.out.println("FALSE");
        }
    }
}
```

Following is the output of the preceding code:

That's interesting because if Java had chosen to evaluate the `if(input.contains(sOne) || input.contains(sTwo))` statement first and then the `&& false` statement, we would have gotten a false result; instead, Java seems to have chosen to evaluate the `(input.contains(sTwo) && false)` statement first and then the `||` statement, that is, `(input.contains(sOne) ||)`. This can make things confusing pretty quick.

Fortunately, just like in algebra, we can ask Java to do operations in a specific order. We do this by surrounding the blocks of our code with parentheses. Blocks of code within parentheses will evaluate before Java leaves the parentheses to evaluate against something else:

```
if((input.contains(sOne) || input.contains(sTwo)) && false)
```

So, after we've surrounded our || statement with parentheses, we'll compute the || statement and then end that result with false:

```
package complexconditionals;
import java.util.*;
public class ComplexConditionals {
    public static void main(String[] args) {
        Scanner reader = new Scanner(System.in);
        String input = reader.next();
        String sOne = "abc";
        String sTwo = "z";
        if((input.contains(sOne) || input.contains(sTwo)) && false)
        {
            System.out.println("TRUE");
        }
        else
        {
            System.out.println("FALSE");
        }
    }
}
```

We will now see that our preceding program always evaluates to false here:

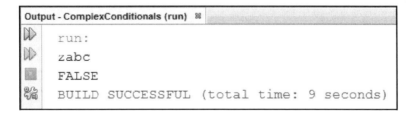

So complex conditionals can get pretty complicated pretty quick. If we come across something like this if statement in code, especially if it's code that we haven't written, it can take us a good while to figure out exactly what's going on.

The boolean variable

To help us with what we discussed in the preceding section, we have the `boolean` variable:

```
boolean bool = true;
```

In the preceding line of code, `boolean` is a primitive type in Java, and a variable of the `boolean` type can have only one of the two values: it can be either `true` or `false`. We can set the value of our Boolean variables to be any conditional statement. So, if we wanted to simplify how our code looks in the actual `if` statement, we could go ahead and store these Boolean values:

```
boolean bool1 = input.contains(sOne);
boolean bool2 = input.contains(sTwo);
```

We need to do this before we actually evaluate the `if` statement, keeping everything much more compact and readable:

```
if((bool1 || bool2) && false)
```

 Remember that the name of the game is keeping our code as simple and readable as possible. A really long conditional might feel great to write, but oftentimes, there's a more elegant solution.

That's the nuts and bolts of complex conditionals in Java.

Switch, case, and break

In this section, we're going to take a look at the `switch` statement, which is another way that we can modify the control flow of our program.

To begin, let's create a new project in NetBeans. At my end at least, I'm going to get rid of all these comments. To demonstrate the power of the `switch` statement, we're going to start by writing a program using only `if` blocks, then we'll convert the program to one that uses `switch` statements. The following are the steps for the program that uses only `if` blocks:

1. To begin, let's simply declare a variable x, (`int x =1;`), and here is our goal: If the value of x is 1, 2, or 3, we'd like to print out the responses RED, BLUE, or GREEN, respectively. If x is not one of those numbers, we'll just print out a default response.

2. Doing this with `if` blocks is pretty straightforward, if not a little tedious:

```
if(x == 1)
{
System.out.println("RED")
}
```

Then, we'll pretty much just copy and paste this block of code and modify it for the blue and green cases:

```
int x=1;
if(x==1)
{
    System.out.println("RED");
}
if(x==2)
{
    System.out.println("BLUE");
}
if(x==3)
{
    System.out.println("GREEN");
}
```

3. For our default case, we simply want to check that x is not equal to 1, x is not equal to 2, and x is not equal to 3:

```
if((x != 1) && (x != 2) && (x != 3))
{
    System.out.println("NONE");
}
```

Let's give our program a very quick run-through:

```
package switcher;

public class Switcher {
    public static void main(String[] args) {
        int x=1;
        if(x==1)
        {
            System.out.println("RED");
        }
        if(x==2)
        {
            System.out.println("BLUE");
        }
        if(x==3)
```

```
        {
            System.out.println("GREEN");
        }
    }
}
```

The following is the screenshot of the expected results:

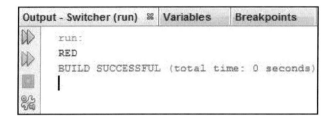

This is a simplified version of something we might logically find ourselves doing in the course of writing a bigger program. While we put together this at a pretty decent clip, it's easy to see how this problem would become extremely unwieldy if we were dealing with many possible cases of x. And, it's also pretty difficult for someone to read and figure out what's going on here. The solution, as you've probably guessed, is to use a switch statement to control our program's flow instead.

Program using switch, case, and break

When we want to execute different lines or blocks of code depending on the value of an individual variable, the switch statement is extremely effective. Now let's rewrite our series of if blocks using a switch statement instead. The syntax is explained in the following steps:

1. We first declare that we're going to use a switch statement, switch being a reserved keyword in Java. Then, we provide the name of the variable that we'd like the switch statement to act on, in this case x because we're going to execute different blocks of code depending on the value of x:

```
package switcher;

public class Switcher {
    public static void main(String[] args) {
        int x=1;

        switch(x)
        {
```

```
        }
      }
    }
```

Then, just like using an `if` or `else` statement, we're going to create a new segment of code using two brackets.

2. Now, instead of creating a series of unwieldy `if` blocks, we create separate blocks in our `switch` statements using the `case` keyword. After each `case` keyword, we give a prescribed value, and the following code will execute if the value of `x` matches with the value of the `case` keyword.

   So, just like when we were doing our `if` blocks, if the value of `x` is 1, we'd like to print out RED. Writing separate cases for each of the possible values now becomes much cleaner and easier to read.

3. The `switch` statements also have a special case, the `default` case, which we pretty much always put at the end of a `switch` statement.

   This case will only execute if none of the other cases have executed, and it means that we don't have to write that complicated Boolean logic for our last `if` block:

```
package switcher;

public class Switcher {
    public static void main(String[] args) {
        int x=7;
        switch(x)
        {
            case 1: case 5: case 7:
                System.out.println("RED");
            case 2:
                System.out.println("BLUE");
            case 3:
                System.out.println("GREEN");
            default:
                System.out.println("NONE");
        }
    }
}
```

If we run the preceding program, we're actually going to see every possible output execute. That's because we've forgotten to do something very important:

The `switch` statements allow us to create complicated logic trees because once a case starts executing, it will continue to execute even through the next cases in the queue. Because we're writing a very simple program where we only want a single case to execute, we need to explicitly end the execution once we enter a case and finish the code.

4. We can do that with the `break` keyword, which exists on a line of code all by itself and simply steps us up and out of the case that we're in:

```
package switcher;

public class Switcher {
    public static void main(String[] args) {
        int x=1;
        switch(x)
        {
            case 1:
                System.out.println("RED");
                break;
            case 2:
                System.out.println("BLUE");
                break;
            case 3:
                System.out.println("GREEN");
                break;
            default:
                System.out.println("NONE");
        }
    }
}
```

Now if we run our program, we'll see the expected results:

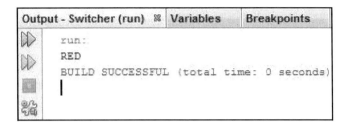

5. In addition to falling through from one case to another, we can increase the complexity and the power of our switch statements by adding multiple cases to a single line. Because the cases freely fall through to each other, doing something like case 1: case 5: case; means that the following block of code will execute if we provide one of these numbers: 1, 5, or 7. So there's the quick and easy way of switch statements:

```
package switcher;

public class Switcher {
    public static void main(String[] args) {
        int x=7;
        switch(x)
        {
            case 1: case 5: case 7:
                System.out.println("RED");
                break;
            case 2:
                System.out.println("BLUE");
                break;
            case 3:
                System.out.println("GREEN");
                break;
            default:
                System.out.println("NONE");
        }
    }
}
```

The following is the output of the preceding code:

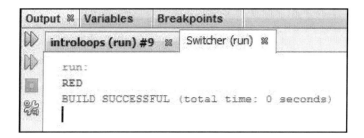

 Switch statements essentially compare the variable or explicit value we're switching and the cases using the equality (==) operator. If elements cannot be compared with the equality operator, the switch statement will not work properly.

As of Java SE v7, you can compare strings with the equality operator so you can use them in switch statements. This was not always the case, and it's still a good idea to avoid using strings with the equality operator in your switch statements. This is because it destroys the backwards compatibility of the code you're writing.

While and do...while loops

Welcome to the introductory lesson on loops. At the end of this section, we'll have command over Java's while and do...while loops. I'm pretty excited about this because loops allow us to execute a block of Java code over and over again as many times as we see fit. This is a pretty cool step in our learning process because the ability to perform small tasks many times in rapid succession is one of the things that makes computers better at certain tasks than humans are:

1. To begin this topic, let's create a new NetBeans project, enter the main method, and simply declare an integer and give it a value. We can choose any positive value. We're going to ask our program to print out the phrase Hello World a number of times equal to the value of our integer.

2. To do this, we'll employ a `while` loop. The `while` loop syntax looks a lot like we're writing an `if` statement. We begin with the reserved `while` keyword and follow it by two parentheses; inside these, we're eventually going to place a conditional statement. Just like it was an `if` statement, the following block of code will only execute if our program reaches our `while` loop and evaluates its conditional statement to true:

```
package introtoloops;

public class IntroToLoops {
    public static void main(String[] args) {
        int i=5;
        while ()
        {
        }
    }
}
```

What separates `while` loops from `if` statements, however, is that when the end of the `while` loop's block of code is reached, our program will basically jump back and execute this line of code again, evaluating the conditional statement and reentering the while loop's block of code if the conditional statement is still true.

Let's start off by setting up the logic for our `while` loop. We have the number of times we would like our loop to execute stored in the value of the integer i, but we're going to need a way to communicate this to our loop. Well, any loop that is not going to run infinite times is going to need to make some control flow changes within the content of the loop. In our case, let's change the state of our program each time the loop runs by decreasing the value of i so that when i reaches 0, we would have ran the loop five times.

3. If that's the case, it means that we only want our loop to execute when the value of `i` is greater than `0`. Let's pause and quickly take a look at this line of code. Here `i = i -1` is a perfectly valid statement, but there's a shortcut we can use that's a little faster and easier to read. We can use `i--` to decrement the value of an integer variable by one. Once we've set this up, the only thing left to do is place the functional code inside of our loop; that's simply a `println` statement that says `Hello world`:

```
package introtoloops;

public class IntroToLoops {
    public static void main(String[] args) {
```

```
int i=5;
while (i>0)
{
    System.out.println("Hello world");
    i--;
}
}
}
```

4. Now, let's run our program and see what happens:

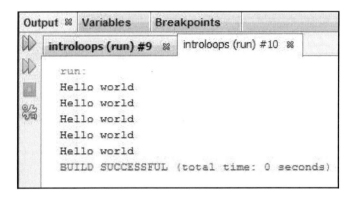

There we go, five `Hello world` instances printed to our console window, just as we intended.

While loops

Often, we allow small programs, such as the ones we're writing here, to end when there's simply no more code for them to execute. However, while we're working with loops, we're probably going to make the mistake of accidentally creating an infinite `while` loop and running a program that has no end:

```
package introtoloops;

public class IntroToLoops {
    public static void main(String[] args) {
        int i=5;
        while (i>0)
        {
            System.out.println("Hello world");
        }
    }
}
```

When this happens, we'll need to turn our program off manually. In NetBeans, there's a handy little feature called Stop at the left-hand side of the output window:

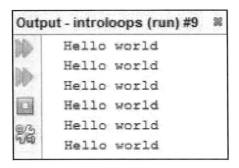

If we're running a program through a Command Prompt, *Ctrl + C* is the common command to cancel the execution of a program. Now that we have a grasp of the basic `while` loop syntax, let's try something a little more complicated and much more dynamic:

1. The program I have in mind is going to need some user input, so let's import `java.util` and set up a new `Scanner` object:

```
public class IntroToLoops {
    public static void main(String[] args) {
        Scanner reader = new Scanner(System.in);
```

2. Rather than gathering user input right away though, we're going to collect new user input every time our `while` loop successfully executes:

```
while(i > 0) {
    reader.nextLine();
    System.out.println("Hello world");
}
```

3. Each time we gather this input, we're going to need somewhere to store it, so let's create a new string whose purpose will be to store the value of the newly acquired input:

```
public class IntroToloops {
    public static void main(String[] args) {
        Scanner reader = new Scanner(System.in);
        String input;
        int i=5;
        while(i>0) {
            input= reader.nextLine();
            System.out.println("Hello world");
```

```
            }
         }
      }
```

This `input` variable's value will change a number of times throughout the execution of our program because at the beginning of every `while` loop, we'll be assigning it a new value. If we were to simply execute this program, it wouldn't be very interesting for us, the user, because the old values of our input string would constantly be lost when we assign it a new value.

4. So, let's create another string whose purpose is to store all the concatenated values that we've gotten from the user. Then, at the end of our program, we'll print out the value of this string so that the user can see we've been storing their input:

```
public class IntroToloops {
    public static void main(String[] args) {
        Scanner reader = new Scanner(System.in);
        String input;
        String all = "";
        int i=5;
        while(i>0) {
            input = reader.nextLine();
        }
        System.out.println(all);
    }
}
```

5. Add the value of the input to the all string on the line illustrated here:

```
while(i>0) {
    input = reader.nextLine();
    all =
}
```

There's a couple of things we can do. We can add strings with the addition operator just fine. So the `all = all + input` statement, with `all` and `input` being strings, and the plus sign are perfectly valid. However, when we add something to itself and work with a primitive or a type that can act like a primitive as a string can, we can also use the `+=` operator, which performs the same function. Also, we cannot forget to reimplement the decrement of the integer value `i` so that our program doesn't run infinitely:

```
package introtoloops;
import java.util.*;
public class IntroToLoops {
    public static void main(String[] args) {
        Scanner reader = new Scanner(System.in);
        String input;
        String all = "";
        int i=5;
        while (i>0) {
            input = reader.nextLine();
            all += input;
            i--;
        }
        System.out.println(all);
    }
}
```

Now, if we run this program and provide five strings of input, we get the output as shown in the following screenshot:

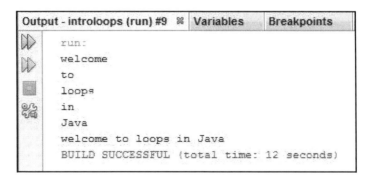

We'll see them all spit back out at us as expected, which is pretty cool, but I've got bigger plans for this program.

Actually, if we'd only wanted to write the program we have right here, a `for` loop, which we'll learn later, might have been completely appropriate. But for what we're about to do, `while` and `do...while` loops are pretty necessary. What I'd like to do is get rid of our counting variable in this program. Instead, we're going to allow the user to tell us when to stop executing our program.

When the user sets the value of the input to the `STOP` string, in all capital letters, we'll quit executing our `while` loop and print out all the strings they've given us so far. So, we only want this `while` loop to run while the value of the input is not the `STOP` value. You'll notice that we'll get a precompiled error as shown in the following screenshot:

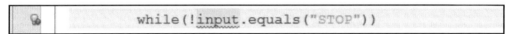

```
while (!input.equals("STOP"))
```

We'll get a full-on compiler error if we do attempt to run our program. That's because our program knows that when we attempt to execute this conditional statement for the first time, the value of the input will not have been set. Even though the nonexistent value of the input is not equivalent to `STOP`, it's a very bad form. In the case of a string here, which is not a primitive, it is not possible for our computer to access any of its methods before it's given any value at all.

One inelegant solution here would be to give the input a start value, like we did with `all`, but there's a better way. Once our loop has executed for the first time, we know that the input will have a proper value given by the user, which may or may not be `STOP`.

The do...while loops

What if instead of checking our conditional at the beginning of our loop, we check it at the end? This is in fact an option. The `do...while` loops operate just like `while` loops, but the first time they run, they won't check to see whether a conditional is true; they'll simply run through and check their conditional statement at the end. We do need to put a semicolon at the end of a conditional statement on the back of the `do...while` loop. I just mentioned this because I always forget it. Now, if we run our program, we can give any number of strings and then type in the `STOP` string to see everything we've typed so far and printed out to the screen:

```
public static void main(String[] args) {
    Scanner reader = new Scanner(System.in);
```

```
    String input;
    String all = "";
    int i=5;

    do
    {
        input = reader.nextLine();
        all += input;
        i--;
    } while(!input.equals("STOP"));
    System.out.println(all);
}
```

The following is the output of the preceding code:

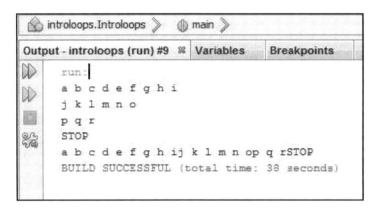

As a last little note, with just about anything followed by its own code block, you'll see a syntax like this, where you will have a keyword and may be a conditional statement and then brackets on the following lines; alternatively, you might see the brackets start on the same line as the keyword and the conditional statement. Both the methods are completely valid, and in fact, the brackets starting on the same line as the keyword is probably quickly becoming more common.

I encourage you to play around with the program we've written. Try executing loops that you think will push the boundaries of how much information a string can hold, or play around with loops that present an enormous amount of information to the screen. This is stuff that computers do that we simply couldn't with pencil and paper, so it's pretty neat.

For loops

In this section, we're going to take a quick look at `for` loops. We use `for` loops to solve a common problem in Java in a very semantically elegant manner. These loops are appropriate when we need to iterate a variable to count how many times we've looped.

To start off, I've written a very basic program using a `while` loop; it prints the values 1 through 100 to the window on our screen. Once you've hashed out in your mind how this `while` loop is working, we'll write the same loop with a `for` loop so that we could see how the `for` loop is more elegant in this particular instance. Let's comment out our `while` loop so that we can still see it as shown in the following screenshot without having it execute any of its code and begin writing our `for` loop instead :

The basic syntax of a `for` loop looks very similar to that of a `while` loop. We have the reserved keyword, two parentheses in which we'll put some information that the loop needs, and the code block that we're going to loop through. Unlike a `while` loop, which just takes a conditional statement between these parentheses, we're going to provide our `for` loop with a bunch of information. Because the `for` loop is designed to handle a specific case, once we give it all this information, it will know exactly what to do with it. This alleviates the need for us to handle code outside of the loop and manually increment or decrement it inside of the loop. It keeps the functional bit of our code, our `println` statement, and in more complicated programs, the more complicated information that may be inside the `for` loop, more isolated.

Our typical `for` loop takes three pieces of input. These are as follows:

1. First, we need to declare the variable that we're going to be incrementing or decrementing to count the number of times we've looped. In this case, we'll use an integer `i` and give it a initial value of `1`. We follow this initial statement with a semicolon. This is not a function call; it's special syntax for the `for` loop.

2. The second piece of information the special syntax requires is the conditional statement that we need to evaluate each time we're going to restart the loop. If this conditional statement is ever not true, then our `for` loop ends and we continue resuming our code after the `for` loop block. In this case, our conditional statement will be the same as it was for the `while` loop. We want our last iteration of the `for` loop to be when `i` is equal to `100`, that is, when we print out `100`. Once `i` is no longer less than or equal to 100, it's time to exit our `for` loop.

3. Just as the first piece of information we specially gave the `for` loop saved us from having to handle a variable outside the scope of our loop, the last piece of information we will give the `for` loop takes the place of us having to manually increment or decrement our counter inside the scope of the loop. This is the special modification code, and whatever we provide the `for` loop here will run at the end of every loop. In this case, we'd just like to increment the value of `i` at the end of each looping through. I think you'll agree that this program is much cleaner than our `while` loop:

```
package forloops;

public class Forloops {
    public static void main(String[] args) {
    /*  int i=1;
        while(i <= 100) {
            System.out.println(i);
            i++;
        }*/
        for(int i=1; i<=100; i++)
        {
            System.out.println(i);
        }
    }
}
```

Now, let's just check that it performs the same task of printing the value of 1 to 100 to our screen, as shown in the following screenshot:

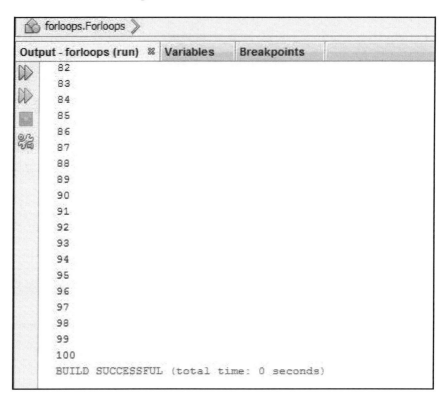

If this statement were to execute at the very beginning of our `for` loop, 0 would have been correct, but this executes at the end.

When we're working with large numbers and increments in Java or any programming language really, we call errors, like what we just ran into, **off-by-one error** (**OBOE**) errors. OBOE are those kinds of little logic mistakes that even experienced programmers can run into if they don't pay attention or just look the wrong way for an instance. Learning to recognize the symptoms of OBOE, for example, one more line outputted than expected, will allow us to track them down and find them much more efficiently.

Summary

In this chapter, we basically saw how to work with conditional `if...else` statements running through the complex conditionals using functions such as `contains`, `complex`, and `boolean`. We went through the intricacies of `switch`, `case`, and `break` with the help of programs; also, we dived deep into how to use the loop functionality using the `while`, `do...while`, and `for` loops.

In the next chapter, we'll look at something called a **data structure**.

4
Data Structures

In this chapter, we are going to learn some of the most important data structures in Java. We'll look at what arrays are and how they are useful when we need to work with sequences of variables. We'll write a program in NetBeans using arrays to understand how they work. This chapter will also walk us through the concept of multidimensional arrays. We'll write a program to create a chessboard using a two-dimensional array.

Next, this chapter will illustrate what ArrayLists are and how they provide increased functionality when compared to arrays. Finally, we'll look at the `Map` data structure and implement it in NetBeans.

More specifically, we'll cover the following topics:

- Arrays and their syntax
- An array example to print the English alphabet
- Multidimensional arrays
- A program to create a chessboard using a 2D array
- ArrayList and its example
- Maps and their implementation in NetBeans

Working with arrays

In this section we're going to learn about Java arrays. Arrays are Java's most basic and commonly used data structure. Data structures are tools that allow us to store and access sequences of information rather than using individual variables. Variables are great when we have one specific piece of information that we need in our local programming space, but data structures are used when we want to store large or complicated sets or series of information. We're going to start this section with some visual learning modes, and then we'll jump into our NetBeans IDE to write some actual Java code and make use of arrays.

Declaring and initializing an array

Let's begin by taking a look at the syntax behind declaring and initializing an array in Java. The following line of code will cause an array to come into being with enough space to hold seven characters:

```
char[] arrayVar = new char[7];
```

To the left of our assignment operator (=), the syntax looks pretty familiar, not unlike the syntax we would use when declaring any other primitive or object. We begin by telling Java what type of element we're going to declare here. In this case, we're declaring a character array. The empty square brackets lets Java know that rather than creating a single character variable, we'd like to declare an array type variable because our array is a variable just like any other. We'll access the elements of the array through the array's variable name itself, not through the individual variable names of the elements, which we don't need to assign as they are being stored in an array. Once we've told Java what type of array we're going to create, we give our array variable a name. I've called this one arrayVar.

To the right of our equality operator, things look a little different. You may have seen the new keyword used in the past when we needed to create a new instance of an object, not a primitive element. When we create a primitive element in Java, Java knows exactly how much memory space is needed to store the primitive element, no matter what its value is. However, objects and arrays can have many different size requirements. Because a single array variable can be assigned to arrays of different lengths, we're going to need to tell Java how much memory to put aside for each of these different length arrays when we create them. When creating an object or an array, therefore, we use the new keyword to tell Java that it should set aside memory space to place what we're about to cause to come into being, and that thing is a character array of length seven.

After declaring and initializing our seven character array, what exists in our program's local memory is something like the following:

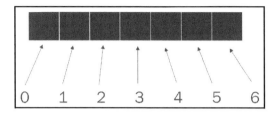

Our array is basically a block of memory large enough to store seven individual characters.

Assigning values to an array

The location of our array is accessed by our program when we call the `arrayVar` variable. This allows us to run lines of code such as the following:

```
arrayVar[2] = 'c';
```

Our `arrayVar` variable gives us access, essentially, to seven different character variables. When we don't want to assign a new array to our `arrayVar` variable, we're probably going to be accessing these character variables as individuals. We do this simply using the variable name of `arrayVar`, following it with square brackets, which include the index of the individual character we'd like to access. Remember, when our computers count indexes, they almost always begin with **0**. So, in Java, our seven-character array has these indexes: **0, 1, 2, 3, 4, 5**, and **6**. If we execute the preceding line of code while setting the value of index 2 in our `arrayVar` to c, we will take the third block of memory and assign its value to the character c, as shown in the following diagram:

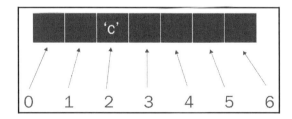

Sometimes when we declare an array, we just want to go ahead and assign values to all of its memory blocks right there in the code explicitly. When we want to do this, rather than using the `new` keyword and having our computer space out the new memory space by telling it how long the array is, we can explicitly declare an array, like we explicitly declare a primitive type. For example, we would do this for our `arrayVar` variable with the following code:

```
arrayVar = {'a', 'b', 'c', 'd', 'e', 'f', 'g'};
```

The preceding statement will create an array of length seven simply because seven elements are declared, and of course, it will map the values accordingly:

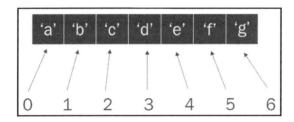

Now, let's jump into some Java code and put arrays to work.

Array example in NetBeans

Alright, I think it's time to employ our newfound knowledge and write a computer program. Arrays allow us to manipulate amounts of information that would be unwieldy to deal with at the individual element level. So, we're going to jump right into hard-hitting stuff and create a cool computer program. Arrays are a big logic step, and if you haven't worked with something like them before, it can take a little time to wrap your head around them. The good news is if you make it through arrays in Java, you're probably going to be just fine with anything else the language can throw at you.

The program I would like to write will print the English alphabet to our screen. We could, of course, do all of this by ourselves by just doing something along the lines of the following code:

```
System.out.println("abcdefg");
```

However, employing this is pretty mind-numbing and it's not going to teach us much. Instead, the program that we're going to write is going to learn, store, and print out the English alphabet.

To do this, we're going to need to employ our newfound knowledge of arrays, our existing knowledge of how characters work and mapping integer values on an ASCII table, and a single `for` loop.

Creating an array

Let's begin our programming by declaring and initializing a character array in which to store the characters of the English language. So, we tell Java that we're going to need a variable to point to an array of characters. I'll call this variable `alpha`. Then we're going to ask Java to set aside memory space by using the `new` keyword for `26` characters, because the English language has 26 letters:

```
char[] alpha = new char[26];
```

Now, if you remember, character values can also map to integer values. To find these, we will look for an ASCII table. (You can access the ASCII table at `www.asciitable.com`.)

Dec	Hx	Oct	Char		Dec	Hx	Oct	Html	Chr	Dec	Hx	Oct	Html	Chr	Dec	Hx	Oct	Html	Chr
0	0	000	NUL	(null)	32	20	040	&#32;	Space	64	40	100	&#64;	@	96	60	140	&#96;	`
1	1	001	SOH	(start of heading)	33	21	041	&#33;	!	65	41	101	&#65;	A	97	61	141	&#97;	a
2	2	002	STX	(start of text)	34	22	042	"	"	66	42	102	&#66;	B	98	62	142	&#98;	b
3	3	003	ETX	(end of text)	35	23	043	&#35;	#	67	43	103	&#67;	C	99	63	143	&#99;	c
4	4	004	EOT	(end of transmission)	36	24	044	&#36;	$	68	44	104	&#68;	D	100	64	144	&#100;	d
5	5	005	ENQ	(enquiry)	37	25	045	&#37;	%	69	45	105	&#69;	E	101	65	145	&#101;	e
6	6	006	ACK	(acknowledge)	38	26	046	&	&	70	46	106	&#70;	F	102	66	146	&#102;	f
7	7	007	BEL	(bell)	39	27	047	'	'	71	47	107	&#71;	G	103	67	147	&#103;	g
8	8	010	BS	(backspace)	40	28	050	&#40;	(	72	48	110	&#72;	H	104	68	150	&#104;	h
9	9	011	TAB	(horizontal tab)	41	29	051	&#41;	)	73	49	111	&#73;	I	105	69	151	&#105;	i
10	A	012	LF	(NL line feed, new line)	42	2A	052	&#42;	*	74	4A	112	&#74;	J	106	6A	152	&#106;	j
11	B	013	VT	(vertical tab)	43	2B	053	&#43;	+	75	4B	113	&#75;	K	107	6B	153	&#107;	k
12	C	014	FF	(NP form feed, new page)	44	2C	054	&#44;	,	76	4C	114	&#76;	L	108	6C	154	&#108;	l
13	D	015	CR	(carriage return)	45	2D	055	&#45;	-	77	4D	115	&#77;	M	109	6D	155	&#109;	m
14	E	016	SO	(shift out)	46	2E	056	&#46;	.	78	4E	116	&#78;	N	110	6E	156	&#110;	n
15	F	017	SI	(shift in)	47	2F	057	&#47;	/	79	4F	117	&#79;	O	111	6F	157	&#111;	o
16	10	020	DLE	(data link escape)	48	30	060	&#48;	0	80	50	120	&#80;	P	112	70	160	&#112;	p
17	11	021	DC1	(device control 1)	49	31	061	&#49;	1	81	51	121	&#81;	Q	113	71	161	&#113;	q
18	12	022	DC2	(device control 2)	50	32	062	&#50;	2	82	52	122	&#82;	R	114	72	162	&#114;	r
19	13	023	DC3	(device control 3)	51	33	063	&#51;	3	83	53	123	&#83;	S	115	73	163	&#115;	s
20	14	024	DC4	(device control 4)	52	34	064	&#52;	4	84	54	124	&#84;	T	116	74	164	&#116;	t
21	15	025	NAK	(negative acknowledge)	53	35	065	&#53;	5	85	55	125	&#85;	U	117	75	165	&#117;	u
22	16	026	SYN	(synchronous idle)	54	36	066	&#54;	6	86	56	126	&#86;	V	118	76	166	&#118;	v
23	17	027	ETB	(end of trans. block)	55	37	067	&#55;	7	87	57	127	&#87;	W	119	77	167	&#119;	w
24	18	030	CAN	(cancel)	56	38	070	&#56;	8	88	58	130	&#88;	X	120	78	170	&#120;	x
25	19	031	EM	(end of medium)	57	39	071	&#57;	9	89	59	131	&#89;	Y	121	79	171	&#121;	y
26	1A	032	SUB	(substitute)	58	3A	072	&#58;	:	90	5A	132	&#90;	Z	122	7A	172	&#122;	z
27	1B	033	ESC	(escape)	59	3B	073	&#59;	;	91	5B	133	&#91;	[	123	7B	173	&#123;	{
28	1C	034	FS	(file separator)	60	3C	074	&#60;	<	92	5C	134	&#92;	\	124	7C	174	&#124;	|
29	1D	035	GS	(group separator)	61	3D	075	&#61;	=	93	5D	135	&#93;	]	125	7D	175	&#125;	}
30	1E	036	RS	(record separator)	62	3E	076	&#62;	>	94	5E	136	&#94;	^	126	7E	176	&#126;	~
31	1F	037	US	(unit separator)	63	3F	077	&#63;	?	95	5F	137	&#95;	_	127	7F	177	&#127;	DEL

The value we're looking for is **97**, the integer value of a lowercase **a**, which is the first character in the English language. So let's create a little comment in our program and store the value `97` for later use:

```
package alphabet;

public class Alphabet {
    public static void main(String[] args) {
        // 97
        char[] alpha = new char[26];
    }
}
```

Creating a for loop

Now let's begin creating our `for` loop. Our `for` loop is going to run 26 times; each time it runs, it will take the next character in the English alphabet and place it in our character array: `alpha`.

To make sure our `for` loop runs exactly 26 times, we should declare a counting variable, say `i`, and set it to 0, that is, (i=0). Next, let's say that our `for` loop should continue to run as long as the value of our counting variable is less than 26, that is, it should take values between 0 and 25 (i<26). Lastly, every time our `for` loop runs, we need to increase the value of our counting variable by one so that it goes up each time, and after 26 iterations, the i<26 statement will no longer be true and our loop will stop at (i++):

```
for(int i = 0; i < 26; i++)
{

}
```

Now, inside our `for` loop, we're going to assign values to the spaces in our character array one by one. To access one of these spaces, we will use the name of the variable assigned to our array, that is, `alpha`, followed by a number (or index) within square brackets to tell Java which character in our array we would like to assign a value to.

The index of our array should be different each time we run through the loop. This is the beauty of `for` loops. By starting our counting variable i at 0, we can use it to map to the index of our array. That is, we can use `alpha[i]` to access elements of the array one by one. Our counting variable's value, as our loop runs, will range from 0 to 25. The index values of our array (because computers start counting at zero) also ranges from 0 to 25.

So, what value do we assign to each character so that our computer will learn the alphabet? Well, I like to think of it this way: when we run through the loop for the first time, the value of the first element of our array, when i is 0, should be 97, which is the integer value of the character **a**. Now, when we should assign 97+i as the value of each character in our array. When we run through our loop the second time, i is incremented by one, and we'll be assigning the value 97 + 1, or **98**, which is the integer value of the character **b**:

```
for(int i = 0; i < 26; i++)
{
    alpha[i] = (char)(97 + i);
}
```

In this instance, Java is asking us to explicitly let it know that we would like to cast this integer value to a character and then store it.

Printing the alphabet

Now, to finish off our program, all we need to do is print out our alpha array. To do this, let's make use of a nifty function in an always accessible object called Arrays. The Arrays.toString() function will convert a single dimension array, which is the kind of array that we've created, that is capable of being converted into a string:

```
public class Alphabet {
    public static void main(String[] args) {
        //97
        char[] alpha = new char[26];
        for(int i = 0; i < 26; i++)
        {
            alpha[i] = (char)(97 + i);
        }
        System.out.println(Arrays.toString(alpha));
    }
}
```

Now, if we run our program, we'll see Java's representation of the English alphabet in array form:

Output - Alphabet (run) ✕	Variables	Breakpoints	

```
run:
[a, b, c, d, e, f, g, h, i, j, k, l, m, n, o, p, q, r, s, t, u, v, w, x, y, z]
BUILD SUCCESSFUL (total time: 0 seconds)
```

If you have followed along with this, you should give yourself a solid pat on the back. That's some heavy lifting we just did.

Default initialization of arrays in Java

Now, let's jump back into theory for the rest of this section. I misled you earlier when I led you to believe that our newly created arrays were filled with empty memory space. In fact, when we declare a new array of a primitive type, that is, characters, integers, Booleans, floats, and so on, Java fills it with default values. For example, our new array of seven characters was filled by seven space characters, that is, what you'd get if you pressed the spacebar on your keyboard:

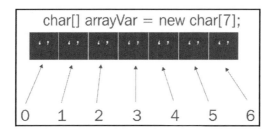

Similarly, an array of integers would be filled with seven zeros:

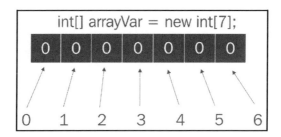

I recommend that you boot up a Java IDE and create some empty primitive arrays and print them out using `println` to see what the default values are.

Now we can create arrays of any object available to us. However, objects, unlike primitives, do not have default values that they set themselves to when they are initialized as part of an array. This is an important thing to realize.

Anything that we would need to use the `new` keyword to create will not default-initialize in an array.

Let's say for some reason we decided that we must have seven `Scanner` objects in an array. The following statement does not create seven `Scanner` objects for us; it simply sets aside memory space:

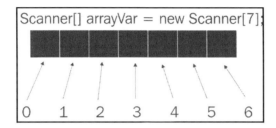

We can create `Scanner` objects and assign them to these memory spaces, but if we try and call one of these memory spaces and use a Scanner-specific function from it before we've assigned a `Scanner` object to the memory location, our program will crash. We'll get what's called `NullReferenceException`, which means that Java asked nothingness to behave like a `Scanner` object.

Multidimensional arrays

In Java, our most basic data structure is the array, which allows us to store sequences of light-typed information and access this through a single location in memory. Sometimes, however, arrays are unwieldy, and we want to use more strongly organized data structures so that they can be easier for humans to understand and write programs around. Oftentimes, what's appropriate here is a multi-dimensional array.

"Multidimensional array" is a pretty scary-sounding name, but in fact the concept behind it is very basic. The question is what happens if we create an array of arrays? The following line of code shows the syntax to do just that:

```
char[][] twoDimArr = new char[3][7];
```

This line of code will create a two-dimensional multidimensional array. You'll see it's very much like the syntax for simply creating an array of characters under normal circumstances, but in every instance where we reference the array variable now, Java is going to need two pieces of information (or two indexes). The preceding line of code will tell Java to create three arrays, each of which has enough space to store seven characters or three arrays of length seven:

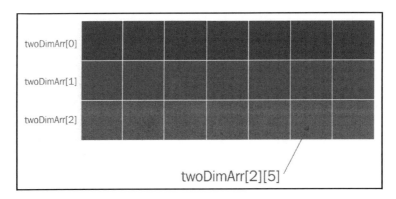

To cement our understanding of this concept, let's write a Java program that utilizes two-dimensional arrays.

A multidimensional array example in NetBeans

While we can use multidimensional arrays to store information in abstract manners, it will probably be easiest for us to learn them by representing an actual two-dimensional object with our two-dimensional array, in this case, a chessboard.

The classic chessboard is divided into black and white squares; it's eight squares in width and eight squares in height. The program we're about to write will store a virtual board in Java with the squares correctly labeled black and white. Then, at the end, we'll have it print this board out to us so that we can check whether we had written to our program correctly.

Creating a multidimensional array

Let's begin by simply declaring and initializing the array we're going to be using. We'll use an array of characters for this task, giving the white squares the character value of W and the black squares the character value of B. Since a chessboard is an eight by eight grid, we're going to want to declare a two-dimensional array of eight arrays, each of which should contain eight characters:

```
char[][] board = new char[8][8];
```

Let's make things even more difficult for someone to inadvertently break in by storing the dimensions of our board in a separate location. To do this, simply create a variable called boardDim, for board dimensions, assign it the value 8, and then reference it when we create our arrays. Arrays will be perfectly happy to use an integer in a variable to initialize themselves, letting us create dynamically linked arrays if our program calls for it. Now, if someone wants to go to this program and scale up our chessboard, they need to only change the value of boardDim:

```
int boardDim = 8;
char[][] board = new char[boardDim][boardDim];
```

In order to assign our squares their proper values, we're going to need to loop through this array to get to each individual node and give it the value we want it to have.

Using nested loops for multidimensional arrays

Loops and arrays get along great because arrays always know how long they are, but a single for loop doesn't allow us to meaningfully loop through a two-dimensional array. A for loop really just goes in one direction, and our two-dimensional arrays have two directions.

To solve this, we're going to make use of nested for loops, or a for loop within a for loop. Our outer for loop will loop through each array in turn, while the job of our inner for loop will be to loop through the nodes that those arrays contain.

A common practice when creating for loops is to use the integer variable i for your initial for loop, and then j, k, and so on for subsequent for loops. However, because we're creating a chessboard, which is an actual object, I'm going to choose the value y as our outer loop's counting variable. This is because what our loop is doing is iterating down the y-axis of our chessboard.

As mentioned earlier, `for` loops and arrays get along great because arrays know how long they are. We could simply state that we would like this loop to run eight times (y<8), but that's not good dynamic programming because if someone were to go along and change the size of our chessboard, our program would now break. We can write this loop such that it will work for a chessboard of any size.

To do this, rather than explicitly saying our loop should run eight times, we should have it start by asking our array how long it is. To ask an array its length, we just need to write `array.length` and this will returns an integer value. This is a two-dimensional array, so simply calling the name of the array to use the `length` variable will get us the length of the array's outermost segment. In this case, we're asking our two-dimensional array, "How many arrays do you have?" To finish off this `for` loop, we simply need to increment `y` after it runs each time. Thus, our outer `for` loop will loop through each array that our 2D array `board` contains:

```
for(int y = 0; y < board.length; y++)
{
}
```

Now, let's do something similar for our inner loop. Because this loop will be iterating through the individual elements of our rows, x for the *x*-axis seems an appropriate variable name to use. Because our array is currently the same length in both its segments, an eight by eight array, simply using the `board.length` statement, would work for now. But once again, it's not good dynamic programming. If someone was to go through and change the size of our board to be eight by ten, this program would no longer execute properly. Instead, at the beginning of this inner `for` loop's execution, let's ask the array that we've currently accessed through the outer loop how long it individually is. This once again makes our program robust and allows us to accommodate multiple sizes for our board:

```
for(int x = 0; x < board[y].length; x++)
{
}
```

OK, the next step in our program is to assign character values to each node in our array: `B` for black squares and `W` for white squares. Let's start off by writing the code to make all the squares white. Our double `for` loop will pass through each node in our two-dimensional array when it executes. So, each time we execute the code in our inner `for` loop, we're executing it in terms of one of the single two-dimensional array nodes. To get this node, we're going to need to ask our `board` array what is located at row `y` and column `x`, and then we'll change the value of that node:

```
for(int y = 0; y < board.length; y++)
    {
```

```
        for(int x = 0; x < board[y].length; x++)
        {
            board[y][x] = 'W';
        }
    }
```

Assigning different colors to our chessboard

The thing is, each time this inner loop executes, we're going to want a different value for the nodes so that we get a chessboard that is alternating white and black squares. To help us do this, let's add another variable to our program. It'll be a Boolean variable, and we'll just call it isWhite. If isWhite is true, then the next square we add will be white; if isWhite is false, the square will be black.

To code this out, let's use some if statements. Firstly, the if(isWhite) code term checks whether isWhite is true. If it is, then we put a W in our square. If isWhite is false, we put a B in the square for black. To check whether something is not true, we can invert any Boolean value with an exclamation point beforehand. This will work for Boolean or even conditional statements.

Next, we simply need to flip the value of isWhite. Well, using our knowledge of the exclamation point operator, which flips the value of Boolean, we can flip the value of isWhite from true to false or false to true by simply setting its value to the knotted version of itself:

```
    public static void main(String[] args) {
        int boardDim = 8;
        char[][] board = new char[boardDim][boardDim];
        boolean isWhite = true;
        for(int y = 0; y < board.length; y++)
        {
            for(int x = 0; x < board[y].length; x++)
            {
                if(isWhite) board[y][x] = 'W';
                if(!isWhite) board[y][x] = 'B';
                isWhite = !isWhite;
            }
        }
    }
```

Unfortunately, this program is not quite perfect. It turns out that if we do this, our chessboard is going to have every single row starting off with a white square, while a real chessboard alternates with every other row with a different colored square.

Fortunately, the outer loop runs once for each row of the chessboard. So if we were to simply add an extra flip to our isWhite Boolean value at the start of every row, we would get alternating row starts as well. If we do it like this, we need to start isWhite off as false because it's going to be immediately changed to true when the outer loop executes for the first time:

```java
public static void main(String[] args) {

    int boardDim = 8;
    char[][] board = new char[boardDim][boardDim];
    boolean isWhite = false;
    for(int y = 0; y < board.length; y++)
    {
        isWhite = !isWhite;
        for(int x = 0; x < board[y].length; x++)
        {
            if(isWhite) board[y][x] = 'W';
            if(!isWhite) board[y][x] = 'B';
            isWhite = !isWhite;
        }
    }
}
```

Printing the chessboard

If you've followed along thus far, let's go ahead and write the final bit of our program, a line of code to print out our chessboard to the screen. Actually, we're going to need a bit more than a line of code. We can use the println() function along with arrays.toString() to print the contents of a single array to the screen, but this technique won't work well with a two-dimensional or higher array.

So, we're going to need to use a for loop again to grab each array in turn, and then print them to the screen. This works pretty well because println will automatically carriage return, or give us a new line between each row we print. Here, let's use the conventional syntax variable i to iterate through our for loop:

```java
for(int i = 0; i < board.length; i++)
{
    System.out.println(Arrays.toString(board));
}
```

You'll notice that Java does not yet understand the `Arrays` keyword as shown in the preceding screenshot; that's because `Arrays` lives in the `java.lang` package. It can be kind of annoying when we call a function or a class and Java doesn't immediately know where to find it, and we have to go online and locate it on Google. If we're working in an IDE, such as NetBeans, sometimes there's a shortcut to find common packages. In this case, if we right-click on the problem statement and go to **Fix Imports**, NetBeans will go through the common packages and check whether it can figure out what we're doing:

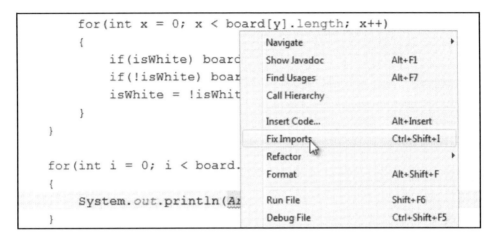

In this case, NetBeans has located the `Arrays` class and added the import statement for us:

```
import java.util.Arrays;
```

Now, because we don't want to attempt to print out the contents of the two-dimensional array each time our `for` loop executes (which wouldn't work very well anyway), we're going to tell our `println` statement to print out the contents of `board[i]`, or the individual array, within the two-dimensional array that we've accessed:

```java
public static void main(String[] args) {
    int boardDim = 8;
    char[][] board = new char[boardDim][boardDim];
    boolean isWhite = false;
    for(int y = 0; y < board.length; y++)
    {
        isWhite = !isWhite;
        for(int x = 0; x < board[y].length; x++)
        {
            if(isWhite) board[y][x] = 'W';
            if(!isWhite) board[y][x] = 'B';
            isWhite = !isWhite;
        }
```

```
    }
    for(int i = 0; i < board.length; i++)
    {
        System.out.println(Arrays.toString(board[i]));
    }
}
```

Now, let's see whether we got everything right the first time through and run our program:

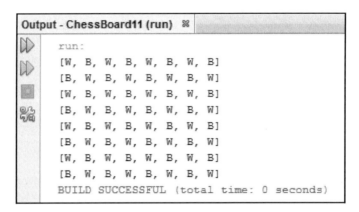

Wow! It looks like we did. There's an alternating white and black representation of a chessboard that begins with a white square and has rows starting in the proper manner. This might not look like much now, but its significance is pretty big. We've essentially taught our program how a chessboard looks. This is our first step toward creating something much bigger, such as a program that plays chess.

Were we to create a program that plays chess (which is a little out of the scope of this section here, but we can talk about it conceptually), we would probably want our individual squares to be able to store more information than just what color they were. For example, we would probably want them to know what piece was on them. To make this happen, we could utilize a three-dimensional array. We could create an array that looks like the following so that each square could store an array that holds two pieces of information, one character for its color and another character to represent what piece it's on:

```
char[][][] board = new char[boardDim][boardDim][2];
```

So that's the basics of multidimensional arrays in Java.

ArrayLists

When we need a Java data structure, we should start by asking ourselves whether a simple array is sufficient. If we can write our program easily and neatly using just an array, that might be our best option to keep our programs simple by extension. If you're writing code that must run as fast as possible and use memory as efficiently as possible, arrays will also have very little overhead. But, in today's development world, where memory efficiency and speed really aren't concerns for your average program, sometimes we need to employ data structures with more built-in functionality, or maybe which are designed for a specific purpose.

A data structure with additional functionality is called an ArrayList. One of the weaknesses of traditional arrays is that when we instantiate them, we have to give them a specific length, so we have to know how large we want our array to be. An ArrayList is basically an array wrapped in some additional code that causes the array to increase or decrease in size to always be the size of the number of elements it contains.

An ArrayList example in NetBeans

To see this in action, let's write a program that would actually be a little more difficult to write if we just used a standard array instead of an ArrayList. I'd like to write a program that will take an input string from the user. It will store this input string with every other input string the user has ever given it, and then print them all out each time the user inputs a new string.

This would be really difficult to do with an array because if the user ever inputs one more string than the array was designed to hold, our array would, in the best-case scenario, not accept the string; in the worst-case scenario, our program might crash. But, our ArrayList object will simply resize to fit the number of strings that it's currently holding.

Creating an ArrayList

We need to begin by importing `java.util`, because `java.util` is where the `Scanner` class, which we'll need to get user input, and the `ArrayList` class itself, live. Once we've declared a `Scanner`, which we'll utilize a bit more later, it's time for us to declare our `ArrayList`:

```
package echo;

import java.util.*;

public class Echo {
    public static void main(String[] args) {
        Scanner reader = new Scanner(System.in);
        ArrayList memory = new ArrayList();
    }
}
```

Simply declaring `ArrayList` looks a lot like declaring any other object. We say what type of object we'd like to create. We give it a name. We use the `new` keyword because Java is going to have to set aside some memory to create this object since it's not a primitive. Then, we tell Java to actually create the object. Even though we're not going to provide any arguments for our `ArrayList` creation, we still need to follow it with the double parentheses. This is actually valid code we've just written, but generally when we create an `ArrayList`, we're going to do a little bit more.

The `ArrayList` memory that we've created will actually store any type of single entity we place within it. This might sound really, really great at first, but honestly, it's not a good thing to have in our program. It's really easy to get confused if we have ArrayLists, or any data structure, really, that's storing just about anything, and if we feel the need to do this, we're either doing something really complicated, or more likely we're not writing our code as cleanly as we should. More importantly, once we store anything in our ArrayList, it's possible for us to sneak by our compiler and create code that compiles OK. However, the other possibility is that it would break at runtime, causing the kind of bugs that are really bad to have in commercial software because they can break when people are actually using it.

To solve this problem, we can tell our ArrayList to only accept information of a certain type. We do this by following our `ArrayList` declaration and instantiation with double character brackets and placing a type within them:

```
ArrayList<String> memory = new ArrayList<String>();
```

We've declared and then caused to come into being an `ArrayList` data structure that will only allow strings to be stored within it.

Getting user input

We're going to need a loop so that our user can input more than one string to the program. For now, let's just use an infinite loop. It will run forever, but while we're building our program and debugging it, we can always just stop it manually:

```
while(true)
{

}
```

Each time our loop runs, we're going to want to use the `nextLine()` function on our Scanner variable, that is, `reader`, to grab a new line of input from the user that we're going to store in our ArrayList.

When we're working with object data structures, that is, data structures that have code wrapped around them, and functions and methods of their own, we're generally not going to have to deal with the individual indices of memory, which can be pretty nice. Instead, we use their provided functions to add, remove, and manipulate the information within them.

In this case, adding something to an ArrayList is pretty easy. The `add()` function in ArrayList will add whatever input we give it, in our case, as long as it's a string, to the end of the array that the ArrayList contains. So, let's add the following line of code that will request a new input string from the user and then put it at the end of our ArrayList inside our infinite `while` loop:

```
memory.add(reader.nextLine());
```

Printing the ArrayList of user input

Now, we can simply use `println` to print our ArrayList out to the user. Note that the `println` code line doesn't know how to take an ArrayList as input. Actually, it might, but we should explicitly use the `toString()` function, which almost every object in Java implements:

```
package echo;

import java.util.*;

public class Echo {
```

```
public static void main(String[] args) {
    Scanner reader = new Scanner(System.in);
    ArrayList<String> memory = new ArrayList<String>();
    while(true)
    {
        memory.add(reader.nextLine());
        System.out.println(memory.toString());
    }
}
}
```

Now, when we run our program, we'll be prompted for some user input, and we'll see the input echoed back out at us. If we give Java some more input, we'll see our more input, and the old input will be stored in our ArrayList:

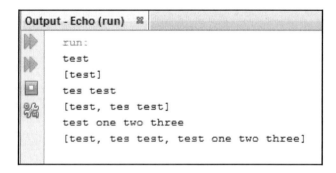

So that's pretty cool! We've built a really basic program that would be more difficult to write with a simple array.

Giving control to the user

ArrayLists have a lot of power contained within them. We can turn them into arrays, create them from arrays, and all sorts of things. If we go to the Java documentation and check under java.util for ArrayList, we can find all of their methodologies. Let's add few more features to our ArrayList program so that I can walk you through some common ArrayList methods.

ArrayLists have a function that takes no input, called `clear()`, which will erase our ArrayList. We can utilize this function to give our users some control over our program. Let's say that if the user inputs the string CLEAR, we would like to erase all of the information in our ArrayList. Well, that's a conditional statement I just made, so we use an `if` statement. We'd utilize the following `if` statement code inside our `while` loop to implement this functionality:

```
if((memory.get(memory.size()-1)).equals("CLEAR")) memory.clear();
```

First, we need to check the item just added to our ArrayList against the string CLEAR. This item will be at the very end, that is, it will be the last item with the highest index value. Unfortunately, there's no `lastItem()` function implemented for ArrayList, but we can essentially create one ourselves by mashing together two ArrayList functions: `get()` and `size()`.

First, in order to get an item from an ArrayList, we utilize the `get()` function. Note that `get()` is very similar to the square brackets we would utilize if we were accessing an item from a traditional array. Also, the `get()` function is going to take an integer value and it's going to map that integer to the index of the array contained within our ArrayList.

So, to get the last item in our ArrayList, we need to know how many items are there in the ArrayList. Then, we want to subtract one from that value, because the last index of an array with the length of, let's say seven, would be six, since the array starts counting at zero. To get how many items are there in our ArrayList, we use the `size()` function, which takes no arguments and simply gives us an integer that is the size of the array, that is, how many items it contains. We subtract 1 from that value so that we can properly access the last index and not the index behind it, which could contain anything. Then, we wrap the whole `memory.get(memory.size()-1)` block, which accesses the last item of our `ArrayList` in parentheses.

This block of our `if` statement we just parenthesized gets for us a string object. We know that we can compare strings by using the `equals()` method. We can actually call that method from the string object that this block of code returns, even though we haven't assigned it a specific variable name yet. Objects exist even if we don't have a name for them, and we can call their methods and do just about anything we like with them if we've just returned them from something else:

```
while(true)
{
    memory.add(reader.nextLine());
    if((memory.get(memory.size()-1)).equals("CLEAR"))
        memory.clear();
    System.out.println(memory.toString());
}
```

So, that's a pretty crazy statement we've just written, but as long as we've written it right, when our user enters CLEAR in the program, we will erase the ArrayList.

Once we've written this code, we can write very similar code to give our user different functionality options. Let's also allow our user to type in END. Currently, we're in a program that will loop infinitely until we manually turn it off. But by using the `break` Java keyword, which will jump us out of whatever loop we're in, or function if we're in a function, we can make this an escapable loop. This way, we let the user essentially turn off our program because once we leave this loop, there's no more code to execute and our program will end:

```
public static void main(String[] args) {
    Scanner reader = new Scanner(System.in);
    ArrayList<String> memory = new ArrayList<String>();

    while(true)
    {
        memory.add(reader.nextLine());
        if((memory.get(memory.size()-1)).equals("CLEAR")) {
            memory.clear();
        }
        if((memory.get(memory.size()-1)).equals("END"))
        break;
    }
    System.out.println(memory.toString());
}
```

Be careful when you're using `break` statements. Make sure it makes sense to do so, because they can be a little confusing if you're going through someone's code. They break and jump the control flow all over the place.

So let's run this program and see what happens. We'll start by giving our program some input and build the ArrayList:

```
Output ✕

▶▶   Echo (run) #4  ✕    Echo (run) #5  ✕

▶▶      run:
□       abc d efg
🧩      [abc d efg]
        h ijkl m
        [abc d efg, h ijkl m]
        no pq
        [abc d efg, h ijkl m, no pq]
        rst uvwxyz
        [abc d efg, h ijkl m, no pq, rst uvwxyz]
```

Now let's try inputting `CLEAR` and check whether it empties our ArrayList. Oh no! I broke it:

```
Exception in thread "main" java.lang.ArrayIndexOutOfBoundsException: -1
        at java.util.ArrayList.elementData(ArrayList.java:418)
        at java.util.ArrayList.get(ArrayList.java:431)
        at echo.Echo.main(Echo.java:18)
C:\Users\nidhishas\AppData\Local\NetBeans\Cache\8.2\executor-snippets\run.xml:53: Java returned: 1
```

This is actually a pretty interesting error that we made. I actually made this error; it wasn't preplanned. I'm going to leave it in because this is a great learning experience for us. It also shows you that even if you're an experienced programmer, you're going to make mistakes. One of the reasons why we should use typed ArrayLists whenever we can, for example, is so that we can easily figure out and fix our mistakes.

Analyzing ArrayIndexOutOfBoundsException

Our program has thrown an `ArrayIndexOutOfBoundsException`. This means that we tried to access memory that our `memory` array did not have access to. Specifically, we tried to look at what was at the index −1 of the array. Since arrays start at index 0, they don't have anything at index −1. Any piece of our computer's memory could be there, and for security reasons, programs aren't allowed to just go looking through a computer's memory because they want to. So, why did this happen? Why did we ask for index −1 of an array, which is never going to be a valid array index?

Well, our first `if` statement that implemented the functionality to clear our ArrayList executed just fine. Our program saw our `CLEAR` command, understood our first look at our array index, and cleared the array.

Immediately following this, we asked our program to again check the last item added to our array, using the second `if` statement. When we did this, we executed `memory.size()−1`. First, we asked Java about the size of our ArrayList. Because we just cleared our ArrayList, Java told us that the size of the ArrayList was zero, that there was nothing in it. Then we subtracted one from that value to get -1. Post this, we ran `memory.get()` on that −1 value. Thus, we asked Java to take a look at what was at index −1 of our array, at which point Java said, "Whoa! What are you doing? It's not cool, I'm going to crash!"

So, how do we solve this? Well, there's a couple of things we could do. We should probably just check and make sure that our arrays are not empty before we run the functions in the second `if` statement. That option looks like a few more lines of code than I want to put. It's not undoable in any sense of the word, and I encourage you to try and implement a better solution than this yourself.

For now, just to get our program quickly up and running without crashing, let's change the pair of `if` blocks to an `if...else` statement as follows:

```
while(true)
{
    memory.add(reader.nextLine());
    if((memory.get(memory.size()-1)).equals("CLEAR")) {
    memory.clear();
    }
    else {
        if((memory.get(memory.size()-1)).equals("END"))
        break;
    }
    System.out.println(memory.toString());
}
```

We've embedded the second `if` statement in the `else` block. This will prevent us from ever running both of the `if` blocks back to back. If our first `if` statement evaluates to be true and our clear statement gets executed, then we will not check for the second `if` statement.

Now, if we run our program and give some gibberish input to build up our ArrayList, and then type in CLEAR, we're going to properly get the response of an empty ArrayList:

```
Output - Echo (run)   %
run:
abc def ghi
[abc def ghi ]
jkl mno pqr
[abc def ghi , jkl mno pqr]
stu vwx yz
[abc def ghi , jkl mno pqr, stu vwx yz]
CLEAR
[]
```

We'll never hit the second `if` statement with an array of size 0 because we're always going to add a line to our array beforehand.

Now, let's cross our fingers and check that the END input works:

```
Output - Echo (run)   %
run:
abc def ghi
[abc def ghi ]
jkl mno pqr
[abc def ghi , jkl mno pqr]
stu vwx yz
[abc def ghi , jkl mno pqr, stu vwx yz]
CLEAR
[]
END
BUILD SUCCESSFUL (total time: 2 minutes 35 seconds)
```

It does! The break command breaks specifically out of loops and functions, so even though we've nested it within an if and else statement, it's still going to break us out of the `while` loop.

I think that little trip up we had was a great learning experience. That's actually a pretty interesting error we ran into. Nonetheless, I hope you've seen how different data structures have different purposes.

Maps

In this section, we're going to take a look at Java's `Map` data structure. I wanted to start with a bunch of already formatted information, so I have created a little program on my own. You will find the following program in the companion files for the book. Take a look through it and make sure you understand how it works:

```java
package maps;
import java.util.*;
public class Maps {
    public static void main(String[] args) {
        String[] allNames =
            //<editor-fold desc="raw names data">
            {"Jane", "Addams",
            "Muhammad", "Ali",
            "Stephen", "Ambrose",
            "Louis", "Armstrong",
            "Joan", "Baez",
            "Josephine", "Baker",
            "Eleanor", "Roosevelt",
            "Frank", "Sinatra"
            };
            //</editor-fold>
        String[] firstNames = new String[allNames.length/2];
        String[] lastNames = new String[allNames.length/2];
        for(int i = 0; i < allNames.length; i++)
        {
            /*This if statement checks if we are in an EVEN
            NUMBERED iteration
            % is the "mod" or "modulus" operator...
            it returns the remainder after we divide number1 by
            number2)*/
            if(i % 2 == 0)
            {
                //We are in an even number iteration - looking at
                a first name
                firstNames[i/2] = allNames[i];
```

```
            }
            else
            {
                //We are in an odd number iteration - looking at a
                last name
                lastNames[i/2] = allNames[i];
            }
        }
        System.out.println(Arrays.toString(firstNames));
        System.out.println(Arrays.toString(lastNames));
    }
}
```

I'm operating on the assumption that we're not yet familiar with file input and output, so I dropped all of the data that we'd normally want to store in a file, or somewhere more manageable, right in the code of our program. I have created a String array that I've called allNames, and what it is a list of names of famous people. Their individual first and last names are also divided. So Jane, Addams comprises the first two elements of the array. Her first name Jane is part of allNames[0], and then Addams, her last name, is at allNames[1], and so on, with every two elements in the array being a single person's first and last name.

This is also a good chance for me to show you a nifty little NetBeans feature that's available in most IDEs. We can talk to our IDEs often if they support features such as these by putting instructions for them in the comments of our code. Because these instructions are commented out, they won't in any way affect the way our Java code compiles and runs, but we can talk to the IDE. The following instruction in the program, paired with its ending instruction, tells NetBeans that we'd like it to section off the code included between them:

```
//<editor-fold desc="raw names data">
.
.
.
//</editor-fold>
```

Now, we can use the little box on the left-hand side of our opening instruction to expand and contract the block of code as shown in the following screenshots:

```
String[] allNames =
    //<editor-fold desc="raw names data">
    {"Jane", "Addams",
    "Muhammad", "Ali",
    "Stephen", "Ambrose",
    "Louis", "Armstrong",
    "Joan", "Baez",
    "Josephine", "Baker",
```

It doesn't make the code go away; it just hides it from us so that we can develop it without cluttering up our screen:

```
public static void main(String[] args) {
    String[] allNames =
        raw names data
    String[] firstNames = new String[allNames.length/2];
```

Now, let's look at a very quick explanation of the program I've written to start this section off. We have an array of strings called `allNames` that contains the first and last names of a bunch of famous people. The program I've written simply loops through this array and determines whether it's looking at the first or last name. Then it places those names in separate arrays of their own. At the end, when we print out these arrays, we have two separate arrays: one of first names and one of last names. The relationship of these arrays, because we've placed them into the two separate arrays (`firstNames` and `lastNames`) in order, is that the indexes of the arrays match up. So, at `firstNames[0]` and `lastNames[0]`, we have the first and last names of Jane Addams.

What I'd like to do now is expand this program and place all of this information in a single data structure: a Java `Map`. While creating such a Map, we let it know the relationship between one set, which we call the keys, and the other set, which we call the values, so that each key maps to the value. This will allow us to ask our program questions, such as, "Given a famous person's last name, what is the first name that is associated with it?"

Creating a Map

To begin, I've gone ahead and imported `java.util` where the `Map` interface lives. Next, I'll get rid of the last two `println` statements that prints the `firstNames` and `lastNames` arrays. Instead, at this point in our code, when our `firstNames` and `lastNames` arrays have been set up, let's start constructing our `Map`. For this, add the following line of code:

```
Map<String, String> famousPeople = new HashMap<>();
```

We begin by using the `Map` keyword and then, as with most data structures, we tell Java what type of information our `Map` is going to take. Maps take two sets of information, so we'll have to give it two information types that are comma-separated. The first information type is the information type for the Map's keys, and the second information type is the type for the Map's values.

We're going to use `lastNames` as our keys because we don't want our `Map` to store multiple values in one key, and it's much less likely that we're going to have multiple identical last names. Additionally, it's a lot more valuable for us to ask for the first name of the famous person named Addams, rather than the last name of the famous person named Jane, of which there are probably more. Anyway, the data type of `lastNames` is `String`, and the data type of `firstNames` is `String`, as well.

Next, we give our new `Map` variable a name: `famousPeople`. Then, we cause our `Map` to come into being by instantiating it. To do this, we use the `new` keyword. `Map` is not an object, actually, it's what we call an interface. For the most part, we interact with interfaces and objects the same way, but we cannot simply declare an instance of an interface. Rather, interfaces are additional wrappings of functionality that we place on top of objects, in the way that ArrayLists add additional functionality to arrays.

So, to create a new `Map`, we need a simpler type of object that we can wrap the `Map` interface around. A great candidate for this is the `HashMap`. Therefore, we create our `HashMap` and assign our Map variable `famousPeople` to it. We'll now interact with this `famousPeople` variable just as if it were an object with all of the `Map` functionality. Additionally, if we would like, we could call only the `HashMap` functionality on this object as well.

While it's a little out of the scope of this particular section, the power of interfaces is that we can assign them to objects of different types, giving common functionalities to otherwise distinct object types. But, for now, we're mostly just interested in the power and function of Java Maps. You'll notice that we didn't have to explicitly tell Java what type our HashMap was going to take. This is a stylistic choice really; if we wanted to, we could explicitly declare the types that the HashMap would take:

```
Map<String, String> famousPeople = new HashMap<String, String>();
```

However, since we're only going to interact with our HashMap in terms of its functionality as a Map, simply protecting us from adding anything but strings when we interact with our HashMap through the variable famousPeople, which is currently our only way to access it, should be just fine.

Assigning values to our Map

Once we set up our Map, it's time for us to go through and fill it with information. For this, I think a for loop will be appropriate:

```
for(int i = 0; i < lastNames.length; i++)
{
    famousPeople.put(lastNames[i], firstNames[i]);
}
```

We're going to need to add a number of pairs of information to our Map, that is, one key and one value, equal to the number of items in either of these arrays. This is because they both have the same length. So let's set up a for loop that iterates through every index from i to the length of (lastNames-1). The i values will map to the indexes of the lastNames array, and because the firstNames array has the same length as the lastNames array, they will map to the indexes of the firstNames array as well.

Now, for each i, we're going to execute our Map's put() function. The put() function is similar to the add() function. It inserts information into our map. However, this function expects two pieces of information. First, it expects our key, which is the value we're currently looking at in lastNames, and then it expects the associated value, which is the value we're looking at in firstNames. Each time we execute the famousPeople.put(lastNames[i], firstNames[i]); line of code in our for loop, we'll be adding a new key value pair to our Map.

Fetching information from our Map

Once we've set up the Map, with all our information already in our program, all we need to do is ask it some questions and make sure we get the right responses:

```
System.out.println(famousPeople.get("Addams"));
```

We use the get() function to ask our Map the basic question that it's designed to answer, "What is the value paired with a given key?" So, let's ask our Map, "What is the value paired with Addams?", or in more understandable English terms, "What is the first name of the person in our Map whose last name is Addams?" When we run this program, we get the expected result, that is, Jane:

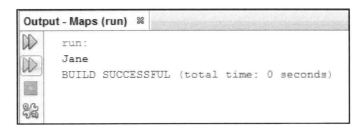

Let's just run it one more time to make sure we haven't made any silly mistakes. Let's see whether our program answers Frank when we input Sinatra:

```
System.out.println(famousPeople.get("Sinatra"));
```

Indeed it does!

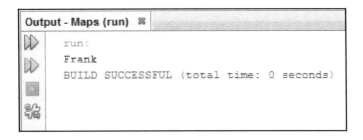

While it's possible for us to write a program like this by simply looping through our arrays when we get user input (finding `lastName`, storing that index, and getting it from `firstNames`), our Map interface essentially does that for us. Perhaps, more importantly than this, when we're working with other programmers or looking at code that we didn't write just yesterday, and we see a `Map`, we understand immediately its intended purpose and what functionality it implements. In almost all cases, just writing code that works is equally important because it makes sense and will be understood by others who might come across the code in the future.

Summary

In this chapter, we looked at arrays and an example that printed the English alphabet by using an array. Next, we looked at multidimensional arrays and wrote a program that created a two-dimensional chessboard.

We walked through what an ArrayList is and how it enhances the functionality of arrays. We also wrote a program using an ArrayList with functionality, which would have been quite difficult to implement using an array. Finally, we looked at Maps and implemented an example to understand this better.

In the next chapter, we'll look at Java functions in detail.

5
Functions

In this chapter, we will start with a discussion of some of the basic concepts and terminologies used in the basics of Java programs. You will learn all these concepts with the help of simple programs. You'll learn about the all-important Java method. If you're an experienced programmer, you've probably run across functions in the past. As you progress with these basic concepts, you will grasp more about advanced Java functions. The following are the topics that we plan to cover in this chapter:

- The basics of a Java function
- Methods
- Advanced Java functions
- Operating Java variables

The basics of Java functions

In Java, the terms "function" and "method" are basically used interchangeably, with "method" being the more technically correct term that you'll see in the documentation.

Methods

Methods are a tool that allow us to break the control flow of our program. They let us declare little **subroutines**, or sometimes we can think of them as smaller programs, that we can reference in our program so that we don't have to write all of our program's logical code in one single block:

```
public class TemperatureConverter {
    public static void main(String[] args) {
```

```
            Scanner reader = new Scanner(System.in);
            char inputType;
            char outputType;
            float inputValue;
            float returnValue;
            System.out.print("Input type (F/C/K): ");
            inputType = reader.next().charAt(0);
            System.out.print("Output type (F/C/K): ");
            outputType = reader.next().charAt(0);
            System.out.print("Temperature: ");
            inputValue = reader.nextFloat();
        }
    }
```

An example of a method is the `.next` method found in the `Scanner` class. Rather than having to teach our `Scanner` object how to acquire the next set of user inputs in this program I've written, I can simply call the `next` method from the class that someone else has written in the past. This turns what would probably be a couple of hundred lines of program into a total of 22 lines approximately, illustrated in the preceding code.

By writing our own methods, we can tackle complicated challenges by breaking them into much smaller and easier-to-manage parts. Programs that are properly modular and make use of methods are also much more human-readable. This is because we can give our methods our own names so our program can be much more self-explanatory and make use of a lot more English(or whatever language you are native to) words. To show you the power of methods right from the start, I've planned a pretty complicated program for us to write today.

Temperature conversion program

Our goal is to create a temperature conversion program, and I've set up the input portion of this program for us already:

```
public class TemperatureConverter {
    public static void main(String[] args) {
        Scanner reader = new Scanner(System.in);
        char inputType;
        char outputType;
        float inputValue;
        float returnValue;
        System.out.print("Input type (F/C/K): ");
        inputType = reader.next().charAt(0);
        System.out.print("Output type (F/C/K): ");
        outputType = reader.next().charAt(0);
```

```
        System.out.print("Temperature: ");
        inputValue = reader.nextFloat();
    }
}
```

So far, this program takes three pieces of information from the user. The first is the temperature type: F for Fahrenheit, C for Celsius, and K for Kelvin. Then it takes another temperature type. This is the type that our user would like us to convert to; once again, it could be Fahrenheit, Celsius, or Kelvin. Finally, we take the value of the initial temperature from the user. With these three pieces of input, our program will convert the given temperature value from Fahrenheit, Celsius, or Kelvin to the temperature type the user desires.

This is a challenging program for two reasons:

- First, there are six possible control flow cases because there are two sets of three user input. This means in the worst-case scenario, we might have to write six if...else blocks, which will get unwieldy pretty quick.
- The second challenge is doing the actual conversion. I've gone ahead and looked up the conversion math for three temperature conversions, namely Fahrenheit to Celsius, Celsius to Kelvin, and Kelvin to Fahrenheit:

```java
package temperatureconverter;

import java.util.*;

// F to C: ((t-32.0f)*5.0f)/9.0f
// C to K: t+273.15f
// K to F: (((t-273.15f)*9.0f)/5.0f)+32.0f

public class TemperatureConverter {
    public static void main(String[] args) {
        Scanner reader = new Scanner(System.in);
        char inputType;
        char outputType;
        float inputValue;
        float returnValue;
```

As you can see, while this isn't difficult math, it's certainly unwieldy and our programs are going to look pretty crazy if we start copying and pasting formula as shown in the preceding comments all over the place. You should also note that with the three conversions in the preceding comments section, we can make any of the possible conversions this program will be asked to do. This is because these three conversions create a circle of conversion, where we can get from a particular type to any other type by passing through one of the interim equations.

With all said and done, let's just jump right into writing our program.

Setting up the control flow

The first thing we need to do is set up some control flow. As I mentioned before, there's six possible cases, and it might be tempting to just set up six `if` statements for each possible pairing of input and output types. This would be a little unwieldy though, so I have a slightly different plan. Instead of handling a different case for each possible pairing of types, the first thing I'm going to do is convert whatever value our user has given as the initial temperature value to a Celsius value. After I've done this, we'll convert that Celsius value to whatever type the user was originally looking for. This can be done using the following code block:

```
System.out.print("Input type (F/C/K): ");
inputType = reader.next().charAt(0);
System.out.print("Output type (F/C/K): ");
outputType = reader.next().charAt(0);
System.out.print("Temperature: ");
inputValue = reader.nextFloat();
```

 Setting up the control flow has the advantage of letting us deal with two pieces of user input in complete isolation. It makes our program more modular because we start and finish one task before we begin the next one.

So to do this initial conversion, where we take whatever the user has given us as input and convert it into a Celsius value, we need to utilize a `switch` statement:

```
public static void main(String[] args) {
    Scanner reader = new Scanner(System.in);
    char inputType;
    char outputType;
    float inputValue;
    float returnValue;
    System.out.print("Input type (F/C/K): ");
    inputType = reader.next().charAt(0);
```

```
        System.out.print("Output type (F/C/K): ");
        outputType = reader.next().charAt(0);
        System.out.print("Temperature: ");
        inputValue = reader.nextFloat();
        switch(inputType)
    }
```

We'll be switching across the `inputType` character variable that tells us what type of temperature-Fahrenheit, Celsius, or Kelvin-our user has given us. Inside the `switch` statement, we'll manipulate `inputValue`, in which the value of that temperature would be stored.

Exploring separate cases - C, K, and F

So I guess we're going to need separate cases for each of the possible or valid input types, that is, capital F for Fahrenheit, C for Celsius, K for Kelvin. We should probably also handle a `default` case. Let's start off by writing the `default` case. We'll use `System.exit` and exit with 1, which is technically an error code:

```
switch(inputType)
{
    case 'F':
    case 'C':
    case 'K':
    default:
        System.exit(1);
```

 `System.exit` basically quits our program. It tells it to stop executing and passes to the operating system or whatever's up in the hierarchy.

In this case, the program will just stop. Because it's the `default` case, we only expect to enter it if the user has failed to enter F, C, or K, which are our valid input types. Now, let's go ahead and handle each of these input types.

Celsius type

We're going to use Celsius as our first point of conversion in all cases, so if our user has inputted a Celsius value, we can just go ahead and break out of this case because the value of inputValue is already OK with us:

```
switch(inputType)
{
    case 'F':
    case 'C':
        break;
    case 'K':
        default:
            System.exit(1);
```

What if the user has given us a Fahrenheit value? Well, let's scroll to the top of the code; you'll see that we have an explicit conversion from Fahrenheit to Celsius:

```
// F to C: ((t-32.0f)*5.0f)/9.0f
// C to K: t+273.15f
// K to F: (((t-273.15f)*9.0f)/5.0f)+32.0f
```

We can take the preceding block of code, which I've made pretty Java-friendly, and just change the value of this input variable to the conversion statement run on its value. So, we'll replace the t placeholder with the input variable:

```
switch(inputType)
{
    case 'F':
        inputValue = ((inputValue-32.0f)*5.0f)/9.0f;
        break;
    case 'C':
        break;
    case 'K':
    default:
        System.exit(1);
}
```

This will properly store the Celsius equivalent of the original Fahrenheit value in this variable.

Kelvin type

We can do something similar for the Kelvin case. We don't have an explicit conversion from Kelvin to Celsius, but we do know how to convert Kelvin to Fahrenheit and then how to convert Fahrenheit to Celsius. So we can get away with doing something like the following:

```
switch(inputType)
{
    case 'F':
        inputValue = ((inputValue-32.0f)*5.0f)/9.0f;
        break;
    case 'C':
        break;
    case 'K':
        inputValue = ((((((inputValue-273.15f)*9.0f)/5.0f)+32.0f) -
        32.0f)*5.0f)/9.0f;
    default:
        System.exit(1);
}
```

In the preceding code, we converted our Kelvin value to a Fahrenheit value, surrounding it in parentheses, and did our Fahrenheit to Celsius conversion on that.

Now this is technically a functional line of code. If we run our program and enter a Kelvin input case, it will properly convert the Kelvin value to a Celsius value. But, let me say that if I'm a programmer and I'm at work and I run across a line of code like this, especially a line of code like this without any comments explaining it, I am not going to be very happy. There are a whole lot of magic numbers in here-numbers are really information in general; that's not in any way self-explanatory. Sure, we as the original programmer, at least when we write it, remember that our goal here is to convert a Kelvin value to a Celsius value; however, that's really not understandable to anyone else going through this program who doesn't really have time to sit down and look through the entire thing. So is there a better way to do this? Yes, there definitely is.

Fahrenheit type

Now let's try to understand the Fahrenheit case. Consider the following code:

```
inputValue = ((inputValue-32.0f)*5.0f)/9.0f;
```

The preceding line of code is a little better than our Kelvin case simply because it contains fewer numbers, but it's still not programmer-friendly by any sense of the word. So what if in our initial implementation of this program, we could provide communication that would really look a lot nicer to a programmer? What if instead of printing out the equation right there, we put the equation somewhere else in our program and call a Fahrenheit to Celsius function?

```
inputValue = fToC(inputValue);
```

We'll just type in `fToC` now to keep things short. This makes a lot more sense to someone looking at our program.

We can do something very similar down here for the Kelvin case:

```
inputValue = fToC(kToF(inputValue))
```

We could call a Kelvin to Celsius function (`kToC`) if we wanted to, or if we don't even want to write that, we can call a Kelvin to Fahrenheit function on our `inputValue` variable and then call the `fToC` function on top of that. That's what we did with all that math initially-conceptually-except that what we've done has abstracted away those numbers and put them somewhere else in our program. This is much more friendly to a programmer. Let's say we made a mistake in our math and another programmer wants to go through and check it. All they would need to do is find the functions that we're about to write, such as `fToC`, and `kToF`, and they can dive into all their dirty details there. So, of course, we do need to write these functions.

When we create a new function, we're actually going to do it outside of the function or method that we're currently in:

```
public static void main(String[] args) {
```

Currently, we're in our program's `main` method, which is a special method where the program begins its execution. So, to write our Fahrenheit to Celsius function, we're going to step out of that method and declare a brand new one; essentially, we're teaching our program how to run a new program called `fToC`:

```
public static fToC()
```

For now, go ahead and use the `public static` keywords in front of your methods. These keywords are going to be very important once we really jump into the object-oriented nature of Java, but for now, we'll utilize them on all the methods we declare.

For a more detailed explanation about what we plan to do next with our program, let's try to see things in much more detail by splitting the program further into two parts.

Executing the first part of the program

Your standard Java method also has one more keyword before we actually give it a name, and that is the type of information this method is going to return:

```
public static float fToC()
{
}
```

For example, we would like to be able to call `fToC` on our Kelvin to Fahrenheit function. When we do this, we're basically treating the result of our Kelvin to Fahrenheit function as a floating-point variable of its own. This is a good sign that the return type we're looking for in these functions is a `float` data type. What this means is when these little programs finish executing, they're going to throw out a floating-point value to our `main` method, which called them. After we name a function, we follow it with two parentheses in the function declaration preceding to it. Between these parentheses, we're going to tell our program what information this function is going to require to run. We do this by basically creating some variables, as shown in the following code block:

```
public static float fToC(fVal)
```

We're going to want a variable that I'll just call `fVal` because we're starting with the Fahrenheit value. We also need to tell our program before each input variable what type of information that's going to be; this way people won't be able to improperly call our function and pass in something like a string, which wouldn't make any sense:

```
public static float fToC(float fVal)
{
}
```

So, we're going to tell our function that in order to run, it needs to be called with a `float` piece of information given as input. In the functions that we wrote before, they actually existed in the program. You'll see that we did this: we provided `inputValue`, or the value of the temperature the user initially gave us, as input to these functions.

Now, we need our `fToC` function, our Fahrenheit to Celsius function, to perform some computation on this `fVal` variable in the code, which will contain the user-inputted temperature value. Since we're going from Fahrenheit to Celsius, we can just copy and paste the string from the top of the program again and substitute the `fVal` with `t`:

```
public static float fToC(float fVal)
{
    fVal = ((fVal-32.0f)*5.0f)/9.0f;
}
```

Now, it may be tempting for us to ask our function to perform this operation to change the value of this variable. While we're certainly allowed to do that, it's not going to give us the result that we require. When our program hits the `inputValue = fToC(inputValue);` code line and runs our `fToC` function, giving `inputValue` as its input variable, this variable is not going to actually drop down to our function's line of code. Rather, Java is simply going to copy the value of `inputValue` and store it in our new variable, as you can see in the following block of code:

```
public static float fToC(float fVal)
{
    fVal = ((fVal-32.0f)*5.0f)/9.0f;
}
```

So changes we make to this `fVal` variable will not map to our `inputValue` variable. Fortunately, we explicitly change the value of `inputValue` to be whatever this function we're writing now returns. Once we're ready to quit the execution of a function, we can have it throw out any value that's equivalent to the value type that we told Java this function would return. We do this with the `return` keyword, followed by any statement that computes to, in our case, a floating-point value. So, when our `fToC` function runs on `inputValue`, it will print out a floating-point number equivalent to the Celsius value of our initial Fahrenheit value stored in the input variable:

```
public static float fToC(float fVal)
{
    return ((fVal-32.0f)*5.0f)/9.0f;
}
```

Once we've written one of these functions, writing other similar functions becomes pretty easy. To write our Kelvin to Fahrenheit function, we're simply going to do the same thing, but in this case take our Kelvin to Fahrenheit conversion equation and change the name of our variable. We could call it `fVal` if we wanted to-`kVal` is just more explanatory-and return that result:

```
public static float fToC(float fVal)
{
    return ((fVal-32.0f)*5.0f)/9.0f;
}
public static float kToF(float kVal)
{
    return (((kVal-273.15f)*9.0f)/5.0f)+32.0f;
}
```

So that's the first half of our program where we convert whatever the user has given us into a Celsius value. So far, this has been much more elegant than six `if` statements, but we have only written half of our program.

Executing the second part of the program

Once we're done with the Celsius conversion, we'll use another `switch` statement. This time, we'll use it on `outputType`, where the user has told us what temperature type they'd like to see the equivalent value of, or see the equivalent value in. Our cases are going to look very similar to the first half of our `switch` statement; however here instead of converting everything to Celsius, we're always going to be converting from Celsius. Once again, that means case `C` can simply break in any instances where we've converted to Celsius and then we no longer need to convert from Celsius:

```
// F to C: ((t-32.0f)*5.0f)/9.0f
// C to K: t+273.15f
// K to F: (((t-273.15f)*9.0f)/5.0t)+32.0f
```

Now, our explicit case here is the Celsius to Kelvin conversion. We know that formula, thanks to our nifty cheat sheet at the top of the code; we can build a function to do this pretty quick. We'll call this function `cToK`; there's our variable name, and there's the logic:

```
public static float fToC(float fVal)
{
    return ((fVal-32.0f)*5.0f)/9.0f;
}
public static float kToF(float kVal)
{
    return (((kVal-273.15f)*9.0f)/5.0f)+32.0f;
```

```
    }
    public static float cToK(float cVal)
    {
        return cVal+273.15f;
    }
```

Once we've declared our cToK function, we can call it on inputValue since inputValue now stores the modified original input value, which will be a Celsius number, to convert to a Kelvin value:

```
case 'K':
    inputValue = cToK(inputValue);
```

Similar to the way we doubled up to convert from Kelvin to Fahrenheit to Celsius, when we make everything Celsius, we can get a Fahrenheit output by getting a Kelvin value from our Celsius value. Then, we can use the Kelvin to Fahrenheit function to convert this Kelvin value into a Fahrenheit one:

```
case 'F':
    inputValue = kToF(cToK(inputValue));
    break;
case 'C':
    break;
case 'K':
    inputValue = cToK(inputValue);
    break;
default:
    System.exit(1);
```

This is the second half of our program. Still, only two real lines of code that might cause anyone to pause, and they're pretty self-explanatory. Yet, all of the logic and functionality of our program is still accessible to a curious programmer who wants to reaccess them:

```
    }
    System.out.println(inputValue);
}
```

Final touch to the program

We can finish up our program here using `println` to throw out `inputValue`, which should now contain the proper conversion. Let's run this program and give some input and output to see how we did:

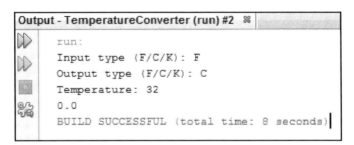

So, when we run our program, it asks what `inputType` we're going to give it. Let's give it a Fahrenheit value. Now let's say we would like to get a Celsius value as the output. Let's see what the Celsius value of 32 degrees Fahrenheit is. We see that the output result of 0. The 32 degrees Fahrenheit is 0 degrees Celsius, so that's a good sign. Let's try some more edge cases. If we attempt to convert Celsius to Celsius, we get the same value as shown in the following screenshot, which is what we would expect:

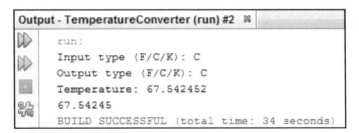

Let's see what the Fahrenheit value of 1 degrees Kelvin is:

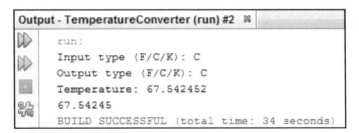

And the good news is that's also the expected value in the preceding screenshot. We've employed functions to make an otherwise very complex and difficult-to-read program much more manageable. The program we've written here is somewhat complicated. It does some math and multifunction statements, so if you weren't 100 percent with us the first time through, I encourage you to go back and check what tripped you up. There's also other ways to approach this problem, and if you had a stroke of inspiration, I encourage you to explore it.

Advanced Java functions

In this section, I'd like you to take a deeper look into Java methods and also learn some really valuable things about how programming languages think about and manipulate information. To help us do this, I'd like to run an experiment of sorts, and to start that experiment off, I've written a really basic Java program:

```
package advancedmethods;

public class AdvancedMethods {
    public static void main(String[] args) {
        int x = 5;
        magic(x);
        System.out.println("main: " + x);
    }
    public static void magic(int input)
    {
        input += 10;
    }
}
```

At the core of this Java program is the `magic` method, which is user-defined following the `main` method. When we come across a new Java method, there's three real things we should notice about it:

1. First, we should ask, "what are its input values?". In the case of our `magic` method, it expects only a single integer as input.

2. Then, we probably want to ask, "what does this method return?". In our case, the method is marked to return `void`. Void methods don't actually return any values at all; they simply execute their code and finish. You'll notice that when we reference `magic` in the main portion of our program, we don't attempt to store its return value in any location. This is, of course, because there would be no return value to store.

3. Then, the third thing to notice about our method is "what does it do?". In the case of our `magic` method, we simply take the value that we've gotten as `input` and increase that value by `10`.

What I'd like to ask you to do right now is take a minute and just look at this program, and try and figure out exactly what the program's output will be when we reach this `println` statement. The challenging question here is what happens to the value of the variable `x` when we run the `magic(x)` line of code and call our `magic` method? Does the variable `x` remain unaffected when we pass it as a value to the `magic` method or does the variable `x` get modified by the input line of the code in the `magic` method such that instead of printing out `5`, we print out the value `15`?

To answer this question, we simply have to run our program, and if we do this, we will see that we get the value of `5`, letting us know that running the `magic` method did not modify the value of the variable `x` within the context of our main method:

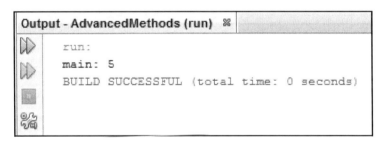

In fact, we'll get the same output if we never run the `magic` method at all. So what does this tell us? This gives us a very important insight into how Java handles method input. To fully understand what's going on here, we need to take a deeper look into how Java variables operate.

Operating java variables

The following is a representation of the information stored by our variable x, that is, the variable in the main method of our Java program:

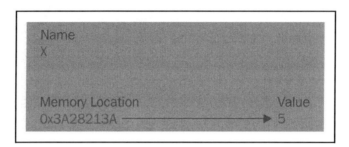

You'll notice that this variable has three core components; let's go through them quickly:

- On the left-hand side, I put this variable's name, which is the keyword that we use to reference it within the scope, and a memory location. Our variables point to a memory location, and in this memory location, we store the variable's value.
- We can think of the name and memory location as being very static; they're not really going to change for this individual variable identifier throughout the course of our program's execution. However, we can, and often do, freely change the value stored in the variable's referenced memory location.

So why is this important? Well, over the course of our program, we're going to have to translate the information stored in our variable x into the information stored in the variable input that our magic method attempted to make use of. If we take a good look at how variables are set up, we quickly see that there's two possible ways to go about doing this:

1. First, we can simply create a brand new variable named input with its own unique memory location, then simply place the same value that we found in the memory location referenced by x as the value in that memory location:

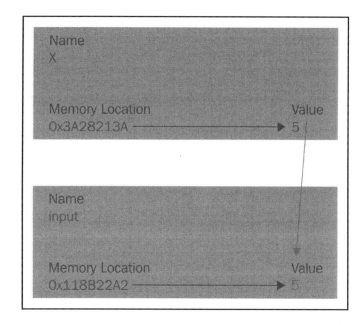

When we pass the variable x to a method, which is the technique that Java uses to create the variable `input`, we can say that Java has passed our variable x by value. This is because only the value is preserved across the creation of the new variable.

2. Another option would be for us to create a brand new variable `input`, but instead of simply copying the value from the variable x to the variable `input`, we could cause `input` to reference the same memory location as x does. This would be called passing the variable x by reference. In this case, because both x and `input` would share a memory location where they would store their values, modifying the value of the variable `input` would also modify the value of the variable x.

So, given what you've just learned about Java variables and taking into account that executing the `magic` method on `magic(x)` code line does not modify the value of the variable x, we can correctly conclude that Java chooses to pass variables to its methods by value rather than by reference.

However, that's not really the end of the story, or rather, this fact has implications that might not be immediately apparent to us. If we were to rewrite our program so that our `magic` method would take character input, boolean input, or really any other primitive type, we would see the same behavior that we've been seeing already. Even if we modify the value of this `input` variable within the scope of the `magic` method, it would not modify the value of the variable x within the scope of the `main` method. So, things are not always so simple.

Using variables in the program

To see this, let's create a brand new method, and in its declaration, we'll have it the same as our existing `magic` method. However, instead of taking a single integer as input, we'll provide it as input in the integer array:

```
package advancedmethods;
public class AdvancedMethods {
    public static void main(String[] args) {
        int[] x = 5;
        magic(x);
        System.out.println("main: " + x);
    }

    public static void magic(int input)
    {
        input += 10;
    }
    public static void magic(int[] input)
    {
        input += 10;
    }
}
```

Remember that our array will be named as a single variable, so all we need to do to let Java know that we'd like to pass an array to the function is inform it that the variable being given is an array of a certain type. You'll also notice that we now have two methods by the name of `magic` within our program. This is called **method overloading**, and it's perfectly legitimate to do this as long as Java has a way of telling the methods apart. In this case, Java can tell the methods apart because both the methods are going to be given different objects as input.

One of our `magic` methods will execute if the input given to the `magic` call is a single integer, and our new `magic` method will execute if the input given to the method is an array of integers. Now, let's write a quick `for` loop so that our new `magic` method will increment the value of every integer contained within our input array by `10`:

```
public static void magic(int[] input)
{
    for(int i = 0; i < input.length; i++)
    input[i] += 10;
}
```

This is extremely similar to the `magic` method we wrote originally, except that instead of operating on a single integer, it's going to operate on any number of them. However, something that may appear weird is going to happen when we modify our `main` method to utilize this new implementation of the `magic` method. In order to make this happen, we need to make a few quick modifications to our program.

Let's change our variable x from an integer to an integer array so that our program will know how to utilize the newly written `magic` method, which runs when we give an integer array as input:

```
package advancedmethods;

import java.util.*;

public class AdvancedMethods {
    public static void main(String[] args) {
        int[] x = {5,4,3,2,1};
        magic(x);
        System.out.println("main: " + Arrays.toString(x));
    }
    public static void magic(int input)
    {
        input += 10;
    }
    public static void magic(int[] input)
    {
        for(int i = 0; i < input.length; i++)
        input[i] += 10;
    }
}
```

We'll also need to modify our `println` statement to make use of `Arrays.toString` so that we display the value stored in the x array properly. We'll import `java.util` so that Java knows about the `Arrays` library:

```java
import java.util.*;

public class AdvancedMethods {
    public static void main(String[] args) {
        int[] x = {5,4,3,2,1};
        magic(x);
        System.out.println("main: " + Arrays.toString(x));
    }
```

Now it's time to ask ourselves another question: when we run the `magic` function on an integer array, will we see the same results we saw when we ran the `magic` function on a single integer value, a primitive type? To answer this question, all we need to do is run our program, and we'll very quickly see that the output, or the final values, stored in the x array are not the same values that we assigned to the x array initially:

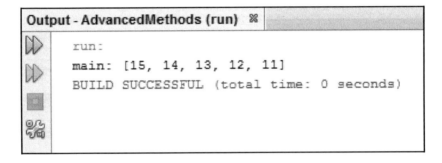

This lets us know that our `magic` method is indeed modifying these values. So this is kind of weird. Why would our `magic` method operate differently depending on whether we gave it a single primitive type as input or an array of primitive types as input? To answer this question, let's take a look at the variable x when it's declared to be an array of integers as opposed to just a single integer as we had it before:

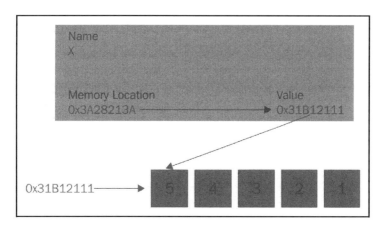

Note that x as an array of integers, as opposed to a single primitive type, still gets a name and memory location to identify it and a place where it can live; however, its value field looks drastically different than it did before. When x was just an integer, we could get away with simply storing an explicit integer in the value field of x, but as an array, x means to be able to reference a number of different values; that's what makes it a data structure. To make this happen, arrays-and really every other element more complicated than a primitive-point to a location in memory as opposed to a single explicit value. For arrays, all we need to do is point to the 0 index of the array in memory. Then, by following from that index, we can store a number of different values that our variable x knows how to access. So why is this important?

Understanding passing parameters

Well, let's take a look at what happens when we pass x to a method by value. As we know, when we pass a variable by value, we're telling Java to create a new variable in the context of the method that's going to have its own unique name and memory location:

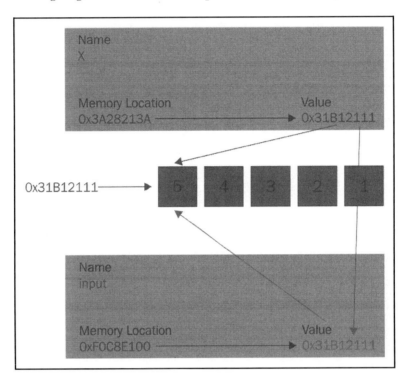

However, this new variable-in our case, `input`-takes the value from the old variable as its own. When we were working with primitive types, these values were completely independent, but now both `input` and x have the values of the same location in memory. So, while modifying the value of input would not change the value of x, modifying the location of memory that input points to would still change that location of memory when x looks at it as well.

Within the context of a method, if we reference an input variable explicitly and then modify that variable, we're going to be modifying only the variable within the context of the function, as we did in our first `magic` method. But, if we have to take an additional step to access the value that we're modifying, as we have to do when declaring an index of an array, then we'll probably have to modify it via a location of memory or by reference. In this instance, we will potentially affect the variable that provided the value for our function variable:

```
package advancedmethods;

import java.util.*;

public class AdvancedMethods {
    public static void main(String[] args) {
        int[] x = {5,4,3,2,1};
        magic(x);
        System.out.println("main: " + Arrays.toString(x));
    }
    public static void magic(int input)
    {
        input += 10;
    }
    public static void magic(int[] input)
    {
        input = new int[] {2,2,2,2,2};
    }
}
```

If our `magic` function that took an array simply attempts to set the value of our integer array to a brand new set of integer values with an all-new starting memory location, we would see that we would no longer be modifying the value of x when we run this function on it:

```
Output - AdvancedMethods (run)  ✖
run:
main: [5, 4, 3, 2, 1]
BUILD SUCCESSFUL (total time: 0 seconds)
```

This is because the creation of a new integer array caused us to explicitly change the value of input. After this line of code, `input` and `x` no longer share a value anymore. Thank you very much for your time. I hope you learned something.

Summary

Are you still with us? If so, congratulations. We started with some of the basic Java functions, such as methods, and then moved on to understand advanced Java functions. That's some complicated stuff we just went over. As you become a more experienced programmer, you'll begin to internalize concepts such as these and you won't have to really think about them explicitly when you're writing day-to-day code. For now, though, there's some logic shortcuts we can use to keep from getting too tripped up.

In the next chapter, you will learn about modeling using object-oriented Java programs in detail.

6

Modeling with Object-Oriented Java

In this chapter, you're going to learn how to create classes and objects in Java. Object-oriented programming allows us to explain highly complicated systems to the computer and also ourselves. In addition, there's a lot more to learn about object-oriented programming in terms of how objects fit together, the kinds of relationships they can have, and what we can do with objects to make our programs easier to write. We will also walk through the topics of creating custom classes, member variables, and member functions. Finally, we will look into a very special member assigned to our custom classes, that is, the constructor, and types of constructor.

We are going to cover the following topics in this chapter:

- Creating classes and objects
- Creating custom classes
- Creating member variables
- Creating member functions
- Creating constructors
- Types of constructors

Creating classes and objects

In this section, you'll take the first real steps of learning object-oriented programming in Java. So I guess the first question to ask is, "What is object-oriented programming?" Well, at a high level, object-oriented programming is the creation of objects, discrete code, and logic entities that are unique and separate from each other but can have complicated relationships.

When we write object-oriented code, we begin to deal with and think about the code as though it were a collection of physical pieces or objects. Java is by its very nature an object-oriented language. So, if you've been learning Java, at the very least, you've been using objects without realizing it.

To see the power of object-oriented programming, take a look at the following program (GettingObjectOriented.java):

```java
package gettingobjectoriented;

import java.util.*;

public class GettingObjectOriented {
    public static void main(String[] args) {
        Scanner reader = new Scanner(System.in);

        System.out.println(reader.next());
    }
}
```

This program is a very basic input/output program, the kind you've probably already written if you've been learning Java. In this program, we make use of a Scanner object that we call reader, and you'll notice that we utilize reader on two lines: on one line, we declare and initialize reader, and on the other line, we call the next() function of reader to acquire some user input.

The important thing I'd like you to notice about the relationship between these two lines of code is that when we declare `reader`, we provide it with some additional information besides simply the command to create a new `Scanner` object. This is interesting because later when we utilize the `next()` function of `reader`, we won't have to retell it what stream it should be reading from; instead, this information is automatically stored and recalled by the `reader` object.

This is the beauty of object-oriented programming: the entities or objects we create can be constructed in such a way that not only do they know what to do with the information given to them and provide us with additional functionality, but also that they know exactly what information to ask to perform their later tasks.

Let's make sure we have our terminology straight. First, let's analyze the `new Scanner(System.in)` part of our code. This command tells Java to create a new object, a new `Scanner` object, for use in our program. This object has location and memory in which it lives, and this location is referenced by the `reader` variable. It would be possible for us to create multiple variables that all point toward the same `Scanner` object; however, in the context of this simple program, `reader` is our only entry point to the object's location in memory. So, we can often get away with referring to an object like this simply by its variable name.

Lastly, different objects operate in a different manner. It is possible for us to create multiple `Scanner` objects; they would not have the same location in memory, but they would share similar functionality. The piece of code and logic that declares what functionality an object has and how that functionality operates is called the object's class. In this case, we're creating an object of the `Scanner` class and pointing to it with the `reader` variable.

This is all well and good, and we can create a whole lot of programs simply using the default standard libraries that Java provides; however, to really open the doors, we're going to need the ability to create custom classes of our own. Let's jump in and create one.

Creating custom classes

Now, we could create a new class within the file we're already working in; however, class declaration code is a little different and logically discrete from something like the executed `main()` method, where the lines are executed one after another in order. Rather, the class we're going to create is going to serve more as a reference for the lines of code, such as the `Scanner reader = new Scanner(System.in);` code line. Generally, when working in an object-oriented language, a high-level object-oriented language such as Java, we simply put each and every new class we create in its own separate file.

To create a new Java file for our class, just right-click on the package name on the left-hand side of the screen, that is, `gettingobjectoriented`. Then, choose **New**, followed by **Java Class**. Post this, we'll just be prompted to give it a name.

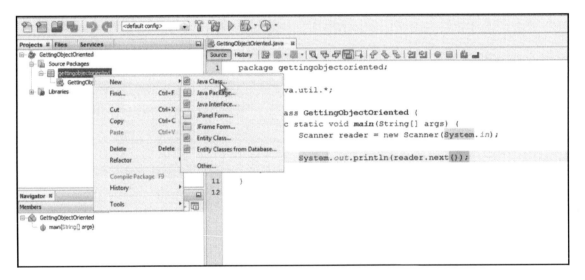

In this instance, we are going to create a class to provide and store some basic information about a person. We'll call it the `Person` class, which creates person objects:

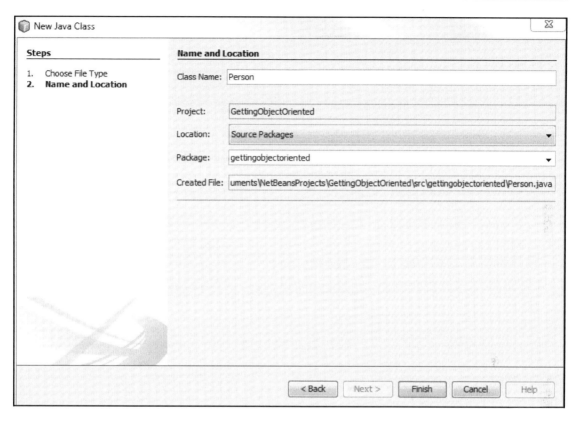

When we press **Finish**, NetBeans is pretty handy and sets up some really basic lines of code for us. It declares this class to be in our local package. This means that when we reference it from our `main()` method, we won't have to import this class like we do with standard library ones. NetBeans is kind enough to create the class declaration for us. This is simply a line of code that lets the Java compiler know that we're about to declare a new class as shown in the following screenshot:

```
package gettingobjectoriented;
public class Person {
}
```

For now, we'll ignore the `public` keyword, but know that it's pretty necessary here. The `class` keyword self-explanatorily lets us know that we're about to declare a class, and then just like everything we create and need to reference at a future date, we give the class a name or a unique keyword.

It's time to write the code to set up our `Person` class. Remember that what we're doing here is teaching future pieces of our program how to create `Person` objects or instances of the `Person` class. So, the code we write here is going to look very different from what we would write in a method that simply executes the lines from start to finish.

The information we place within a class declaration is going to fall into one of these two categories:

- The first category is us telling Java what information a `Person` class should be able to store
- The second category is us teaching Java what functionality a `Person` object should expose

Creating member variables

Let's start with the first category. Let's tell Java what information we'd like to store in `Person`:

```
package gettingobjectoriented;

public class Person {
    public String firstName;
    public String lastName;
}
```

Telling Java what information to store is a lot like declaring variables in any other piece of code. Here, we've given the `Person` class two member variables; these are pieces of information that we can access in any `Person` object.

Just about everything we declare in a class declaration needs to be given a protection level. When we become more advanced Java users, we'll begin to use different protection levels, but for now, we're simply going to declare everything "public."

So, as we've set it up here, every `Person` object has `firstName` and `lastName`. Remember, these member variables are unique to each instance of a `Person` object, so different persons do not necessarily share first and last names.

To make things a little more interesting, let's also assign birthdays to people. We'll need to import `java.util` because we're going to use another class for this, the `Calendar` class:

```
package gettingobjectoriented;
import java.util.*;
public class Person {
    public String firstName;
    public String lastName;
    public Calendar birthday;
}
```

Calendars are basically points and times or dates with a whole lot of functionality wrapped around them. The cool thing is that `Calendar` is a class of its own. So we're placing a class within our `Person` class; `String` is a class too, but Java considers it a little special.

Now, let's head back to the `main()` method in the `GettingObjectOriented.java` file and see what it looks like to create a brand new person. For now, we'll leave this line of code so we can use it as a template. We'd like to create a new instance of our `Person` class or create a new `Person` object. To do this, we're first going to tell Java what type of object we'd like to create.

Because we've declared the `Person` class within the package that we're using, Java will understand the `Person` keyword now. Then, we need to give a name to the variable that we will assign our new person to; let's name the person `john`. Creating a new person is as simple as creating a new `Scanner` object. We use the `new` keyword to let Java know that we're creating something brand new that doesn't exist yet, then we ask it to create a person:

```
package gettingobjectoriented;

import java.util.*;

public class GettingObjectOriented {
    public static void main(String[] args) {
        Scanner reader = new Scanner(System.in);
        Person john = new Person();
        System.out.println(reader.next());
    }
}
```

Here, `Person john = new Person();` will cause the person pointed to by the variable `john`, who we'll just think of as a person John, to come into being. Now `john` already has some basic functionality just by the fact that we've declared some member variables for the `Person` class, so even our rudimentary declaration of the `Person` class has given John some member variables that we can work with.

For example, `john` has `firstName` that we can access as a variable with the dot(.) operator, and we can go ahead and assign a value to this variable. We can do the same thing with John's last name and also, of course, his birthday:

```
package gettingobjectoriented;
import java.util.*;
public class GettingObjectOriented {
    public static void main(String[] args) {
        Scanner reader = new Scanner(System.in);
        Person john = new Person();
        john.firstName = "John";
        john.lastName = "Doe";
        john.birthday =
        System.out.println(reader.next());
    }
}
```

Now, I had mentioned that `birthday` was going to be a little different from `firstName` and `lastName` by the time we reach this point. While strings are technically classes in Java, Java also gives them the special privilege of being able to be assigned to an explicit value or a string explicit. Calendars, of course, don't have this unique special privilege, so we're going to need to create a new `Calendar` object to place within our object, that is, `john`.

Now, `Calendar` is one of those classes that we can assign instances of; however, when we want to create a brand new one, we would need to create something more specific that is also a calendar. So, for this instance, we'll use `GregorianCalendar`. Then, let's assign `birthday` to `john`, say, `1988, 1, 5`. Then, to see that everything is being assigned as expected, simply print out John's first and last names.

There we go! When we run the following program:

```
package gettingobjectoriented;
import java.util.*;
public class GettingObjectOriented {
    public static void main(String[] args) {
        Scanner reader = new Scanner(System.in);
        Person john = new Person();
        john.firstName = "John";
        john.lastName = "Doe";
        john.birthday = new GregorianCalendar(1988,1,5);
        System.out.println(john.firstName + john.lastName);
    }
}
```

We see `John Doe` not really properly formatted but printed to the screen, as expected:

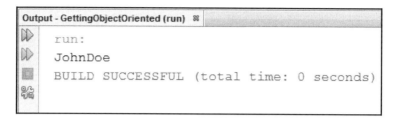

We've successfully stored information in our `john` object. If we wanted to, we could create a brand new person "Jane" who would have `firstName`, `lastName`, and `birthday` of her own; her member variables being completely separate from that of John's.

Creating member functions

Let's go back to our `Person` class, that is, the `Person.java` file, and provide people with some more functionality. So, the beauty of object-oriented Java is that we're already beginning to think about instances of our `Person` class as physical objects. This makes anticipating the questions that will be asked of them much easier.

For example, when I meet someone new, I'd either want to know their first name or their full name in most cases. So wouldn't it be nice if our person stores a string called `fullName` that people could just ask of rather than having to individually acquire their first and last names?

Now, of course, simply adding another member variable like this is unwieldy because the people creating a new instance of `Person` will need to set `fullName`. Also, if the person's first name, last name, or full name were to ever change, their `fullName`, `firstName`, and `lastName` variable might not match up properly. But what if instead of a member variable, we provide a member method?

When we create methods within the context of a class, we have access to the class's member variables. We can modify them if we want, or if we're doing something like we just did, we can simply utilize their values, in this case return this person's dynamically constructed full name:

```
package gettingobjectoriented;
import java.util.*;
public class Person {
    public String firstName;
    public String lastName;
    public Calendar birthday;
```

```
        public String fullName()
        {
               return firstName + " " + lastName;
        }
   }
```

There's another question that I anticipate this person being asked, and that is how old are you? This will be a lot like the method we just wrote, with one exception. In order to know how old this person is, this person will need to be told what today's date is because that's not information that this person already stores.

To do this, we'll ask people to pass this information when they call this method, and we'll simply return the difference between today's year and the birthday year of this person.

Now, the syntax for getting a year from a calendar is a little wonky, but I think we should be able to follow it. We simply use the `get` method, which has a number of uses, and then we need to tell the method exactly what we'd like to get from it, and what we'd like to get is a calendar year(`Calendar.YEAR`). So, let's make sure to save this file and jump over to our `main` method and make use of one of these new methods that we've just added to `Person` instances:

```
   package gettingobjectoriented;
   import java.util.*;
   public class Person {
        public String firstName;
        public String lastName;
        public Calendar birthday;
        public String fullName()
        {
               return firstName + " " + lastName;
        }
        public int age(Calendar today)
        {
               return today.get(Calendar.YEAR) - birthday.get(Calendar.YEAR);
        }
   }
```

So, we've set up `john`. He has a birthday. Let's ask John how old he is, right in our `println` statement here. To do this, we're simply going to call John's `age` method and create a new `Calendar` object to pass in. I think the new `GregorianCalendar` instance will be set to the current date and time by default.

If we run the following program:

```
package gettingobjectoriented;
import java.util.*;
public class GettingObjectOriented {
    public static void main(String[] args) {
        Scanner reader = new Scanner(System.in);
        Person john = new Person();
        john.firstName = "John";
        john.lastName = "Doe";
        john.birthday = new GregorianCalendar(1988,1,5);
        System.out.println(john.age(new GregorianCalendar()));
    }
}
```

We see that John is 29 years old:

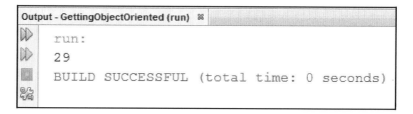

So there you have it. That's our basic introduction to object-oriented Java, but it's all going to boil down to the basics that you just learned.

Creating constructors

In this section, you're going to learn about a very special member we can assign to our custom classes, that is, the constructor. To start off, let's take a look at the following code:

```
package gettingobjectoriented;

import java.util.*;

public class GettingObjectOriented {
    public static void main(String[] args) {
        Scanner reader = new Scanner(System.in);
        Person john = new Person();
        john.firstName = "John";
        john.lastName = "Doe";
        john.birthday = new GregorianCalendar(1988,1,5);
        System.out.println(
```

```
            "Hello my name is " +
            john.fullName() +
            ". I am " +
            john.age(new GregorianCalendar()) +
            " years old.");
        }
    }
```

This program creates an instance of our custom class `Person` and immediately assigns some values to member variables of `Person`: `firstName`, `lastName`, and `birthday`. Then, we utilize some of the member functions of `Person` to print out some information about the values we've just assigned.

While this is a decent program, which we've just written, it's easy to see someone make a mistake while writing even this simple program. For example, what if I had forgotten, or simply didn't realize, that `birthday` was one of the member variables of `Person`? If I don't assign a birthday to a person right away and then attempt to use the `age()` member method as shown in the following code block:

```
package gettingobjectoriented;

import java.util.*;

public class GettingObjectOriented {
    public static void main(String[] args) {
        Person john = new Person();
        john.firstName = "John";
        john.lastName = "Doe";
        //john.birthday = new GregorianCalendar(1988,1,5);
        System.out.println(
        "Hello my name is " +
        john.fullName() +
        ". I am " +
        john.age(new GregorianCalendar()) +
        " years old.");
    }
}
```

Our program would crash when it attempts to access that birthday variable that has not been set to anything as shown in the following screenshot:

```
Output - GettingObjectOriented (run)

  run:
  Exception in thread "main" java.lang.NullPointerException
          at gettingobjectoriented.Person.age(Person.java:13)
          at gettingobjectoriented.GettingObjectOriented.main(GettingObjectOriented.java:15)
  C:\Users\nidhishas\AppData\Local\NetBeans\Cache\8.2\executor-snippets\run.xml:53: Java returned: 1
  BUILD FAILED (total time: 0 seconds)
```

This is a very reasonable mistake for a programmer to make, both in terms of not knowing that they should set this member variable to a value and also in assuming that this member variable would have a value because what person doesn't have a birthday? Fortunately, there's a system in place where we can demand information from the user before we allow them to even create an instance of our object. So, let's jump into the code that declares the `Person` class and set this class up so that a person can only be created if it's given all of the necessary information right from the start. To do this, we're going to use a constructor.

A constructor declaration looks a lot like a normal method declaration, except for one thing. Where a normal method would have a return value, even the value null if it wasn't designed to return anything, constructors don't even have that. Also, the name of the constructor method is the same name that we've assigned to our class; however, just like normal methods, we can give input to constructors.

To start off, let's assume that all persons have `firstName`, `lastName`, and `birthday`; otherwise, they simply shouldn't exist. When we create a new instance of the `Person` class and the `Person` class has a constructor defined, we will always create an instance of the class using the `Person` constructor:

```java
package gettingobjectoriented;

import java.util.*;

public class Person {
    public String firstName;
    public String lastName;
    public Calendar birthday;
    public Person(String firstName, String lastName, Calendar birthday)
    {

    }
    public String fullName()
    {
        return firstName + " " + lastName;
```

```
    }
    public int age(Calendar today)
    {
          return today.get(Calendar.YEAR) - birthday.get(Calendar.YEAR);
    }
}
```

If we save this update to our `Person` class declaration and then go back to the `main` method of our program, we'll get a compiler error as shown in the following screenshot:

```
import java.uti   constructor Person in class Person cannot be applied to given types;
                  required: String, String, Calendar
                  found: no arguments
public class Ge   reason: actual and formal argument lists differ in length
                  ....
     public stat  (Alt-Enter shows hints)

          Person john = new Person();    I
```

That's because we've modified the `Person` class to demand that our newly created constructor be used. This constructor takes three input values: a string, a string, and a calendar. So, instead of modifying the member variables of `Person` in these three lines of code, what we're going to do is pass these three variables as arguments to our constructor method:

```
package gettingobjectoriented;

import java.util.*;

public class GettingObjectOriented {
    public static void main(String[] args) {
        Person john = new Person("John", "Doe",
newGregorianCalendar(1988,1,5));

        System.out.println(
        "Hello my name is " + john.fullName() + ". I am " + john.age(new
        GregorianCalendar()) +
        " years old.");
    }
}
```

Now, as far as the main method in our program is concerned, the syntax of our program is once again valid. Of course, if we run this program, we're going to run into some trouble because while we pass these arguments to the Person constructor, we haven't yet done anything with them.

Now, it needs to be the job of our Person constructor here, as opposed to the main method in our Java program, to translate these parameters into the values of the member variables of Person. So, let's do that. Let's change our Person class's firstName, or rather set its value, to the variable passed to this function:

```
package gettingobjectoriented;
import java.util.*;
public class Person {
    String firstName;
    String lastName;
    Calendar birthday;
    public Person(String firstName, String lastName, Calendar birthday)
    {
        firstName = firstName;
    }
    public String fullName()
    {
        return firstName + " " + lastName;
    }

    public int age(Calendar today)
    {
        return today.get(Calendar.YEAR) - birthday.get(Calendar.YEAR);
    }
}
```

Now, this is a technically correct syntax that we have here; it will do what we want it to do.

The firstName = firstName code line is really weird, and it's pretty ambiguous if you go about reading it. After all, which firstName variable are we talking about in each of these instances? Are we talking about Person.firstName, the member variable of this class, or are we talking about firstName that was passed in as an argument to the constructor method? To disambiguate this, we can do a couple of things.

First off, we could simply change the name we assign to our method arguments to something that's not identical to the local member name; however, sometimes, it just makes sense to explicitly ask for firstName. It can be a lot easier for people who are going to use the constructor. When we need to explicitly tell our program that we're using one of Person class's member variables, we should provide a path for it properly. The this keyword will allow us to access the class that we're currently operating in, or rather its object instance, when the program runs. So, this.firstName will always reference the member variable as opposed to the one passed in as an argument. Now that we have the syntax, we can quickly assign the argument values to the values of our member variables:

```java
public Person(String firstName, String lastName, Calendar birthday)
{
    this.firstName = firstName;
    this.lastName = lastName;
    this.birthday = birthday;
}
```

Now when we save this file and go back to our main method—that is, GettingObjectOriented.java—and run our program, we'll get the original output showing us that our Person constructor has properly mapped these input values to the values stored in our Person object:

```
Output - GettingObjectOriented (run)  ✕

run:
Hello my name is John Doe. I am 29 years old.
BUILD SUCCESSFUL (total time: 0 seconds)
```

So this is pretty cool. We've modified our Person class so that it's much more difficult for a programmer to make an obvious mistake and call these methods when they're bound to fail. A programmer could still get into trouble if they did something along the lines of modifying one of the member variables after our person has been created.

However, there's a system in place for us to protect our classes, if we choose to, from having their members modified without going through a proper protocol. Let's say that we'd like to change our `Person` class so that the only time these members are ever changed is once at the very beginning when the constructor calls. If you remember, we've been tagging all the members of our classes with this `public` protection tag. Something that's tagged `public` is basically viewable anytime by any piece of our program that has access to its container.

However, we can use a couple of other different protection tags. If we were to tag all our member variables `private`, then they would only be viewable within the context of their current class. So, we could still use the member variables in our `Person` constructor and in our `fullName` and `age` methods, but when we attempt to access `lastName` outside of the actual class declaration, then it would be invalid:

```
package gettingobjectoriented;

import java.util.*;

public class Person {
    private String firstName;
    private String lastName;
    private Calendar birthday;
```

We can tag members `private` and then create public methods to modify their values when appropriate. By doing so, we will protect our objects from ever being given invalid values.

Types of constructors

Now, let's go back to talking about constructors before we wrap up. As with normal methods, we can override constructors and have more than one option for our programmer to choose from.

For example, let's say that sometimes in our program, we want to create new people who have just been born. In this instance, it might make a lot of sense for us to construct a person by simply giving `firstName` and `lastName` to our constructor and then having `birthday` as new `Gregorian Calendar`, which will default to today's date:

```
package gettingobjectoriented;

import java.util.*;

public class Person {
    private String firstName;
    private String lastName;
```

```
    private Calendar birthday;
    public Person(String firstName, String lastName)
    {
        this.firstName = firstName;
        this.lastName = lastName;
        this.birthday = new GregorianCalendar();
    }
    public Person(String firstName, String lastName, Calendar
    birthday)
    {
        this.firstName = firstName;
        this.lastName = lastName;
        this.birthday = birthday;
    }
```

If we wanted to use this constructor in our program instead, we'd simply call the constructor with only two string arguments. This would map to the newly created constructor that we've declared here.

Consider the following program:

```
package gettingobjectoriented;

import java.util.*;

public class GettingObjectOriented {
    public static void main(String[] args) {
            Person john = new Person("John", "Doe");
            System.out.println(
                    "Hello my name is " +
                    john.fullName() +
                    ". I am " +
                    john.age(new GregorianCalendar()) +
                    " years old.");
    }
}
```

When we run it, since the birth date has been set to the current date and time, we will see that John Doe is now 0 years old, as shown in the following screenshot:

```
Output - GettingObjectOriented (run)  ✖

    run:
    Hello my name is John Doe. I am 0 years old.
    BUILD SUCCESSFUL (total time: 0 seconds)
```

Lastly, we can give someone the option of utilizing one of our constructors or simply creating an instance of the class without doing anything, simply by declaring a constructor that is empty. Then, the syntax will look just like the creation of John we participated in earlier:

```
public Person()
{

}
```

Generally, we don't want to do this, though. What we want to do if we have an empty or default constructor is to assign default values to our member variables so that at the very least, we're still not breaking our program. So, it might make a lot of sense for our default constructor to assign empty strings and maybe today's date to our firstName, lastName, and birthday fields:

```
public Person()
    {
        firstName = "";
        lastName = "";
        birthday = new GregorianCalendar();
    }
```

Then, even if our programmer doesn't properly assign values to John's fields after creating them, there's still going to be some valid values in those fields to protect us from actually throwing an error when we run the following program:

```
package gettingobjectoriented;

import java.util.*;

public class GettingObjectOriented {
    public static void main(String[] args) {
            Person john = new Person();
            System.out.println(
                    "Hello my name is " +
                    john.fullName() +
```

```
                                ".  I am  " +
                                john.age(new GregorianCalendar()) +
                                " years old.");
                }
        }
```

The following is the output of the preceding code:

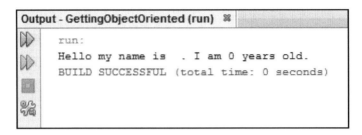

So that's the skinny on constructors, another tool that helps us protect and make the code we've already written more robust.

Summary

In this chapter, we saw how to create classes and objects and how we can create member variables and functions that will make our code less complicated. You also learned about creating constructors assigned to the class and types of constructors.

7

More Object-Oriented Java

In this chapter, we're going to explore the topic of inheritance in Java by creating a superclass and subclass and understanding the relationship of "is-a" between them, using concepts such as overriding, data structures, the abstract method, and the protected method. We'll also delve into the concept of an Abstract class.

We'll cover the following concepts in detail:

- Inheritance
- Abstract

Inheritance

Rather than starting with a high-level description, I think it'll be best if we jump right into a problem.

To get us started, I've created a basic Java program, which we can access from the given code files. In this program, we declare two Java classes: a `Book` class and a `Poem` class. Both the `Book` and `Poem` classes store a number of attributes; for example, Book can have a title, an author, a publisher, and a genre. It takes all these attributes as constructor input and provides a single `public` method; we can use the `Print` method in our main program to print out information about any books we create.

The Poem method does something very similar. It has a couple of attributes and a `Print` method, and we set its attributes through its constructor. I've whipped up a really quick main function to utilize the `Book` and `Poem` classes. This function creates a new book and poem and then prints them out:

```
package inheritance;
public class Inheritance {
    public static void main(String[] args) {
        Book a = new Book(
                "The Lord Of The Rings",
                "J.R.R. Tolkein",
                "George Allen and Unwin",
                "Fantasy");
        Poem b = new Poem(
                "The Iliad",
                "Homer",
                "Dactylic Hexameter");

        a.Print();
        b.Print();
    }
}
```

The preceding program works fine, but it's much more complicated than it needs to be.

If we take a look at our `Book` and `Poem` classes side by side and just look at their member variables, we'll see that both `Book` and `Poem` share two member variables, namely `title` and `author`:

Inheritance.java Book.java ✖

Source History

```java
 2    public class Book {
          private String title;
          private String author;
          private String publisher;
          private String genre;

 8        public Book(String title, String author, String publisher, String genre)
 9        {
10            this.title = title;
11            this.author = author;
12            this.publisher = publisher;
13            this.genre = genre;
14        }

16        public void Print()
17        {
18            System.out.println(title);
19            System.out.println("\tWritten By: " + author);
20            System.out.println("\tPublished By: " + publisher);
21            System.out.println("\tIs A: " + genre);
22        }
23    }
```

Poem.java ✖

Source History

```java
 1    package inheritance;
 2    public class Poem {
          private String title;
          private String author;
          private String style;

 7        public Poem(String title, String author, String style)
 8        {
 9            this.title = title;
10            this.author = author;
11            this.style = style;
12        }

14        public void Print()
15        {
16            System.out.println(title);
17            System.out.println("\tWritten By: " + author);
18            System.out.println("\tIn The Style Of: " + style);
19        }
20    }
```

The actions they take with the member variables, namely printing them to the screen, are performed and achieved in a very similar manner in both classes:

```
Inheritance.java    Book.java ✳
Source   History

16          public void Print()
17          {
18              System.out.println(title);
19              System.out.println("\tWritten By: " + author);
20              System.out.println("\tPublished By: " + publisher);
21              System.out.println("\tIs A: " + genre);
22          }
23      }
```

```
Poem.java ✳
Source   History

14          public void Print()
15          {
16              System.out.println(title);
17              System.out.println("\tWritten By: " + author);
18              System.out.println("\tIn The Style Of: " + style);
19          }
20      }
21
```

It's a good sign that Book and Poem inherit from one common class. This becomes easy for us to see when we think about books and poems as the physical objects that they represent. We can make the statement that both books and poems are forms of literature.

Creating a superclass

Once we've come to the conclusion that books and poems share certain fundamental attributes, the attributes of all literature, we can start breaking down these classes into component parts. Our `Book` class, for example, has two real variables. It has a `title` variable and an `author` variable, which are attributes we associate with all literature. It also has a `publisher` variable and a `genre` variable, which may not be unique only to books and which we don't necessarily consider all forms of literature to have. So how can we exploit this knowledge? Well, we can build our `Book` and `Poem` classes so that they share their nature as pieces of literature at a fundamental level. But to make this happen, we're first going to have to teach our program what a piece of literature is. The following is a step-by-step procedure for doing this:

1. We'll create a brand new class and call it `Literature`.

2. We'll assign to this class the attributes that the pieces of literature share, which we've so far declared. In our case, books and poems are already declared as pieces, with shared titles and authors. It makes some logical sense to make a statement that all pieces of literature will have a title and an author:

```
package inheritance;
public class Literature {
    protected String title;
    protected String author;
```

3. From here, we'll flesh out our `Literature` class like we would any other. We'll give it a constructor; in this case, our constructor will take two variables: `title` and `author`. Then, we'll assign them to the fields, much like we did with our `Poem` and `Book` classes:

```
package inheritance;
public class Literature {
  protected String title;
  protected String author;

  public Literature(String title, String author)
  {
     this.title = title;
     this.author = author;
  }
```

4. While we're at it, let's give `Literature` a similar `Print` method, as the one we assigned to the `Book` and `Poem` classes:

```
public void Print()
{
    System.out.println(title);
    System.out.println("\tWritten By: " + author);
}
```

Now if we wanted to, we could go to our `main` method and declare an object of the `Literature` class, but that's not the point. This is not the reason we've created the `Literature` class. Rather, our goal is to make use of this `Literature` class as a base that we'll build on to declare more specific types of literature, such as poems or books. To make use of our `Literature` class, let's see how it applies to the existing `Poem` class.

The is-a relationship

Our `Literature` class contains the declarations and all of the functionality needed to manage a piece of literature's title and author. If we let Java know that there is an inheritance relationship between `Poem` and `Literature`, we should be able to remove all the real references from the title and author of the following `Poem` class:

```
package inheritance;
public class Poem extends Literature{
    private String title;
    private String author;
    private String style;
```

First, let's talk about the declaration of the `Poem` class that we've modified. When we say that one class extends another, we're saying that there is an is-a relationship between them such that I can logically make the statement, "A poem is a piece of literature." In more Java terms, we're saying that the `Poem` subclass extends or inherits from the `Literature` class. This means that when we create a `Poem` object, it will have all the members and functionality of the class that it extends:

```
package inheritance;
public class Poem extends Literature {
    private String style;

    public Poem(String title, String author, String style)
```

In our case, two of these members are `title` and `author`. The `Literature` class declares these members and does a good job of managing them throughout the class's functionality. So, we can remove these members from our `Poem` class and we'll still be able to access them within the `Poem` class's methods. This is because the `Poem` class simply inherits its declaration from `Literature`. We do need to make a slight modification to get this `Poem` class working as intended, though. When we construct an object of a class that inherits from another class, by default the constructor of the subclass, as in the preceding screenshot, will begin by calling the constructor of the superclass:

```
package inheritance;
public class Literature {
    protected String title;
    protected String author;

    public Literature(String title, String author)
    {
        this.title = title;
        this.author = author;
    }
}
```

This confuses Java as we have it set up right now because the `Poem` constructor takes three variables as input whereas the `Literature` constructor is only expecting two. To solve this, explicitly call the `Literature` constructor within the `Poem` constructor, using the following steps:

1. When we're in a subclass, we can call the methods of our superclass using the `super` keyword. So in this case, we're going to begin our `Poem` constructor by simply calling the `super` constructor, or the `Literature` constructor, and passing to it the attributes that we'd like it to know about:

```
public Poem(String title, String author, String style)
{
    super(title, author);
    this.style = style;
}
```

2. We can do something very similar in our `Print` method because our `Literature` class, our superclass, knows how to print out a title and author already. There's no reason for the `Poem` class to implement this functionality:

```
public void Print()
{
    super.Print();
    System.out.println("\tIn The Style Of: " + style);
}
```

We'll get the same behavior from our `Print` method if we begin it by calling `super.Print`, instead of the original explicit printing lines shown in the preceding screenshot. Now, when the Poem's `Print` method runs, it will begin by calling the superclass's, that is, the `Literature.java` class's `Print` method. It will finally print out the `Poem` class's style, which is not shared across all pieces of literature.

While our `Poem` constructor and `Literature` constructor have different names and even different styles of input, the two `Print` methods shared between `Poem` and `Literature` are exactly the same. We'll talk about this a little more later, but for now you should know that we've made use of a technique called **overriding** here.

Overriding

When we declare that a subclass has a method that's identical to one of its superclass methods, we've overridden the superclass method. When we do this, it's a good idea to use the Java `Override` indicator:

```
@Override public void Print()
```

This is an indicator to future coders and some more arcane elements of our compiling suite that this particular method, given in the preceding screenshot, is hiding a method beneath it. When we actually run our code, Java gives preference to the lowest or subclassed version of a method.

So let's see whether we've declared our `Poem` and `Literature` relationship successfully. Let's go back to the `main` method of our program in the `Inheritence.java` class and see whether the poem portion of this program executes as it did before:

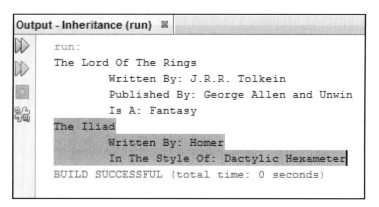

```
Output - Inheritance (run)  ✕

run:
The Lord Of The Rings
        Written By: J.R.R. Tolkein
        Published By: George Allen and Unwin
        Is A: Fantasy
The Iliad
        Written By: Homer
        In The Style Of: Dactylic Hexameter
BUILD SUCCESSFUL (total time: 0 seconds)
```

When we run this program, we get the exact same output as we did previously, which is a great sign that we've set up our `Poem` class to inherit from `Literature` in a logical manner.

Now we can jump to our `Book` class. We'll set it up as an is-a relationship between the `Book` and `Literature` class using the following steps:

1. First, we'll declare that `Book` extends the `Literature` class; then, we'll remove references to title and author in our `Book` class because now the `Literature` class, the superclass, will take care of this:

```
package inheritance;
public class Book extends Literature{
private String publisher;
private String genre;
```

2. As with the `Poem` class, we're going to need to explicitly call the `Literature` class's constructor and pass `title` and `author` to it:

```
public Book(String title, String author, String publisher, String
genre)
{
    super(title, author);
    this.publisher = publisher;
    this.genre = genre;
}
```

3. Then, we can make use of our superclass's `Print` method to simplify the printing of our `Book` class:

```
@Override public void Print()
{
    super.Print();
    System.out.println("\tPublished By: " + publisher);
    System.out.println("\tIs A: " + genre);
```

4. Once again, let's jump back to our `main` method and run it to make sure that we've done this successfully:

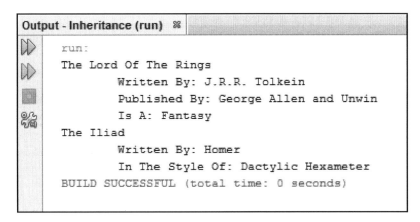

There we go: `The Lord of the Rings` output, just as we saw it before. Style-wise, this change is really great. By adding the `Literature` class and then subclassing it to create `Book` and `Poem` classes, we've made our `Book` and `Poem` classes much more bite-sized and easier for a programmer to go through and figure out what's going on.

However, this change is not purely stylistic. By declaring an is-a relationship between the `Book`, `Poem`, and `Literature` classes, where `Book` and `Poem` inherit from the `Literature` class, we've given ourselves actual functionality that we didn't have before. Let's take a look at this in action. If we go back to our `main` method, let's pretend that, rather than dealing with a single `Book` and `Poem` class, we're dealing with a vast network that we need to store in some sort of a data structure. With our original implementation, this would be a real challenge.

Data structure

There's no easily accessible data structure that will happily store both books and poems. We'd probably have to use two data structures or break strong typing, which is the whole point of Java:

```
Book[] books = new Book[5];
```

However, with our new implementation, where Book and Poem both inherit from Literature, we can store them in the same data structure. This is because inheritance is an is-a relationship, meaning that we can, once we've inherited from something, make claims such as book is literature and poem is a literature too. If that's true, then an array of Literature objects should be able to store both Book and Poem within it. Let's go through the following steps to illustrate this:

1. Create an array of Literature objects:

   ```
   Literature[] lits = new Literature[5];
   lits[0] = a;
   lits[1] = b;
   ```

   The fact that we get no compile errors when we build this project is a really good sign that we're doing something legal.

2. For the sake of our demonstration, let's flesh out our array here to contain the number of books and poems:

   ```
   Literature[] lits = new Literature[5];
   lits[0] = a;
   lits[1] = b;
   lits[2] = a;
   lits[3] = b;
   lits[4] = a;
   ```

   We'll modify our main method to print out directly from the array. Now, when we utilize our subclasses as though they were objects of their superclass, we do have to be aware that we're now referencing them as objects of that superclass. For example, when we go through and acquire an element from our Literature array, irrespective of whether that element is a Book class, we will still not be able to access things such as its genre field even if this field is public:

   ```
   Literature[] lits = new Literature[5];
   lits[0] = a;
   lits[1] = b;
   ```

```
lits[2] = a;
lits[3] = b;
lits[4] = a;
for(int i=0; i< lits.length; i++)
{
        lits[i].Print();
}
```

This is because the `Literature` class that we're now using as an object (as given in the preceding screenshot) does not have a `genre` member variable. But what we can do is call methods from our superclass that are overridden by the subclasses.

3. We can call the `Literature` class's `Print` method within our `for` loop. Java will prioritize the `Print` methods of our subclasses:

```
for(int i=0; i< lits.length; i++)
{
        lits[i].Print();
}
```

This means that, when we run this program, we'll still get the specially formatted output that we have attributed to `Book` and `Poem`, not the simplified version that we stored in our `Literature` class:

```
public void Print()
{
        System.out.println(title);
        System.out.println("\tWritten By: " + author);
}
```

The abstract method

We may sometimes see methods that exist only to be overloaded by subclasses. These methods don't do anything, and we can tag them with the `abstract` keyword, that is, `public abstract void Print()`, in the superclass (`Literature.java`). Of course, if a class has methods declared `abstract`, it's probably a good sign that an instance of such a class should never be explicitly created. If our `Literature` class's `Print` method is abstract, we should never declare objects that are only Literature. We should only use objects that are one of the subclasses of `Literature`. If we're going to go down this route, we should declare `Literature` to be an `abstract` class as well:

```
package inheritance;
public abstract class Literature {
```

If we did this, of course, we'd have to get rid of the references to the Literature class's super method, so let's undo these changes for now.

Let's take a look at a minor mistake we made when building this program initially. When creating our Literature class, we declared that title and author were `public` member variables. As you may know, generally we do not declare member variables public if we don't have a good reason to. It doesn't make a lot of sense for a piece of literature to change its author after it's been declared already, so `author` and `title` should be `private` member variables that are set in the `Literature` class's constructor whose values should never change. Unfortunately, if we make this change to our Literature class, we're going to limit the functionality of our Poem and Book classes.

Let's say, for example, that we wanted to modify the `Print` function of our `Poem` class so that it wouldn't have to explicitly call the `Print` function of the `Literature` class:

```
@Override public void Print()
{
    System.out.println(title);
    System.out.println("\tWritten By: " + author);
    System.out.println("\tIn The Style Of: " + style);
}
```

Maybe we want to start it by telling it that we're declaring a `Poem` class here:

```
System.out.println("POEM: " + title);
```

Unfortunately, because we've made `title` and `author` private to the `Literature` class, the `Poem` class, even though it is a subclass of `Literature`, will not be able to access these member variables in its explicit code. This is kind of annoying, and it seems like there is some sort of protection setting between `private` and `public` where it's private for every class, except for the subclasses of the class. In fact, there is a protection setting available.

The protected method

The `protected` method is the protected protection setting. If we declare that member variables are `protected`, it implies they're private and not accessible by anyone, except the class and it's subclasses:

```
package inheritance;
public class Literature {
    protected String title;
    protected String author;
```

Just to reassure ourselves, everything we've been doing here is legitimate. Let's run our program again and make sure the output looks good, which is the case. After this, we should have a pretty good grasp of inheritance. We can develop a lot of systems that really mimic their real-world counterparts, and we can write very elegant and functional code using inheritance and small classes that don't do a lot of complicated things in and of themselves.

Abstract

In this section, we'll take a quick look at an important idea that relates to inheritance in Java. To wrap our heads around what we're going to talk about, I think it's best if we start an existing project in the system. So let's take a look at the code we have in the code files.

So far, we've done the following:

- The `main` method of our program creates a list of objects. These objects are either of the type `Book` or `Poem`, but we've placed them in a list of `Literature` objects, leading us to believe that the `Book` and `Poem` classes must inherit from or extend the `Literature` class.
- Once we've built this array, we simply iterate through it using a `for` loop and call the `Print` method of this `for` loop on each object.
- At this point, we're dealing with objects as `Literature` objects, not the Books or Poems that they are at the lowest level. This leads us to believe that the `Literature` class itself must implement a `Print` method; if we jump into the class, we'll see that this is true indeed.

However, if we run our program, we will quickly see that Books and Poems execute their `Print` method slightly differently, displaying different information for each of them. This is explained when we look at the `Book` and `Poem` classes, which do indeed extend the `Literature` class, but each of these classes overrides the `Literature` class's `Print` method to provide its own functionality. This is all well and good and is a pretty elegant solution, but there's an interesting case that we should take a look at and discuss. Because `Literature` is itself a class, it's perfectly valid for us to declare a new `Literature` object, just as we could for `Book` or `Poem`. The `Literature` class's constructor first expects the `title` of the piece of literature and then the `author`. Once we've created a new instance of the `Literature` class, we could put that instance into our list of `Literature` classes, just like we've been doing with instances of the `Book` and `Poem` classes:

```
Literature l= new Literature("Java", "Zach");
Literature[] lits = new Literature[5];
```

```
lits[0] = a;
lits[1] = b;
lits[2] = l;
lits[3] = b;
lits[4] = a;
for(int i=0; i< lits.length; i++)
{
     lits[i].Print();
}
```

When we do this and run our program, we'll see the `Literature` class's `Print` method get executed, and the new `Literature` object we have created will display alongside our list of books and poems:

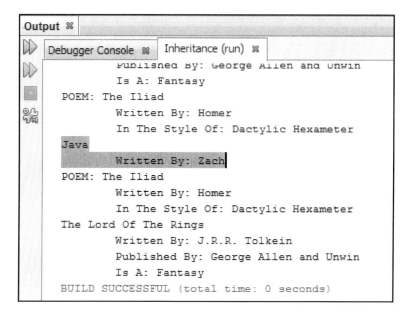

So what's the problem here? Well, depending on the true nature of the software we're trying to design, this may or may not make a lot of sense. Let's say we're doing this as part of a library system, providing someone with just the information that something called Java was written by some guy called Zach, without telling them whether it's a book or a poem or any other information that we've decided to associate with specific types of literature. This may simply not be useful at all and is something that should never be done.

If this is the case, Java provides us with a system to create classes that we can use for inheritance purposes, but we will never be able to legally instantiate them on their own, as we've done before. If we want to mark a class to be of that type, we're going to call it an abstract class, and in the class's declaration, we simply use the abstract keyword:

```
public abstract class Literature {
```

Once we've marked a class abstract, it's no longer a legal operation to instantiate this class. At face value, this is a really simple thing and primarily a "protect our code from ourselves and other programmers" kind of deal, but that's not entirely true; rather, it is true but it's not the only purpose of declaring a class as abstract.

Once we've told Java that we can never create an instance of just Literature, of classes that use Literature as their superclass, we're no longer as restricted when setting up the Literature class. Because we've declared Literature to be an abstract class, we and Java will know that Literature will never be instantiated on its own, only when it is a superclass of a class being instantiated. When this is the case, we can get away without having portions of this class that most Java classes have to have. For example, we don't need to actually declare a constructor for Literature. If Literature was a standard Java class, Java would not be okay with this because if we did try to instantiate Literature, it would have no idea of what to do. There would be no constructor to call. But because Literature is abstract, we can be confident that Literature's subclasses will have constructors of their own. Of course, if we do make this change, we're going to have to get rid of the references to the Literature constructor in our subclasses, that is, by deleting the super method from the subclasses. Therefore, there's definitely a trade-off associated with this change. It requires more code in our subclasses to have less code in our Literature superclass. In this particular instance, this trade-off probably isn't worth it because we're duplicating code between our Book and Poem constructors, but if the constructors for Literature subclasses could be assumed to do very different things, not declaring a common base constructor would make a lot of sense.

So, in a nutshell, when we architect our program, or a larger solution, so that we have classes that make a lot of sense for architecture purposes but should never be created all on their own, we should declare those classes as abstract. Sometimes, we'll really know we've come across a class like this when certain common class functionalities, such as having a constructor, just don't make sense for this class.

Summary

In this chapter, we got to know some intricacies of object-oriented programming, using the concept of inheritance precisely by creating something called a superclass and subclass and establishing an "is-a" relationship between them. We also discussed the usage of some key aspects, such as overriding a subclass and superclass, data structures, and the `protected` method. We also got to know how an `abstract` method works in detail.

In the next chapter, you'll learn about useful Java classes.

8
Useful Java Classes

Once we've achieved a level of confidence with the basics of Java, both the Java syntax and the basic object-oriented concepts that Java was built around, we can then take a look at Java's API and the class libraries that are immediately and easily accessible to us for writing Java programs. We want to do this because we're going to be using these class libraries to speed up our programming and to make use of the work of programmers who have written really great stuff.

Also, taking a look at the Java class libraries, or the class libraries of any programming language really, is also a great way to see how the programming language is designed for use and what optimal coding in that language should look and feel like.

So, in this chapter, we will look at the `Calendar` class and how it works. We will take an in-depth look at the `String` class and a couple of its interesting methods. Next, we will walk through how to detect exceptions, that is, exceptional cases in our program, and how to handle them. We'll look at the `Object` class, which is the superclass of all classes in Java. Lastly, we'll look at the primitive classes of Java in brief.

The following are the topics that this chapter will cover:

- The `Calendar` class
- The `String` class and the difference between using `String` objects and literals
- Exceptions and how to handle them
- The `Object` class
- Primitive classes of Java

The Calendar class

In this section, we're going to take a look at Java's `Calendar` class. When writing Java code, we generally use the `Calendar` class to refer to a specific moment in time.

The `Calendar` class is actually a relatively new addition to the Java API. Previously, we used a class called `Date` to perform the similar functionality. If you end up working on older Java code or are writing Java code that deals with a SQL or MySQL database, you'll probably end up using the Java `Date` class at least occasionally. If this happens, don't panic; consult the Java documentation and you'll discover that there are some really great functions for swapping between `Calendar` and `Date` objects.

To see the power of Java's `Calendar` class, let's jump into a Java program and instantiate it. Let's create a new program; first, import all the classes from the `java.util` package because that's where the `Calendar` class lives.

Next, we declare a new `Calendar` object; I'm going to call it `now` because our first goal is to set the value of this `Calendar` object as the current moment in time. Let's set the value of `now` as the default value of a `Calendar` object and see what it gives us. To do this, I suppose we're going to need to use the `new` keyword. While we haven't actually looked it up in the documentation, this seems like a reasonable starting or default date for a `Calendar` instance.

Lastly, let's set up our program so that we can print out the information contained in our `now` object:

```
package datesandtimes;

import java.util.*;

public class DatesAndTimes {
    public static void main(String[] args) {
        Calendar now = new Calendar();
        System.out.println(now);
    }
}
```

Perhaps, surprisingly, this basic program actually fails when we attempt to compile it:

```
Output
Debugger Console    DatesAndTimes (run)
run:
Exception in thread "main" java.lang.RuntimeException: Uncompilable source code - java.util.Calendar is abstract; cannot be instantiated
        at datesandtimes.DatesAndTimes.main(DatesAndTimes.java:7)
C:\Users\nidhishas\AppData\Local\NetBeans\Cache\8.2\executor-snippets\run.xml:53: Java returned: 1
BUILD FAILED (total time: 1 second)
```

Our error is on `Calendar`, where we have instantiated the `Calendar` class, according to the error shown in the console. The error is `Calendar is abstract; cannot be instantiated`.

If you recall, abstract classes are those that are designed purely to be subclassed, and we can never declare an instance of an abstract class all by itself. So what good is Java's `Calendar` class if we can never instantiate one? Of course, that's not a fair question because we definitely can create `Calendar` objects; they just have to be a specific type of `Calendar` object. We're almost always going to make use of `GregorianCalendar`.

Subclasses of Calendar

Let's take a step back and assume, perhaps rightfully so, that we didn't know what `Calendar` options were available to us. This is one of the times when working with an **IDE (Integrated Development Environment)**, such as NetBeans here, can be really amazing.

Normally, at this point in time, we'd have to take a trip to the Java documentation to see exactly what subclasses of `Calendar` are available for us to instantiate. But because our IDE knows some metadata about the packages that we've already imported, we can ask our IDE what it thinks might be a possible solution for our code. If you're working in NetBeans, you can get these kinds of suggestions very often by checking some of the **Code Completion** options from **Tools | Options | Code Completion**.

However, to keep code completion from popping up all the time, I'm going to make use of a NetBeans shortcut on this occasion. This shortcut, by default, is the key combination *Ctrl +* space, which will prompt a code completion pop-up window for the current location of our cursor, as shown in the following screenshot:

The **Code Completion** option in NetBeans is excellent. NetBeans has given us three possible suggestions: the abstract Calendar class, BuddhistCalendar, and GregorianCalendar. We already know we don't want to use the Calendar class because we can't actually instantiate an abstract class. The BuddhistCalendar and GregorianCalendar certainly look like subclasses of Calendar.

If we select GregorianCalendar, we'll see that it is a subclass of Calendar. So let's go ahead and attempt to create a brand-new GregorianCalendar instance with default settings and values:

```
package datesandtimes;

import java.util.*;

public class DatesAndTimes {
    public static void main(String[] args) {
        Calendar now = new GregorianCalendar();
        System.out.println(now);
    }

}
```

If we run this Java program, we do get some output:

```
Output - DatesAndTimes (run)
run:
java.util.GregorianCalendar[time=1505395515055,areFieldsSet=true,areAllFieldsSet=true,lenient=true,zone=sun.util.calendar
BUILD SUCCESSFUL (total time: 0 seconds)
```

This output means two things:

- Our syntax is correct because we compiled successfully
- We can see what values Java puts in a brand new Calendar object

One of the great things about Java is how extensive and demanding it is that new objects implement the toString() method used by println(). This means that most Java standard library objects are capable of printing themselves out in some sort of human-readable format when we ask them to.

Our new Calendar class printed out here isn't exactly easy to read, but we can go through it and see that values have been assigned to many of its fields, and we can also see what the fields, which a Calendar class has, actually are (such as areFieldsSet, areAllFieldsSet, and so on).

Fetching the current day, month, and year

Let's see how to get just one piece of information from `Calendar` class. Let's see whether it is actually set to the value of today. Let's print the day, month, and year on three separate `println` lines to keep things simple. To access the current day, month, and year, we'll need to get those fields from the `Calendar` object `now`. If our `Calendar` object represents a specific moment in time, it should have fields for day, month, and year, right? Well, if we open up our autocomplete option, we can take a look at all the fields and methods available to us, exposed by our `Calendar` object as shown in the following screenshot:

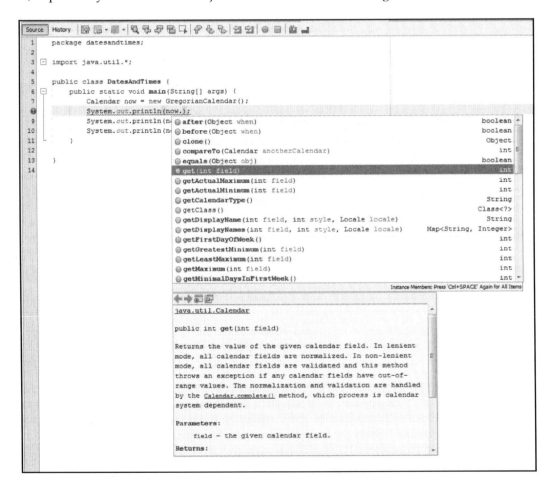

We're not going to find an easily accessible day, month, and year field, and this might start to disenfranchise us from `Calendar`; however, we're just not going enough levels deep.

The `Calendar` class exposes the `get()` method that allows us to acquire the fields that describe the specific `Calendar` instance or moment in time. It's a function that takes an integer as a parameter. To some of us, this might look a little confusing at first. Why would we provide `get()` with an integer to tell it what `Calendar` field we're looking for?

This integer is actually an enumerator, which we'll think about for now as a static string exposed by the `Calendar` class itself. If, for the parameter of `get()`, we type in the `Calendar` class name like we wanted to get a static member variable and then go back to autocomplete, we see a list of options that we can utilize in this instance, as shown in the following screenshot:

Some of these options don't make a lot of sense. We have to remember that autocomplete is just telling us what Calendar exposes; it's not giving us the solution because it has no idea what we're trying to do. For example, we wouldn't want to use our Calendar instance now to get its value of May; this wouldn't make any sense. But, we can use our Calendar instance to get the current month (MONTH). Similarly, what we really want is the day of the month (DAY_OF_MONTH) and the current year (YEAR). Let's run the following program:

```
package datesandtimes;

import java.util.*;

public class DatesAndTimes {
    public static void main(String[] args) {
        Calendar now = new GregorianCalendar();
        System.out.println(now.get(Calendar.MONTH));
        System.out.println(now.get(Calendar.DAY_OF_MONTH));
        System.out.println(now.get(Calendar.YEAR));
    }

}
```

If we run the preceding program, we get the output 9, 12, 2017:

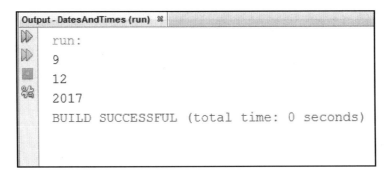

I'm writing this book on October 12, 2017, so this is actually a little confusing because October is the tenth month of the year.

Fortunately, there's a reasonable explanation for this. Unlike the day of the year and year, which makes sense to store as integer variables, most implementations of `Calendar` and classes similar to `Calendar` in most programming languages, not just Java, choose to store months as an array. This is because in addition to a numeric value, each month also has a corresponding string: its name.

Since arrays are zero-indexed, our month appears, in case you forget about this, one month lower than it should be. Our `println()` function should probably look like the following:

```
System.out.println(now.get(Calendar.MONTH) + 1);
```

I got the following output. You'll have to trust me on this; it is today's date:

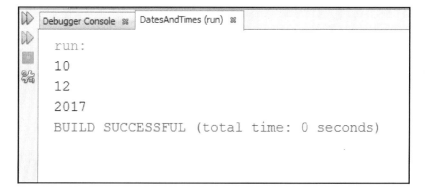

So `Calendar` has a whole lot of methods associated with it. In addition to just setting `Calendar` to the current point of time and reading from it with our `get()` function, we can set `Calendar` to points in time using the `set()` function. We can add or subtract using negative values to point in time, using the `add()` function. We can check whether points in time are before or after other points of time, using the `before()` and `after()` functions.

How Calendar works

If you're like me though, you'd like to know a little bit about how this `Calendar` object is really operating. Is it storing the month, day, and seconds of time in separate fields, or is there one big number that contains all of this information?

If we spend some time and take a look at the methods available to us in the `Calendar` class implementation, we'll find these two methods: `setTimeInMillis()` and its sister method `getTimeInMillis()` as shown in the following screenshot:

The fact that these methods are specially set aside is a really great window of opportunity for us to see how the `Calendar` class really thinks.

Let's begin our exploration by calling the `getTimeInMillis()` function and printing out its output:

```
System.out.println(now.getTimeInMillis());
```

We get a really large integer number, which is presumably the time in milliseconds since some particular point in time:

If we were to do the math on this though, we would discover that this point in time is not actually the year 0; rather, it's a time much closer than that. This point in time is referred to by the `Calendar` class as the **epoch**, and it's the point in time when we start counting from when we store a time in Java in terms of how many milliseconds it's been since the epoch.

We could whip out our calculator and through a pretty painstaking process figure out exactly what this point in time was, or we could do it in our native Java environment with a lot less pain. Let's simply change the value of `now`, originally set to the default or current moment in time, to be the time when milliseconds is set to `0`. We'll do this with `setTimeInMillis()` and provide `0` as an argument:

```
package datesandtimes;

import java.util.*;

public class DatesAndTimes {
    public static void main(String[] args) {
        Calendar now = new GregorianCalendar();
        now.setTimeInMillis(0);
        System.out.println(now.getTimeInMillis());
        System.out.println(now.get(Calendar.MONTH) + 1);
        System.out.println(now.get(Calendar.DAY_OF_MONTH));
        System.out.println(now.get(Calendar.YEAR));
    }

}
```

When we run our program again, we get the same output fields:

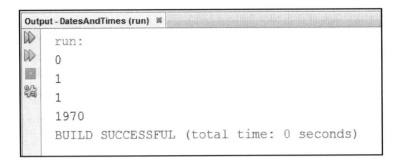

The first number in our output is our confirmation that milliseconds has been set to 0. Now our `Calendar` moment in time is January 1, 1970. So once we start adding days to our object, we'll be counting from January 2, 1970. This point in time is referred to by the Java `Calendar` as the epoch.

Why is this a really interesting thing for us to know? It means that we can convert our `Calendar` classes to these millisecond values and then add, subtract, and I guess multiply and divide them as integer values. This allows us to use all sorts of operations on them in the native format of mathematics.

Lastly, I'd like to show you one more thing because it's a bit of syntax that you may not be familiar with and may not immediately recognize when you come across it. If you recall at the beginning of this section, we said `Calendar` is an abstract class; we can only instantiate specific types of `Calendar` classes. However, oftentimes, we won't specify exactly what type of calendar we're looking for; we'll ask the `Calendar` class to decide this.

As we saw with our enums, in addition to having object-level methods, the `Calendar` class does provide some static methods that we can use just by referencing the `Calendar` type name. One of these methods is `Calendar.getInstance()`, which will create for us the best fit `Calendar` class that Java can figure out:

```
Calendar now = Calendar.getInstance();
```

In this case, it's going to be that same `GregorianCalendar` class that we have created already.

String functionality

Working with strings in Java can be a little confusing at first because they really are a special case. Strings have associated with them this concept of a string literal, that is, a sequence of characters between double quotation marks. We can just put it right into our Java programs and Java will understand it, just like it would understand an integer number or a single character.

Unlike integers, characters, and floats, Java doesn't have a primitive keyword associated with this string literal. About the closest we could get if we wanted to is a character array; however, generally, Java likes us to associate string literals with the String class. To understand the String class better, look at the following program:

```
package strings;

public class Strings {

    public static void main(String[] args) {
        String s1 = new String
          ("Strings are arrays of characters");
        String s2 = new String
          ("Strings are arrays of characters");
        System.out.println("string1: " + s1);
        System.out.println("string2: " + s2);
        System.out.println(s1 == s2);


    }
}
```

The String class in Java is special. In some ways, it's just like any other class. It has methods, and as we can see in the code lines, where we defined the variables s1 and s2, it has a constructor. But, we can use operators on the String class that are normally only reserved for literals and primitives. For example, in the preceding program, we added s1 to the string literal string 1: to get a meaningful result. This is not normally an option when dealing with a Java object.

String literals versus String objects

Java's decision to use objects of the String class as either string literals or genuine objects interchangeably is really powerful. It gives us way more options to manipulate text than we would otherwise have, but it does come with some trade-offs. While dealing with a String object, it's very important that we understand whether we're dealing with its string value or with the object itself. This is because we can get radically different behaviors. The preceding program we saw is designed to illustrate one of these instances.

It's a pretty simple program. Let's step through it and attempt to anticipate its output. We start off by declaring and instantiating two String objects: s1 and s2. We use the String constructor (we'll talk about why that's important here soon), and we simply pass in the same string literal value to each of these new objects. Then, we ask our program to print out these values just so we can compare them visually. But then, we also ask our program to carry out this interesting task: compare using the double equal sign comparison operators s1 and s2. Before you run this program, take a second and ask yourself, "What do you think the result of this comparison is going to be?".

When I run this program, I see that Java does not believe that the comparison of s1 and s2 returns true. I get the result false:

```
Output - Strings (run) ⌗
run:
string1: Strings are arrays of characters
string2: Strings are arrays of characters
false
BUILD SUCCESSFUL (total time: 0 seconds)
```

Depending on what we were thinking about s1 and s2 at the time, the output either makes sense or is confusing. If we were thinking of s1 and s2 as string literals being compared by the comparison operator, it would be very confusing to us. We'd wonder why we didn't get the result true since the string literals assigned to both s1 and s2 are the same.

However, if we were thinking of `s1` and `s2` as the objects that they are, the `false` result makes a lot more sense because what we're asking Java is, "Are these two objects the same?" They're clearly not because they're both the result of creating two different new objects.

This is why we like to use the `equals()` method when we can in Java. Almost every object implements an `equals()` method, and the `equals()` method should be written for every object so that it could logically compare the value of these objects.

If we compare our strings using the `equals()` method, we also compare the string literal values they contain:

```
System.out.println(s1.equals(s2));
```

Now if we execute our program, we get the result `true`, as opposed to the `false` we got when we were trying to see whether they were actually the same objects stored in the same location of memory:

```
Output - Strings (run)  ✕
run:
string1: Strings are arrays of characters
string2: Strings are arrays of characters
true
BUILD SUCCESSFUL (total time: 0 seconds)
```

String functions

So what powers does this `String` implementation give us? Well, we know that we can add or concatenate strings together because we can manipulate them as literals. In addition to this literal manipulation, we can also make use of all the functionality provided by the `String` class itself. We can go to the Java documentation to see what functionality is available for us, or we can always check using the code completion feature of NetBeans. I should probably point out here that we can even use the `String` class functionalities on string literals, as shown in the following screenshot:

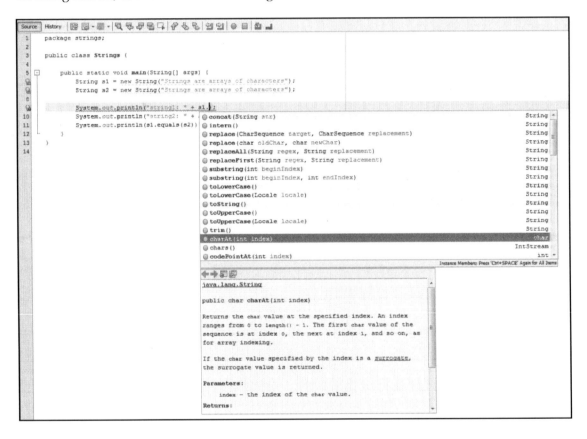

The replace() function

A lot of the methods you'll see in the methods list are pretty self-explanatory (toLowerCase(), toUpperCase(), and so on). But just to make sure we're all on the same page, let's make use of one of them. Let's use replace(). The replace() function takes two arguments, and these arguments can either be single characters or a character sequence of which a string qualifies. This method simply replaces all the instances of the first string or character with the second string or character. Let's look at the following replace() example:

```java
package strings;

public class Strings {

    public static void main(String[] args) {
        String s1 = new String
        ("Strings are arrays of  characters");
        String s2 = new String
        ("Strings are arrays of characters");

        System.out.println
        ("string1: " + s1.replace("characters", "char"));
        System.out.println("string2: " + s2);
        System.out.println(s1.equals(s2));
    }
}
```

When we run our program, we see that we've modified its output:

```
Output - Strings (run)  ⬚
run:
string1: Strings are arrays of char
string2: Strings are arrays of characters
true
BUILD SUCCESSFUL (total time: 0 seconds)
```

Most of these methods simply modify the value being returned. We can see that our program still finds that s1 equals s2 at this last line of code, showing us that the value of s1 hasn't been modified by our call to the replace() method. The replace() method has simply returned the modified value for our println() function to utilize.

The format() function

Perhaps, the most interesting of the String class's methods is actually one of its static methods: String.format(). To show you the power of String.format(), I'd like to create a brand new functional class for our project. So right-click on the Project name in the filesystem, shown on the left-hand side of the screen, create a new class, and call it CustomPrinter.java:

```
package strings;

public class Strings {

    public static void main(String[] args) {
        CustomPrinter printer = new CustomPrinter("> > %s < <");
        String s1 = new String
        ("Strings are arrays of characters");
        String s2 = new String
        ("Strings are arrays of characters");
        printer.println
        ("string1: " + s1.replace("characters", "char"));
        printer.println("string2: " + s2);
    }
}
```

So that you can see what we're doing when we set the CustomPrinter class up, let's look at the prewritten code we're going to use in our main() method. The idea behind the CustomPrinter class is that it will have a constructor that takes a string as input. This input string will format, or wrap around, any strings that we print out to our console using the CustomPrinter instance. We will implement System.out.println() within CustomPrinter, so we can just call printer.println() when we want to utilize it for formatting our text.

When we format a string in Java, we use some special syntax. Within our format string, we can preface the characters f or d or s most commonly with a percentage symbol (like we used %s in our code). In terms of the String.format() function, Java understands these as areas in our format string where we're going to insert other information.

The format string that we've used in our code will wrap any string output we create with caret brackets. This is more complicated than simply appending and prepending to a string, and we could certainly create an implementation that would allow us to add multiple pieces to our formatted strings.

Let's edit our `CustomPrinter.java` file next. We know that we're going to need a `CustomPrinter` constructor, which takes a format string as input. Then, we're probably going to need to store this `format` string. So let's just have our constructor take the provided format string and store it for later use in the `formatString` variable:

```
package strings;

public class CustomPrinter {
    private String formatString;
    public CustomPrinter(String format)
    {
        formatString = format;
    }
}
```

We also declare a `println()` function, which presumably is going to be a `void` function; it's just going to utilize `system.out.println()` to print something to the screen. What that *something* is, is going to be a little complicated. We need to take our given format string and replace `%s` with the input provided to our `println()` function.

We do this with the awesome `String.format()` static function that takes two parameters: a format string and the data to be formatted. If our format string had multiple strings to format, we could provide multiple fields in `String.format()`. It's a function that can take any amount of input. But, to keep everything simple and moving along, we're simply going to assume that our format string only has one input instance.

Once we've successfully formatted this string using the `String.format()` function, we'll simply print it out to the screen, as we did earlier:

```
package strings;

public class CustomPrinter {
    private String formatString;
    public CustomPrinter(String format)
    {
        formatString = format;
    }
    public void println(String input)
    {
        String formatted = String.format(formatString, input);
        System.out.println(formatted);
    }
}
```

When we run this program (we need to run the class where we have our `main()` method), we see that all of our output gets properly wrapped in caret brackets:

```
Output - Strings (run)
run:
   > > string1: Strings are arrays of char < <
   > > string2: Strings are arrays of characters < <
   BUILD SUCCESSFUL (total time: 0 seconds)
```

Extending a custom printer like this, of course, to take a higher amount of varied input and to be much more dynamic than the quick thing we created, is the basis for anything, such as a logging system, or a terminal system, where you will be able to see the same pieces of information wrapped around messages. We could use a custom printer like this, for example, to place dates and times after any message we send to the user. However, details would need to be properly formatted so that they're not just tacked on at the end but have proper spacing between them and stuff like that.

I hope you have learned something about strings. The way Java handles them is really powerful, but as with most powerful things in programming, you will need to understand them at a basic level before you can be sure that they're not going to come back and bite you.

Exceptions

Sometimes, there is a possibility that our code might fail. It might be our fault for making a programming error, or it might be an end user using our system in a way we didn't anticipate. Sometimes, it might even be a hardware failure; a lot of errors can't really be attributed to any one single source, but they are going to happen. The way that our program handles the error case is often just as, if not more, important as how it handles ideal use cases.

In this section, we're going to take a look at Java exceptions. Using Java exceptions, we can detect and catch, and in some cases recover from, errors that occur within our program. As we go through exceptions, there's something really important to keep in mind. Exceptions are called exceptions because they exist to handle exceptional cases, things that we either couldn't handle or couldn't anticipate when originally writing our code.

Exceptions modify the control flow of our program, but we should never use them for anything other than catching and handling or passing exceptions. If we attempt to use them to implement logic, we'll make a program that will quickly become very confusing for us and will be immediately very confusing for any other programmer who attempts to understand it.

To help us explore Java exceptions, I've set up a basic program for us to play with; it is something that can fail. It's an eternal loop that does two real things. First, it takes input from the user using the `nextFloat()` function of `Scanner`, then it prints that input back to the user:

```
package exceptions;

import java.util.*;

public class Exceptions {
    public static void main(String[] args) {
        Scanner reader = new Scanner(System.in);
        while(true) {
            System.out.print("Input a number: ");
            float input = reader.nextFloat();
            System.out.println("You input the number: " + input);
            System.out.println("\r\n");
        }
    }
}
```

If we accurately assign floating-point values as input to this program, then the program will theoretically run forever, as shown in the following screenshot:

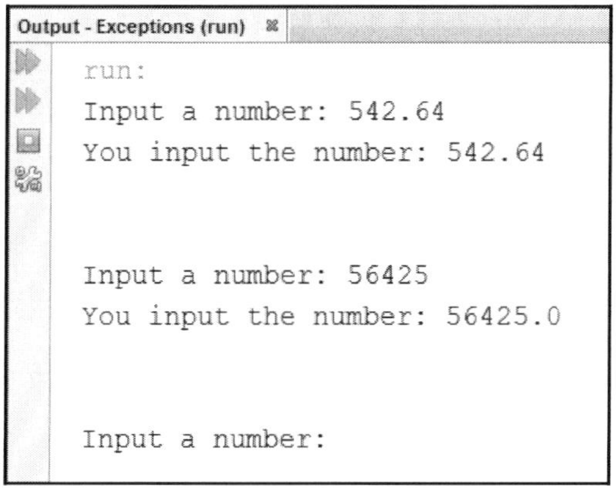

However, if we make a mistake and give this program a string as input, the `nextFloat()` function will not know what to do with it and an exception will occur:

```
Output - Exceptions (run) #2
run:
Input a number: fail
Exception in thread "main" java.util.InputMismatchException
        at java.util.Scanner.throwFor(Scanner.java:864)
        at java.util.Scanner.next(Scanner.java:1485)
        at java.util.Scanner.nextFloat(Scanner.java:2345)
        at exceptions.Exceptions.main(Exceptions.java:11)
C:\Users\nidhishas\AppData\Local\NetBeans\Cache\8.2\executor-snippets\run.xml:53: Java returned: 1
BUILD FAILED (total time: 5 seconds)
```

When this happens, we get red text in our console. This red text is actually going to the `System.err` stream.

Analyzing the console exception messages

Let's walk through the output text and understand what it means. There are two important sections in it. The first part of the output text, the bit that's not tabbed in, is the identifier of this exception. It lets us know that an exception has been thrown and where it has occurred. Then it tells us what type of exception has occurred. You'll notice that this exception is found in the `java.util` path (this part of the output looks very similar to whether we were importing something into our code or directly pathing to an external library). That's because this exception is actually a Java object, and our output text is letting us know exactly what type of object it is.

The second bit of this exception test (the part that is tabbed) is what we call a stack trace. It's basically the pieces of our program that Java has jumped through. The very bottom of our stack trace is the location where the exception was originally thrown; in this case, it is `Scanner.java` and it is on line `909`.

That's not our code; that's the code written for `Scanner.java`, presumably where the `nextFloat()` method lives or code that the `nextFloat()` method calls.

Stack traces are layers of code, so once `InputMismatchException` occurs, Java begins to jump through these layers of code or bracketed areas until it eventually reaches the top layer where the code resides, that's `Exceptions.java` in our case. It's the file we've created, and it's at the top of the stack trace. Line 11 of our `Exception.java` code file is the last place where Java was able to handle or throw this exception.

Once line 11 was reached and the exception was still propagating upwards, there was nothing else to handle because it had reached the top of our program. So the exception ended by getting printed to our System.err stream and our program terminated with result 1, which is a failure case.

This is great for debugging purposes; we knew where we had to go to figure out what went wrong in our program, line 11 of Exceptions.java. But, if we were creating a program that we were looking to release for some reasonable purpose, we generally don't want our program to crash whenever a minor error were to occur, especially an input error such as this, which is perfectly reasonable for a user to make from time to time. So let's explore how we can handle exceptions.

Handling exceptions

When Java is told to throw an exception, it stops executing the current code block and begins jumping up levels until the exception is handled. That's how we moved from deep within the Scanner.java class' 909 line to line 11 of Exceptions.java, the piece in our code where, as far as we're concerned, the exception occurred. If our code were executed by another block of code, because we haven't handled this exception, instead of printing out to System.err, we'd simply throw the exception up another level. Due to this, they'd see line 11 of Exception.java in their stack trace.

However, sometimes it doesn't make sense to keep throwing an exception. Sometimes, we want to handle the exception case because we know what to do with it or because, as in the case we're dealing with right now, there are nicer ways to inform the user of what went wrong than just providing the stack trace and exception name.

Additionally, if we handle this exception here, there's no reason that we can't resume our while loop as though nothing had happened. One failed case of this while loop isn't necessarily a reason to terminate our program. If we're going to handle exception cases, we're going to make use of the try...catch code blocks.

The try and catch blocks

In any block of code where we think an exception might be thrown and we'd like to handle the exception, we're going to wrap that line of code in a try block. For the most part, this doesn't affect how this code is executed unless an exception occurs within the try block. If an exception is thrown within the try block, instead of propagating that exception upward to the next level, the code within the following catch block will immediately get executed.

Note that `catch` blocks require a little more information before they can execute; they need to know what exactly they're going to catch. We can catch all exceptions by simply catching anything of the `Exception` class, but this may not be a fair thing to do. There's a lot of different schools of thought on exception handling, but generally, people will agree that you should only catch and handle exceptions that you, to some degree, expected might occur.

In the example we saw, we know that `InputMismatchException` is thrown if we give invalid information through user input. Because we're going to be printing out a message when this exception occurs, which specifically tells the user `Please enter a float number.`, we certainly don't want to be catching any exceptions that are not `InputMismatchException`. So, we use the following code to catch `InputMismatchException`:

```
package exceptions;

import java.util.*;

public class Exceptions {
    public static void main(String[] args) {
        Scanner reader = new Scanner(System.in);
        while(true) {
            try{
                System.out.print("Input a number: ");
                float input = reader.nextFloat();
                System.out.println("You input the number: " + input);
                System.out.println("\r\n");
            }
            catch(InputMismatchException e)
            {
                System.out.println
                ("Please enter a float number.");
                System.out.println("\r\n");
            }
        }
    }
}
```

When we run this program, first we must quickly test that it works in a good use case, as it did before. Then, if we cause `InputMismatchException` to be thrown by providing the string input, we should see our catch block execute, and we should get the `Please enter a float number.` response:

```
Output - Exceptions (run)   ✖

    Input a number: Please enter a float number.


    Input a number: Please enter a float number.


    Input a number: Please enter a float number.


    Input a number: Please enter a float number.
```

Now, as you can see, we do get that response, but unfortunately, we're getting that response over and over again. We've inadvertently introduced an even worse bug. Now, instead of throwing an exception and crashing, our program just enters an infinite loop.

Here's why this happens: our `Scanner` object `reader` is a stream reader, which means there's a buffer of input that it picks to read from. In a normal use case, when our infinite `while` loop executes, our user adds floating-point numbers to that buffer of input. We pick these out, print them, and go back to the start of the loop and wait for another. However, when a string is found in that buffer, the line of code where we call the `nextFloat()` function throws an exception, which is fine because we catch it with our catch block.

Our catch block prints out the line of text telling the user that he/she gave invalid input and we go back to the beginning of the while loop. But, the bad string in our `reader` objects buffer is still there, so when we catch our exception, we will need to clear out that stream.

Fortunately, this is something we can handle. Once we've caught and handled our exception, we need to clear out the stream reader by simply grabbing its next line and doing nothing with its information. This will flush the `Please enter a float number.` line from the reader:

```
catch(InputMismatchException e)
{
    System.out.println("Please enter a float number.");
    System.out.println("\r\n");
}
```

If we run our program now, we'll see that it handles and recovers from a failed input where we give it a string, which is pretty cool:

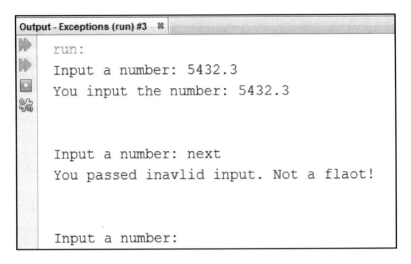

Let's go over a couple of more things we can do with exceptions. For one, clearing out our reader at the end of an exception case makes a lot of sense, but it might make even more sense to clear out our reader at the end of any attempted case. After all, we're entering this `while` loop with the assumption that there's no new line in the reader. So, to implement this, we have the `finally` block.

The finally block

If we'd like to execute a case always, no matter whether we did or did not succeed in our `try` block, we can follow our `catch` block with the `finally` block. The `finally` block executes no matter what, whether an exception was or was not caught. This exists so that you can put cleanup code in your system. An example of cleanup code is clearing out our `reader` objects buffer so that there's nothing there to confuse ourselves later or other programmers.

Exceptions are more than a simple object that gets thrown; they can contain a lot of really important information. As we saw earlier, exceptions can contain a stack trace. Let's quickly modify our program so that while it still gives user-friendly `Please enter a float number.` information, it also prints out the stack trace so that a programmer can debug our program.

Generally, when we're writing finished code that a user is going to utilize, we never want a case where they would be able to see something as deep as a stack trace. It's confusing for most computer users and can be a security risk in some instances, but as a feature in a debug mode or for developers, detailed exceptions such as these can be very useful.

The `Exception` class exposes a method called `printStackTrace()`, which requires a stream as input. We've been using `System.out` for all of our output so far, so we'll provide the `printStackTrace()` method with `System.out` as its stream:

```
catch(InputMismatchException e)
{
    System.out.println("Please enter a float number.");
    e.printStackTrace(System.out);
    System.out.println("\r\n");
}
```

Now when we run our program and give it a bad string, we get our initial friendly exception text code. However, we still have the stack trace, so we can exactly see where the errors are coming from:

```
Output - Exceptions (run) #6

run:
Input a number: fail
You passed inavlid input. Not a flaot!
java.util.InputMismatchException
        at java.util.Scanner.throwFor(Scanner.java:864)
        at java.util.Scanner.next(Scanner.java:1485)
        at java.util.Scanner.nextFloat(Scanner.java:2345)
        at exceptions.Exceptions.main(Exceptions.java:12)
```

As I mentioned earlier, exception handling is an extremely deep topic in modern software development, but at the end of this section, you should have a firm hand on the basics. When you come across exceptions in code or when you're writing your own code and feel that you need exception handling, you should be well prepared.

The Object class

In this section, we're going to learn some very important things about how Java has chosen to implement object-oriented programming. We're going to be exploring the Object class itself. To get us started, I've written a really basic program:

```
package theobjectclass;

public class TheObjectClass {
    public static void main(String[] args) {
        MyClass object1 = new MyClass("abcdefg");
        MyClass object2 = new MyClass("abcdefg");
        object1.MyMethod();
        object2.MyMethod();
        System.out.println("The objects are the same: " +
        (object1 == object2));
        System.out.println("The objects are the same: " +
        object1.equals(object2));
    }

}
```

This program utilizes a custom class called MyClass and creates two instances of this class: object1 and object2. We then call a void MyMethod method on each of these objects, which simply prints out the value that we've given them to contain. Then, the program compares these objects.

We first compare using the comparison operator (==) that checks whether these two objects are actually the same object. We know that this will not be true because we can see that the objects were instantiated completely independent of each other. They share a class, but they are two different instances of the MyClass class. We then compared these objects using the equals() method, which we'll be talking about a lot in this section.

When we run this program, we see that the objects are found not to be the same when compared by the comparison operator, which is what we would expect. But, we also see that when they're compared using the equals() method, the objects are found not to be equal, even though the objects were both created under the same parameters and had the exact same things done to them from their creation to this point in time. Following is the output of the preceding code:

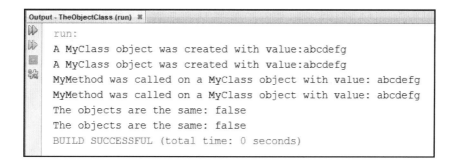

So, what does it mean when objects are not found to be equal by the `equals()` method? The first question we should ask ourselves is, where does this `equals()` method come from or where is it implemented?

If we go by the definition of the `MyClass` class, we don't actually find an `equals()` method, which is pretty weird because `MyClass` is not declared to be inheriting from any superclass, but `equals()` is called directly on the `MyClass` instance. In reality, `MyClass`, as with all Java classes, does inherit from a superclass. At the very top of every class inheritance tree, there is the `Object` class, even though it's not explicitly declared in our code.

If we head to the Java documentation (`docs.oracle.com/javase/7/docs/api/java/lang/Object.html`) and look up the `Object` class, we will find this definition: "Class `Object` is the root of the class hierarchy. Every class has `Object` as a superclass. All objects, including arrays, implement the methods of this class." Then, if we scroll down the page, we get a short but very important list of methods:

Modifier and Type	Method and Description
protected Object	clone() Creates and returns a copy of this object.
boolean	equals(Object obj) Indicates whether some other object is "equal to" this one.
protected void	finalize() Called by the garbage collector on an object when garbage collection determines that there are no more references to the object.
Class<?>	getClass() Returns the runtime class of this Object.
int	hashCode() Returns a hash code value for the object.
void	notify() Wakes up a single thread that is waiting on this object's monitor.
void	notifyAll() Wakes up all threads that are waiting on this object's monitor.
String	toString() Returns a string representation of the object.
void	wait() Causes the current thread to wait until another thread invokes the notify() method or the notifyAll() method for this object.
void	wait(long timeout) Causes the current thread to wait until either another thread invokes the notify() method or the notifyAll() method for this object, or a specified amount of time has elapsed.
void	wait(long timeout, int nanos) Causes the current thread to wait until another thread invokes the notify() method or the notifyAll() method for this object, or some other thread interrupts the current thread, or a certain amount of real time has elapsed.

Because all Java objects inherit from the `Object` class, we can safely assume that any Java object we're dealing with implements each of the methods here. Among these methods is the `equals()` method that we were just talking about and trying to figure out where it came from. This makes it very clear to us that `MyClass` is inheriting the `equals()` method from its `Object` superclass.

The definition of the `equals()` method at the object level is very vague. It says, "Indicates whether some other object is **equal** to this one." To some degree, this vagueness leaves it up to us, as programmers, to determine what equality really means on a class-by-class basis.

Let's say we come to the decision, the reasonable decision, that `object1` and `object2` should be determined to be equal to each other if the values they contain are identical. If we make this decision, then the current implementation of our program is not quite correct because it's currently telling us that `object1` and `object2` are not equal. In order to change this, we're going to need to override the `equals()` method in `MyClass`.

Overriding the equals() method

Overriding an `Object` class method is no more difficult than overriding the method for any other superclass. We simply declare an identical method, and this specific method will be used when appropriate, when we're dealing with a `MyClass` object. It's important for us to notice that the `equals()` method does not take a `MyClass` object as input; it takes any object as input. So, before we can go ahead and compare this object's value with the value of our current `MyClass` objects, we need to protect ourselves and make sure that the object given as input is actually a `MyClass` object.

To do this, let's check some bad cases where we would want our program to simply go ahead and return `false` without even comparing the inner values of these objects:

1. If we've been given an object that hasn't actually been instantiated, a pointer, or a null pointer, we'd simply want to return `false` because our instantiated `MyClass` object is not equivalent to nothing at all.
2. The more difficult question is this: Is the object that we've been given to compare, an instance of `MyClass`? Let's check the opposite of this; let's confirm that this object is not an instance of `MyClass`. The `instanceof` keyword lets us see what classes an object has within its repertoire. If our `instanceof` statement does not evaluate to `true`, we simply want to return `false` because we'd be comparing a `MyClass` object with an object that is not a `MyClass` object.

Once we've made it through these hoops successfully, it's safe for us to assume that we can cast a given object to a `MyClass` object. Now we can simply compare the value fields they contain and return the appropriate value. Let's write the following code to our `MyClass.java` file and jump back to our `main()` method to run it:

```
package theobjectclass;

public class MyClass {
    public String value;
    public MyClass(String value)
    {
        this.value = value;
        System.out.println
        ("A MyClass object was created with value:" + value);
    }
    public void MyMethod()
    {
      System.out.println
      ("MyMethod was called on a MyClass object with value: " +
      value);
    }
    @Override
    public boolean equals(Object obj)
    {
       if(obj == null)
         return false;
       if(!(obj instanceof MyClass))
       return false;
       return value.equals(((MyClass)obj).value);
     }
}
```

When we run this program, we will see that `object1` and `object2` are found to be equal to each other:

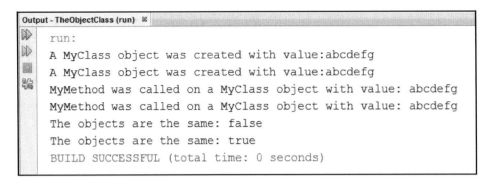

```
Output - TheObjectClass (run)
run:
A MyClass object was created with value:abcdefg
A MyClass object was created with value:abcdefg
MyMethod was called on a MyClass object with value: abcdefg
MyMethod was called on a MyClass object with value: abcdefg
The objects are the same: false
The objects are the same: true
BUILD SUCCESSFUL (total time: 0 seconds)
```

Other Object methods

The `Object` class declares a number of methods. In addition to `equals()`, some important methods are `hashCode()` and `toString()`. We're not going to implement `hashCode()` in this section because it requires us to do a little more math than is really wieldy, but I would very much recommend that you check out how `hashCode()` works by going to the documentation and exploring it.

For now, let's just know that an object's `hashCode()` method should return an integer value that describes that particular object. In all instances, if two objects are found to be equal through the `equals()` method, their `hashCode()` functions should also return the same integer value. If two objects are not equal, as far as the `equals()` method is concerned, their `hashCode()` functions should return different values.

At this point in time, we should be familiar with the `toString()` method. This is also a method in the `Object` class, meaning that we can call the `toString()` method on any single object. But, in our custom objects, until we've overridden `toString()`, it's probably not going to return meaningful, human-readable information.

As you learn Java, I highly recommend that you implement `equals()` and `toString()`, even on the small little test classes you write while learning. It's a great habit to get into, and it keeps you thinking about object-oriented programming in the same way that Java does. When we create finalized software projects where we have public classes that other programmers may someday be using, we should be very careful that all our classes properly implement these methods in an understandable manner. This is because Java programmers will expect to be able to utilize these methods to manipulate and understand our classes.

Primitive classes

In this section, I'd like to take a very quick look at the primitive classes available to us in Java. In Java, we often say that strings are special because they have a literal interpretation identified by these double quotation marks; however, we still interact with them primarily through the `String` class, rather than a `string` primitive type that is not actually available to us.

In the case of a standard Java primitive, however, we generally interact with it through its primitive typing method. For every primitive type, we do have a corresponding primitive class. These are the `Integer`, `Character`, and `Float` classes and so on. For the most part, the explicit uses of these classes where we create an instance of them and then call methods on that instance are not very useful unless we're overriding them to create a class of our own. Let's look at the following program:

```
package the.primitiveclasses;

public class ThePrimitiveClasses {

    public static void main(String[] args) {
        String s = "string";
        Character c = 'c';
    }
}
```

The methods given to us by the instance c of the `Character` class are primarily conversion methods as shown in the following screenshot that would happen automatically or that we could simply cast to:

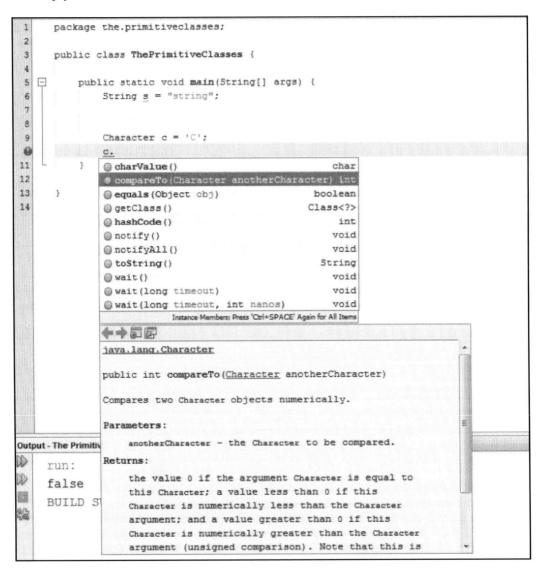

Note that `compareTo()` is sometimes useful, though. It returns an integer value 0 if the other character given is equivalent and less than 0 or greater than 0, depending on which side of the integer conversion scale the two characters fall in relation to each other.

However, often we may find ourselves using the static methods of these primitive classes to manipulate or get information from instances of the primitive types. For example, if I want to know whether our character C is lowercase, I can certainly convert it into an integer value, check an ASCII table, and then see whether that integer value falls between the range of lowercase characters. But, that's a whole lot of work:

The `Character` primitive class provides a static function for me, `isLowercase()`, as shown in the preceding screenshot, which will tell me whether a character is lowercase or not. Let's run the following program:

```
package the.primitiveclasses;

public class ThePrimitiveClasses {

    public static void main(String[] args) {
        String s = "string";
        Character c = 'c';
        System.out.println(Character.isLowerCase(c));
    }
}
```

Following is the output of the preceding code:

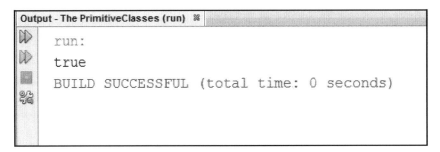

That's really the gist of primitive functions. We can interact with the other literal types and their primitive types in the same manner: interact with strings using a class if we so choose.

When we don't need the functionality of a primitive class, we should continue using primitive types (for example, use `char` instead of `Character`). The presence of the syntax highlighting feature and universal look of these primitive types across languages makes them much more friendly for programmers to work with.

Summary

In this chapter, we looked at the `Calendar` class of Java to work with dates and times. We saw the `String` class in detail. We also saw what exceptions are and how to handle them to make our programs more robust. Then, we walked through the `Object` class and some of its methods. Finally, we looked at the primitive classes of Java.

In the next chapter, we'll look at how to process files using Java.

9
File Input and Output

The file I/O function is an extremely powerful tool that can make one of the most difficult and frustrating tasks of modern programming, namely transferring information between logically separate entities of code, much easier than it would otherwise be. Having said that, in this chapter, you will learn how to write and read data files using the `FileWriter` and `BufferedWriter` and `FileReader` and `BufferedReader` classes. We'll also look at the usage of the `close ()` method and the `Scanner` class. Then you'll learn about exception handling. Finally, we will see one more aspect of I/O: the `Serializable` class.

Specifically, we'll cover the following topics in this chapter:

- Writing data to files
- Reading data from files
- The Serializable class

Writing data to files

This will be an exciting chapter. First we'll take a look at how to write to files using Java. To do this, we'll declare a mathematical sequence for the first 50 numbers of the mathematical sequence in which each number will be the sum of the previous two numbers. When we run the following program we will see these 50 numbers printed out to our `System.out` stream, and we will be able to view them in our console window:

```
package writingtofiles;

public class WritingToFiles {
    public static void main(String[] args) {
        for(long number : FibonacciNumbers())
        {
            System.out.println(number);
```

```
        }
    }
    private static long[] FibonacciNumbers()
    {
        long[] fibNumbers = new long[50];
        fibNumbers[0] = 0;
        fibNumbers[1] = 1;
        for(int i = 2; i < 50; i++)
        {
            fibNumbers[i] = fibNumbers[i - 1] + fibNumbers[i - 2];
        }
        return fibNumbers;
    }
}
```

However, when we close the console for good, these numbers will be lost. To help us with this task, we're going to make use of the `java.io` library; here, `io` stands for **input and output**:

```
import java.io.*;
```

We'll utilize a class that lives in this library: `FileWriter`.

The FileWriter class

The `FileWriter` class and its usage could be explained as follows:

1. Let's declare a new `FileWriter` class, and for reasons that will become apparent a little later on, let's explicitly set this `FileWriter` class to null:

```
public class WritingToFiles {
    public static void main(String[] args) {
        FileWriter out = null;
```

2. Once we do this, we can go ahead and instantiate it. In order to write to a file, we're going to need to know two important things:
   - First, of course, we'll need to know what to write to the file
   - Second, our `FileWriter` class will need to know what file it should write to

3. When we use a `FileWriter` class, we associate it with a specific file, so we pass into its constructor the name of the file we would like it to write to. Our `FileWriter` class is capable of creating a file if none exists, so we should just pick a name that ends with `.txt` so that our operating system will know we're creating a text file:

```
public class WritingToFiles {
    public static void main(String[] args) {
        FileWriter out = null;
            out = new FileWriter("out.txt");
```

Even though we've called the `FileWriter` constructor with valid arguments, NetBeans will still let us know that we'll get a compiler error in this code. It'll tell us there's an unreported exception, an `IOException` error that can be thrown here. Many exceptions in Java are marked as handled exceptions. These are exceptions that a function explicitly states it may throw. `FileWriter` is a function that explicitly states that it can throw an `IOException` error. So, as far as Java is concerned, it is an error for our code not to explicitly handle this possible exception.

4. To handle this, of course, we're simply going to wrap the portions of our code where we use our `FileWriter` class with a `try...catch` block that catches `IOException` errors:

5. If we do catch an `IOException` error, it's probably a good time to print out a helpful message to the **error stream**:

```
catch(IOException e)
{
    System.err.println("File IO Failed.");
}
```

Then, our program will finish running and will terminate because it would have reached the end of the `main` method. With this exception caught, the instantiation of `FileWriter` is now valid and legal, so let's put it to use.

We no longer need our program to print out numbers to our console, so let's comment out our `println` statement, as shown in the following code block:

```
for(long number : FibonacciNumbers())
{
    // System.out.println(number);
}
```

We're going to do the same logical thing with our `FileWriter` class:

```
try{
    out = new FileWriter("out.txt");
    for(long number : FibonacciNumbers())
    {
        // System.out.println(number);
    }
```

The `FileWriter` class doesn't have a `println` statement, but it does have the `write` method. Each time our `foreach` loop executes, we'd like to write the number to our file using the `out.write(number);` syntax.

6. Unfortunately, the `write` method doesn't know how to take a `long number` as input; it can take a string and it can also take an integer. So let's use the static `String` class method `valueOf` to acquire the value of our `long number` to print out the number to our file:

```
for(long number : FibonacciNumbers())
{
    out.write(String.valueOf(number));
    // System.out.println(number);
}
```

So, we should now have all the pieces of a successful program here:

- First we declared and instantiated our `FileWriter` class, giving it a filename
- Then, we looped through our Fibonacci sequence of numbers, and told our `FileWriter` class to write each of these numbers to `out.txt`

Nevertheless, the question is where is `out.txt`? We haven't given the `FileWriter` class a full system path, just the name of a file. We know that the `FileWriter` class is capable of creating this file if it does not exist, but where in our system's directories will this `FileWriter` class choose to create the file?

To answer this question, we need to know where NetBeans will create the `.jar` file for our compiled program. To find this out, we can open the console window and build our program. Here, NetBeans will tell us where it's creating all its files. For example, in my case, it's a folder called `WritingToFiles`; if we navigate to this folder, we'll see our project files. One of these files is `dist`, short for **distributable**, and this is where our JAR file will be compiled to:

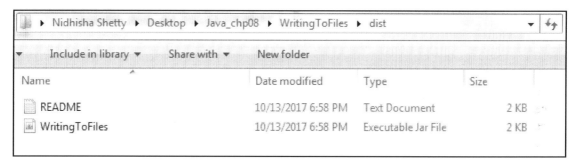

JAR files are as close as we're going to get to an executable with raw Java code. Because Java code must be interpreted by the Java virtual machine, we can't actually create Java executables; however, in most operating systems where Java is installed, we can run a JAR file by simply double-clicking on it, like how we would run an executable. We can also tell the Java virtual machine to boot up and run a JAR file using the Java command line `-jar` command, followed by the name of the file we would like it to execute, of course:

When we submitted this command, the Java virtual machine interpreted and executed our `WritingToFiles.jar` program. It looks like it worked because a new file was created in the directory, as shown in the preceding screenshot. This is the working directory, and until we move it, this is where the command that executed the JAR file will execute from. So that's where our `FileWriter` class chose to create `out.txt`.

Relieving resources using the close() method

Unfortunately, when we open up `out.txt`, there's nothing for us to see. This leads us to believe that our file writing probably didn't work. So what went wrong? Well, there's an important piece to using a `FileWriter` that we failed to take into account. When our `FileWriter` is created, it opens a file, and whenever we open a file, we should make sure that we close it in the end. This is pretty easy to do from a code standpoint; we simply call the `close` method on our `FileWriter`:

```
public class WritingToFiles {
    public static void main(String[] args) {
        FileWriter out = null;
        try{
            out = new FileWriter("out.txt");
            for(long number : FibonacciNumbers())
            {
                out.write(String.valueOf(number));
                // System.out.println(number);
            }

        }
        catch(IOException e)
        {
            System.err.println("File IO Failed.");
        }
        finally{
            out.close();
        }
    }
}
```

There's a familiar error message that appears, as shown in the following screenshot; `out.close` can also report an `IOException` error:

```
catch(IOEx  unreported exception IOException; must be caught or declared to be thrown
    System
                Dereferencing possible null pointer
}
                ----
finally{     (Alt-Enter shows hints)

    out.close();

}
```

We could put `out.close` within another `try...catch` block and handle this `IOException` error, but if our file cannot be closed, that's a sign that something is very seriously wrong. In this case, it might be appropriate for that exception to keep propagating upwards and that we pass it on to a more robust piece of code rather than our fairly contained `WritingToFiles` program. This will happen by default if we don't handle this exception, but we do need to let Java know that this exception propagating upwards from our current code is a possibility.

When we declare our `main` method, we can also let Java know what exception types might be thrown by this method:

```
public static void main(String[] args) throws IOException
```

Here, we tell Java that under some circumstances, our `main` method may not execute perfectly and will instead throw an `IOException` error. Now, anyone who calls the `main` method of `WritingToFiles` will need to handle this exception themselves. If we build our Java program and then execute it again, we'll see that `out.txt` has been properly printed. Unfortunately, we forgot to put new lines in our output, so there's no distinguishable spacing between the numbers. When we write, we will need to append `\r\n` to each number. This is a new line escape character syntax that's going to be visible to just about every operating system and environment:

```
for(long number : FibonacciNumbers())
{
    out.write(String.valueOf(number) + "\r\n");
    // System.out.println(number);
}
```

Again, it's time to build, run, and take a look at out.txt, which is now starting to look pretty useful:

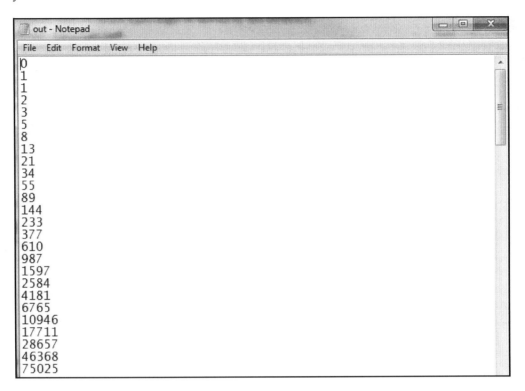

So this was our initial stated goal: print this Fibonacci sequence out to a file. A few quick things before we're finished here, though. Let's take a look at what happens if we run our program again, and then take a look at our output text file. The text file looks the same as it does before, which may or may not be expected. It seems like it's a kind of a toss-up whether FileWriter would clear this file and write brand new text, which is what it appears to have done, or whether it would put the appended text after the existing text in the file. By default, our FileWriter will clear the file before it writes to it anew, but we can toggle this behavior through a parameter in the FileWriter constructor. Say, we set its append behavior to true:

```
try {
    out = new FileWriter("out.txt", true);
```

Now build the project, run it, and take a look at out.txt; we'll see twice as much information as there was before. Our text is now appended at the end.

The BufferedWriter class

Lastly, there's a lot of different writers available to us in Java, and `FileWriter` is just one of them. I decided to show it to you here because it's pretty simple. It takes some text and prints it to a file. Very often, however, you'll see `FileWriter` wrapped around by the `BufferedWriter` class. Now the declaration of the `BufferedWriter` class will look like the one given in the following code block, where `BufferedWriter` is created and given `FileWriter` as its input.

The `BufferedWriter` class is pretty cool because what it does is it intelligently takes all the commands you give it and attempts to write the content to a file in the most efficient way possible:

```
package writingtofiles;

import java.io.*;

public class WritingToFiles {
    public static void main(String[] args) throws IOException {
        BufferedWriter out = null;
        try {
            out = new BufferedWriter(new FileWriter
              ("out.txt", true));

            for(long number : FibonacciNumbers())
            {
                out.write(String.valueOf(number) + "\r\n");
                //System.out.println(number);
            }
        }
        catch(IOException e) {
            System.err.println("File IO Failed.");
        }
        finally{
            out.close();
        }
    }
}
```

The program we've just written is from our point of view, doing the same thing as our existing program has been doing. However, in instances where we make many small writes, `BufferedWriter` can be significantly faster because where appropriate, it will intelligently collect the write commands we give it and perform them in proper blocks to maximize efficiency:

```
out = new BufferedWriter(new FileWriter("out.txt", true));
```

For this reason, very often you'll see Java code that looks like the preceding code block, instead of the `FileWriter` being used in isolation.

Reading data from files

A common task we'll need to perform as programmers is reading input from a file. In this section, we're going to take a quick look at how to acquire text input from files.

 We've gone ahead and told Java that sometimes our `main` method will simply throw `IOException` errors. Both the `FileWriter` and `FileReader` objects in the following code block can create a number of `IOException` errors for a number of reasons, for example, if they can't connect to the files they're supposed to.

```java
package inputandoutput;

import java.io.*;

public class InputAndOutput {
    public static void main(String[] args) throws IOException {
        File outFile = new File("OutputFile.txt");
        File inFile = new File("InputFile.txt");
        FileWriter out = new FileWriter(outFile);
        FileReader in = new FileReader(inFile);

        //Code Here...
        out.close();
        in.close();
    }
}
```

When writing actual programs for actual applications, we should always make sure that we catch and handle our exceptions in a reasonable manner, throwing them upward if it's truly necessary. But we're going to throw everything here because we're doing this to learn and we don't want to be bogged down right now by wrapping all of our code in `try...catch` blocks.

The FileReader and BufferedReader class

Here, you will learn about the `FileReader` class with the help of the code we already have (see the preceding code). Firstly, go through the following steps:

1. I've declared `FileWriter` and `FileReader` objects for us. `FileReader` is a sister class of `FileWriter`. It's capable of, believe it or not, reading text input from files, and it's constructed in a very similar manner. It expects to be given a file to be associated with throughout its life when it's constructed.

2. Rather than simply giving the `FileReader` and `FileWriter` paths to these files, I've chosen to create `File` objects. The Java file object is simply a reference to an existing file, and we tell that file what file it will reference when it's created as shown in the following code block:

```
package inputandoutput;

import java.io.*;

public class InputAndOutput {
    public static void main(String[] args)
      throws IOException {
        File outFile = new File("OutputFile.txt");
        File inFile = new File("InputFile.txt");
        FileWriter out = new FileWriter(outFile);
        FileReader in = new FileReader(inFile);

        //Code Here...
        out.write(in.read());
        out.close();
        in.close();
    }
}
```

In this program, we're going to use `InputFile.txt`, which contains some information. Also, we're going to use `OutputFile.txt`, which currently contains no information. Our goal is to move the information from `InputFile` to `OutputFile`. Both `FileWriter` and `FileReader` have methods that are going to be useful here.

Our `FileWriter` class has the `write` method, which we know can be used to put information into a file. Similarly, `FileReader` has the `read` method, which will allow us to acquire information from a file. If we simply call these methods in sequence and run our program, we'll see that information will be taken from `InputFile` and put into `OutputFile`:

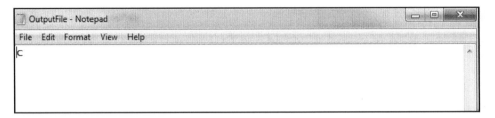

Unfortunately, only one character appears in `OutputFile`: the first character of the `InputFile` text. It would appear that our `FileReader` class's `read` method only acquires the smallest acquirable piece of text information. This is not a problem for us though because we are programmers.

3. We can simply loop through the file using the `in.read` method to acquire all of the information available to us in that `InputFile` file:

```
String input = "";
String newInput;
out.write(in.read());
```

4. However, we can make life a little easier by wrapping `FileReader` with a `BufferedReader` class. Similar to the way we wrap `FileWriter` with `BufferedWriter`, wrapping `FileReader` with `BufferedReader` will allow us to collect varying lengths of input at any given time:

```
FileWriter out = new FileWriter(outFile);
BufferedReader in = new BufferedReader(new FileReader(inFile));
```

Even more so than wrapping our `FileWriter` class, it's almost always a good idea to wrap our `FileReader` class The `BufferedReader` class also serves to protect the `FileReader` class from files that are too large for the `FileReader` class to hold in memory at one time. This doesn't happen very often, but when it does happen, it can be a pretty confusing bug. This is because `BufferedReader` looks at the portions of the file only at one time; it's protected from that instance.

The `BufferedReader` class is also going to let us use the `nextLine` method so that we can collect information from `InputFile` on a line-by-line basis instead of a character-by-character basis. Either way though, our `while` loop is going to look pretty similar. The only real challenge here is that we need to know when to stop looking for information in our `InputFile` file. To figure this out, we're actually going to put some functional code in the conditional portion of our `while` loop.

5. We're going to assign a value to this `newInput` string variable and that value is going to be `in.readLine`. The reason we want to do this assignment in the conditional portion of our `while` loop is so that we can then check what value was assigned to `newInput` string. This is because if `newInput` string were assigned no value at all, it would mean that we'd reach the end of our file:

```
while((newInput = in.readLine()) !=null)
{

}
```

If `newInput` does have a value, if the variable is not null, then we would know that we've read in legitimate text from our file, an entire line of legitimate text actually, because we're using the `readLine` method.

6. In such a case, we should add a new line of text, which is `input +=` `newInput;` to our input string. When we're finished executing our `while` loop, when `newInput` string is assigned the value `null` because there's nothing else for our reader to read, we should print out the string we've been building:

```
while((newInput = in.readLine()) != null)
{
    input += newInput;
}
out.write(input);
```

7. Now, because our `BufferedReader` class's `readLine` method specifically reads lines of text, it doesn't append the end line character at the end of these lines, so we'll have to do this on our own:

```
while((newInput = in.readLine()) != null)
{
    input += (newInput + "\r\n");
}
```

So, we've executed this program. Let's go to our directory and see what's been copied over to `OutputFile`:

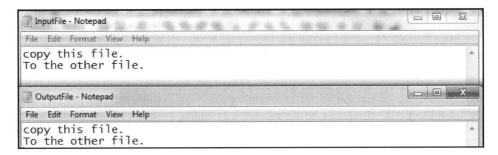

There we go; `InputFile` and `OutputFile` now have identical content. That's really all there is to basic file reading in Java.

A couple of other things to note, though. Just as we can wrap `FileReader` with `BufferedReader`, we can wrap `BufferedReader` with `Scanner` if we import `java.util`:

```
Scanner in = new Scanner(new BufferedReader
(new FileReader(inFile)));
```

This would allow us to use the `Scanner` class's methodologies to acquire only those portions of the text we were reading that match certain patterns. It's also important to note that the `FileReader` class and it's wrapping classes are only appropriate when we're reading text from a Java file. If we want to read binary information, we're going to use different classes; you'll see more on this when you learn about serializing objects in Java.

The Serializable class

Often, when we're dealing with information outside of our actual code, we're dealing with human-readable text that we've gotten from a file or are writing to a file or from an input or output stream. However, sometimes, human-readable text is just not convenient, and we'd like to use information that's more computer friendly. Through a process called **serialization**, we can take some Java objects and convert them into a binary stream that we could transfer across programs. This is not a human-friendly approach, as we'll see in this section. A serialized object looks like complete gibberish to us, but another Java program that knows about that object's class can recreate an object from that serialized information.

Not all Java objects can be serialized, though. In order for us to serialize an object, it needs to be marked as an object that can be serialized, and it needs to only contain members that themselves can be serialized. For some objects, those that depend on external references or those that simply haven't had all their members marked as serializable, serialization is just not appropriate. Refer to the following code block:

```
package serialization;

public class Car {
    public String vin;
    public String make;
    public String model;
    public String color;
    public int year;
    public Car(String vin, String make, String model, String
     color, int year)
    {
        this.vin = vin;
        this.make = make;
        this.model = model;
        this.color = color;
        this.year = year;
    }
    @Override
    public String toString()
    {
        return String.format
         ("%d %s %s %s, vin:%s", year, color, make, model, vin);
    }
}
```

The class in the given program (in the preceding code block) is a prime candidate for serialization. Its members are a number of strings and integers, both of which are classes that Java has marked as serializable. However, in order for us to transform a Car object into a binary representation, we will need to let Java know that the Car object is serializable as well.

We can do this by going through the following steps:

1. We're going to need the io library for this, then we're going to let Java know that our Car object implements Serializable:

   ```
   import java.io.*;
   public class Car implements Serializable{
   ```

   This is telling Java that all the elements of the Car object can be converted into binary representations. We should never tell Java that an object implements Serializable unless we've looked at the object and thought it out and determined that this is a safe assumption to make.

   So, we've now marked Car as a Serializable class, but that is, of course, the easy part of this section. Our next goal is to make use of this new functionality to create a Car object, serialize it, print it out to a file, and then read it back.

2. To do this, we're going to create two new Java classes: one to serialize our object and print it to a file and another class to deserialize our object and read it from a file.

3. In both these classes, we're going to create main methods so that we can run our classes as separate Java programs.

Serializing an object

Let's begin with the Serialize class, as follows:

1. The first thing we're going to need is an object for us to serialize. So let's go ahead and instantiate a new Car object. The Car class takes four strings and an integer for its variables. It takes a vehicle identification number, make, model, color, and a year. So we'll give it all of that, respectively:

   ```
   package serialization;
   public class Serialize {
       public static void main(String[] args) {
   ```

```
Car c =  new Car("FDAJFD54254", "Nisan", "Altima",
"Green", 2000);
```

Once we've created our `Car` object, it's time to open up a file and serialize this `Car` for output. When we open up a file in Java, we'll use some different managers, depending on whether we'd like to write formatted text output to this file or whether we're just planning on writing raw binary information.

2. Serialized objects are binary information, so we're going to use `FileOutputStream` to write this information. The `FileOutputStream` class is created with a filename to associate itself with:

```
FileOutputStream outFile = new FileOutputStream("serialized.dat");
```

Because we're writing raw binary information, it's not that important that we specify it as a text file. We can specify it to be really whatever we would like. Our operating system really isn't going to know what to do with this file if it tries to open it anyway.

We're going to want to surround all of this information in a `try...catch` block because whenever we're dealing with external files, exceptions can definitely be thrown. If we do catch an exception, let's just simply print an error message:

```
try{
    FileOutputStream outFile =
    new FileOutputStream("serialized.dat");
}
catch(IOException e)
{
    System.err.println("ERROR");
 }
```

Notice that we are required to add a lot of input here; let's just import the entirety of the `java.io` library, that is, lets import the `java.io.*;` package.

Now I think we're good to move along. We've created our `FileOutputStream` class, and this stream is pretty good. However, we can wrap it with another string that's more specialized for the act of serializing a Java object.

3. This is `ObjectOutputStream` class, and we can construct `ObjectOutputStream` object by simply wrapping it around an existing `FileOutputStream` object. Once we've created this `ObjectOutputStream` object and associated a file with it, serializing our object and writing it to this file becomes extremely easy. We simply need to use the `writeObject` method and provide our `Car` class as the object to be written.

4. Once we write this object to our file, we should be responsible and close our output string:

```
try{
    FileOutputStream outFile = new
    FileOutputStream("serialized.dat");
    ObjectOutputStream out = new ObjectOutputStream(outFile);
    out.writeObject(c);
    out.close();
}
catch(IOException e)
{
    System.err.println("ERROR");
}
```

Now I think we're good to run our following program. Let's see what happens:

```
package serialization;

import java.io.*;

public class Serialize {
    public static void main(String argv[]) {
        Car c = new Car("FDAJFD54254", "Nisan", "Altima",
        "Green", 2000);

        try {
            FileOutputStream outFile = new
            FileOutputStream("serialized.dat");
            ObjectOutputStream out = new
            ObjectOutputStream(outFile);
            out.writeObject(c);
            out.close();
        }
        catch(IOException e)
        {
            System.err.println("ERROR");
        }
    }
}
```

We have multiple `main` methods in this Java project. So as far as NetBeans is concerned, when we run our program, we should make sure to right-click on the class whose `main` method we want to enter with and run that file specifically. When we run this program, we don't really get any meaningful output because we didn't ask for any, at least an error wasn't thrown. But, when we head to our directory in which this project lives, we'll see a new file: `serialize.dat`. If we edit this file with Notepad, it looks pretty ridiculous:

```
serialized.dat
1  ¬íNULENOsrNULDC1serialization.CarAT#Ü:ÉNUL{STXNULENOINULEOTyearLNULENOcolort
   NULDC2Ljava/lang/String;LNULEOTmakeqNUL~NULSOHLNULENOmodelqNUL~NULSOHLNULETXv
   inqNUL~NULSOHxpNULNULBELDtNULENOGreentNULENONisantNULACKAltimatNULVTFDAJFD542
   54
```

This is certainly not a human-readable format, but there are some words, or fragments of words, that we recognize. It certainly looks like the correct object was serialized.

Deserializing an object

Let's begin by heading to our other class, that is, the `DeSerialize` class, and attempt to write a method that will pull the `Car` object out from that file that we've written its serialized information to. The steps for doing this are as follows:

1. Once again, we're going to need a `Car` object, but this time, we're not going to initialize it with a constructor value; rather, we're going to set its value to be the object we read back from our file. The syntax we're going to use in our deserializer is going to look very similar to the syntax that we used in our `Serialize` class `main` method. Let's just copy the code of the `Serialize` class so that we can see mirrored similarities as we build our `main` method of `DeSerialize` class.

    In the previously discussed `Serialize` class, we made kind of an irresponsible error in the `Serialize` class's method. We closed `ObjectOutputStream` but we did not close `FileOutputStream`. This isn't really a big deal because our program immediately opened these files, performed its functionality, and upon terminating Java, it destroyed these objects and the files knew that nothing else was pointing to them. So, our operating system is aware that these files are closed and can now be freely written. But, in a program that continues for a long time, or even indefinitely, not closing a file can have some very weird consequences.

When we're nesting `FileInput` or `Output` classes like we've done in this program, we're generally going to close our files in reverse order in which we accessed them. In this program, it wouldn't make sense for us to call `outFile.close` before `out.close` because for a brief moment, our `ObjectOutputStream` object would be referencing a file that it could no longer access because the inner `FileOutputStream` class would have been closed. Now delete `Car c = new Car("FDAJFD54254", " Nisan", "Altima", "Green", 2000);` in the current `DeSerialize.java` class.

With that out of the way, we've copied our code over and now we're going to make some modifications to it. So instead of serializing our object to a file, we are now reading the serialized object from a file.

2. Therefore, instead of a `FileOutputStream` class, we're going to use its sister class, namely `FileInputStream`:

   ```
   FileInputStream outFile = new FileInputStream("serialized.dat");
   ```

3. Let's import `java.io` again. We want to be referencing the same filename as given in the preceding code; also, let's intelligently name our variables.

4. In a similar manner, we're going to wrap `FileInputStream` with `ObjectInputStream` instead of `ObjectOutputStream`, which is still referencing the same file:

   ```
   ObjectInputStream in = new ObjectInputStream(outFile);
   ```

   Of course, this time we have no interest in writing an object to this file, and that's good because our `InputStream` class does not have the permissions or the know-how to write to this file; what it can do, however, is read an object from the file.

5. `ReadObject` doesn't take any parameters; it's simply going to read whatever object happens to be in that file. When it reads that object, assign it to our `Car` object. Of course, `ReadObject` only knows it's going to acquire an object from the file; it has no idea what type of object that will be. One of the weaknesses of serialization is that we really are forced to take a leap of faith and cast this object to the expected type:

   ```
   c = (Car)in.readObject();
   ```

6. Once we've done this, it's simply time to close our file readers in reverse order:

```
try {
    FileInputStream inFile = new FileInputStream("serialized.dat");
    ObjectInputStream in = new ObjectInputStream(inFile);
    c = (Car)in.readObject();
    in.close();
    inFile.close();
}
```

7. There's another type of handled exception being thrown now, namely ClassNotFoundException:

> unreported exception ClassNotFoundException; must be caught or declared to be thrown
> ----
> (Alt-Enter shows hints)

This is thrown if our readObject method fails.

So, let's catch ClassNotFoundException, and to keep things simple and moving, we'll just throw or print out an error message like we did with the previous I/O exception:

```
catch(ClassNotFoundException e)

{
    System.err.println("ERROR");
}
```

8. Now we need a way to tell whether our program worked or not. So, at the very end, let's attempt to print out our car's information using its custom toString function, that is, System.out.println(c.toString()); statement. NetBeans is letting us know that the variable c might not be initialized at this point in time as shown in the following screenshot:

```
catch(ClassNotFoundException e)
{
    System.err.prin
}
                  variable c might not have been initialized
                  ----
                  (Alt-Enter shows hints)
System.out.println(c.toString());
```

Some programming languages will let us make this mistake, and our `Car` object might not have been initialized because this `try` block could have failed. To let NetBeans know that we're aware of this case, or rather, to let Java know that we're aware of this case, we should initialize our `Car` object. We can simply initialize it to the value `null`:

```
public class DeSerialize {
    public static void main(String[] args) {
        Car c = null;
        try {
            FileInputStream inFile = new
            FileInputStream("serialized.dat");
            ObjectInputStream in = new
            ObjectInputStream(inFile);
            c = (Car)in.readObject();
            in.close();
            inFile.close();
        }
        catch(IOException e)
        {
            System.err.println("ERROR");
        }
        catch(ClassNotFoundException e)
        {
            System.err.println("ERROR");
        }
        System.out.println(c.toString());
    }
}
```

Now it's time for our moment of truth. Let's execute the main method. When we run our file in our console, we get the output as a pin number: 2000 Green Nisan Altima with vin: FDAJFD54254. This is illustrated in the following screenshot:

```
Output - Serialization (run)  ✖
  ▷▷   run:
  ▷▷   2000 Green Nisan Altima, vin:FDAJFD54254
  ▬    BUILD SUCCESSFUL (total time: 0 seconds)
  ✂    |
```

That's the same car we declared in the `main` method of the `Serialize.java` class and serialized to the file. Clearly, we have been successful. Serialization of objects is one of the things that Java does really elegantly and really well.

Summary

In this chapter, we went through the process of writing and reading data files, where we saw the usage of `FileWriter` and `FileReader` classes and how to relieve resources that use the `close()` method. We also saw how to catch an exception and handle it. Then, you learned how to use the `BufferedWriter` and `BufferedReader` classes to wrap the `FileWriter` and `FileReader` classes, respectively. Finally, we saw one more aspect of I/O: the `Serializable` class. We analyzed what serialization is and its usage with respect to serializing and deserializing objects.

In the next chapter, you'll learn about basic GUI development.

10
Basic GUI Development

Sometimes, we write programs that are all about raw functionality. However, we often write programs that are generally used by us or other users who expect the process of their interaction with us to be streamlined. In this chapter, we will see the basic functions of the **Graphical User Interface (GUI)** in NetBeans. A couple of things that define truly amazing software programs are their GUI and user experience. You will learn how to create an application window with the JFrame class by setting its size, adding labels to it, and closing the application on the whole. Then comes the topic of the GUI editor, that is, palette; here, we'll see a working instance of palette and the components available in it. Finally, you'll learn how to trigger events by adding a button and adding functionality to it.

We'll cover the following topics in this chapter:

- Swing GUIs
- A visual GUI editor tool – palette
- Event handling

Swing GUIs

NetBeans is a powerful program that offers a lot of functionality, and we access this functionality through a GUI and the menus and buttons provided by NetBeans. In theory, we could have chosen to operate NetBeans as a command-line program, but in order to use NetBeans like that, we would have to memorize or look up a large library of specific commands for every action we would want to take. A powerful and well-written application has a streamlined interface that will guide us toward important functionality and make it easy for us to access it. The JDK contains a Java extension library, the swing library, which makes it very easy for us to wrap our own code in GUIs like the one NetBeans has.

The JFrame class

To start off on this track, we're going to write a program that will open up a new GUI window. The steps are as follows:

1. At the heart of the `swing` Java GUIs is the `JFrame` class. In our case, this class will be the actual window object that our operating system will handle and that we could move around our screen. We can create a new `JFrame` class as we might create any other object. We can even pass some parameters to this `JFrame` class's creation. If we just give it a string parameter, we'll be telling the `JFrame` class what to present as its name:

```
package GUI;
import javax.swing.*;

public class GUI {
    public static void main(String[] args) {
        JFrame frame = new JFrame("Hello World GUI");
    }
}
```

2. Once we've declared a `JFrame` class, it's simply going to exist in Java's memory like any other object. It won't present itself to the user until we explicitly tell it to. It will simply be a function call to the `setVisible` function and we will assign the value `true` to this function, pretty easy right:

```
frame.setVisible(true);
```

3. There's one more thing we should do before we make JFrame window visible and that's to call the `pack` method:

```
frame.pack();
```

When we create more complicated frames, they may contain a lot of information, and in a GUI, much of this information takes up visible space. The `pack` method basically prebuilds the physical relationships between the objects in the frame and ensures that the frame doesn't behave oddly when it actually appears visible to the user. So we've written a really simple program so far – only three lines of code and no real thought required on our part:

```
package gui;
import javax.swing.*;

public class GUI {
```

```
public static void main(String[] args) {
    JFrame frame = new JFrame("Hello World GUI");
    frame.pack();
    frame.setVisible(true);
}
}
```

When we run this program, it might appear that nothing has happened, but something has. In the top left-hand corner of the screen, a new window has appeared. If we click on the right-hand side of this window, we can, in theory, drag it around or just resize the window:

This is a fully fledged window that our operating system can now handle, allowing us to move around; it even supports dynamic resizing. You'll see that our header has also been appended to our window. So that's super basic.

Setting the size of our window

Now let's see what else we can do with our existing JFrame class. When our JFrame window appeared, it was very small and hard to see. A program window of such a size is never really going to be useful to anyone, so let's see what powers `frame` gives us in terms of setting the window's size. Often, we're going to use the `setPreferredSize` method to apply a size to our JFrame class. There is also a `setSize` method, but this method will not give us exactly what we expect it to at all times. This is because right now our JFrame class is set to be resizable, and it's not appropriate for us to explicitly assign a size to it; rather, we should instruct it that given no other input from the user, meaning resizing JFrame window, the window should be a certain size.

We can store, manipulate, and create size information using the `Dimension` class. To construct a new dimension, we can simply give it a width and height. So let's set JFrame class's preferred size, the size it would like to be until we stretch it, to `400 x 400`:

```
frame.setPreferredSize(new Dimension(400, 400));
```

The `Dimension` class lives in another library, so we'll have to import the `java.awt.*;` package, then we should be able to build and compile our project and once again open up our new GUI:

Now we get a nice squared GUI to start with; however, it's still pretty useless as there's nothing contained within this GUI.

Adding a label

Now let's take a quick look at how to add elements to our GUI from a programming standpoint. Quite possibly the simplest element that we could put inside JFrame is JLabel. Labels are responsible for containing text, and instantiating them is extremely simple. We simply tell them what text they should contain. Of course, in more complicated programs and GUIs, this text can become dynamic and may change, but for now, let's just get some text to display:

```
JLabel label = new JLabel("Hi. I am a GUI.");
```

Simply declaring that we have a JLabel class is not enough. We have not yet associated this label object in any way with our existing frame. Our frame, as you can probably tell by the vast array of methods and members it exposes, has a whole lot of components, and we need to know in which of these components we need to place our new JLabel class:

```
package gui;
import javax.swing.*;
import java.awt.*;
public class GUI {

    public static void main(String[] args) {
        JFrame frame = new JFrame("Hello World GUI");
        frame.setPreferredSize(new Dimension(400, 400));
        JLabel label = new JLabel("Hi. I am a GUI.");

        frame.pack();
        frame.setVisible(true);
    }
}
```

One of the components within our `JFrame` class is `contentPane`; that's the area that we visibly see inside the window where things normally go in a program's GUI. This seems like a reasonable place for us to add a new component, in this case, `label`. Once again, let's build our program, kill the old instance, and run the new program:

There we go! Now we have text in our GUI; we've successfully added an element to the content of our JFrame window.

Closing our application

One thing that's kind of annoying is that our program is continuing to run even after we close the associated GUI. That's a little silly. When I press the close button on the NetBeans GUI, NetBeans closes itself and stops running as a process on my system. We can instruct our frame to terminate the associated process using its `setDefaultCloseOperation` method. This method has the return type `void` and takes an integer as a value. This integer is an enumerator, and there's lots of options available to us. All of these options are statically declared by the `JFrame` class, and the one we're probably looking for is `EXIT_ON_CLOSE`, which will exit our application when we close our window. Build and run the program, and terminate the GUI, and there goes our process, which is not quietly running in the background anymore:

```
frame.setDefaultCloseOperation(JFrame.EXIT_ON_CLOSE);
```

That's our basic introduction to GUIs in Java. Creating a GUI is complicated, but it is exciting as well because it's visual and immediate; also, it is really powerful.

As our program stands right now as shown in the following code block, it's functional, but were we to extend it, we might eventually run into some very odd and confusing issues. What we've done now flies in the face of the recommended practices when creating a new GUI. These recommended practices are in place to protect us from some very low-level issues that can occur when our programs become multithreaded.

What does it mean when we say that our program is multithreaded? Well, when we create our GUI, when we cause it to come into being, our program goes from performing a single task, which is simply executing the `main` method from start to finish, to performing multiple tasks. This is because we are now executing the following code:

```
package gui;
import javax.swing.*;
import java.awt.*;
public class GUI {
    public static void main(String[] args) {
        JFrame frame = new JFrame("Hello World GUI");
        frame.setDefaultCloseOperation(JFrame.EXIT_ON_CLOSE);
        frame.setPreferredSize(new Dimension(400, 400));
        JLabel label = new JLabel("Hi. I am a GUI.");
        frame.getContentPane().add(label);
        frame.pack();
        frame.setVisible(true);
    }
}
```

However, in addition, the code is also managing the new window we've created and any functionality performed by that window. To protect ourselves from the complexities of multithreaded code, it's recommended that we create our new Swing GUI by allowing one of the Swing utilities to construct this GUI for us asynchronously.

In order to make this happen, we're actually going to need to pull all of the code we've written out of our `main` method and place it in one place where we can reference it from our `main` method. This will be a new function as shown in the following code line:

```
private static void MakeGUI()
```

We can just paste all of this code back to our new function:

```
private static void MakeGUI()
{
    JFrame frame = new JFrame("Hello World GUI");
    frame.setDefaultCloseOperation(JFrame.EXIT_ON_CLOSE);
    frame.setPreferredSize(new Dimension(400, 400));
    JLabel label = new JLabel("Hi. I am a GUI.");
    frame.getContentPane().add(label);
    frame.pack();
    frame.setVisible(true);
}
```

The SwingUtilities class

Now, let's take a look at how Swing recommends we cause our GUI to come into being. As I said, the `swing` package provides us some functionality that will perform this vast amount of work and thinking for us. The `SwingUtilities` class has a static `invokeLater` method that will create our GUI when no other thread really needs to be processed or when all of the other thinking is done for a bit:

```
SwingUtilities.invokeLater(null);
```

This `invokeLater` method expects us to pass in a `Runnable` object to it, so we're going to have to create one of the `Runnable` objects for ourselves:

```
Runnable GUITask = new Runnable()
```

The `Runnable` objects are those that can be converted into a thread of their own. They have a method that we're going to override, called `run`, and the `SwingUtilities.invokeLater` method will call the `run` method of `Runnable` when appropriate. When this occurs, all we want it to do is call our `MakeGUI` method and begin executing the code that we've just tested out, the one that will create a GUI. We'll add the `Override` notation to be good Java programmers and pass our new `Runnable` object to the `invokeLater` method of `SwingUtilities`:

```
public static void main(String[] args) {
    Runnable GUITask = new Runnable(){
        @Override
        public void run(){
            MakeGUI();
        }
    };
    SwingUtilities.invokeLater(GUITask);
}
```

Run the preceding program and there we go! The functionality is exactly the same, and what we've done could arguably be overkill for a program this small; however, it's really good for us to take a look at what we should expect to see in a larger software project, where things such as multithreading could become a concern. We went through this a bit quickly, so let's stop and take a look at this section once again:

```
Runnable GUITask = new Runnable(){
    @Override
    public void run(){
        MakeGUI();
    }
};
```

What we've done in this bit of code is create an anonymous class. While it looks like we've created a new `Runnable` object, we've really created a new subclass of the `Runnable` object with its own special overridden version of the `run` method, and we just put it right in the middle of our code. This is a powerful methodology that allows us to cut down on the amount of code needed. Of course, if we overuse it, our code can quickly become very complicated for us or another programmer to read and understand.

A visual GUI editor tool – palette

The Java programming language, a GUI extension library such as Swing, and a development environment – a powerful one such as NetBeans – can be a really strong combo. Now we're going to take a look at how to create GUIs using a GUI editor like the one found in NetBeans.

 To follow along, I highly recommend that you utilize the NetBeans IDE for this section.

So, to get started, let's create a Java application like we normally would and give it a name and we're good to go. We're going to start off by simply deleting the default Java file that NetBeans provides and instead ask NetBeans to create a new file. We're going to ask it to create a **JFrame Form** for us:

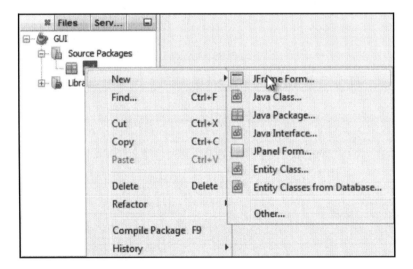

We'll give this JFrame form a name and keep it in the same package. When NetBeans creates this file, even though it's a .java file, the window that pops up will look really different to us. In fact, our file is still just Java code. Click on the **Source** tab to see the code as shown in the following screenshot:

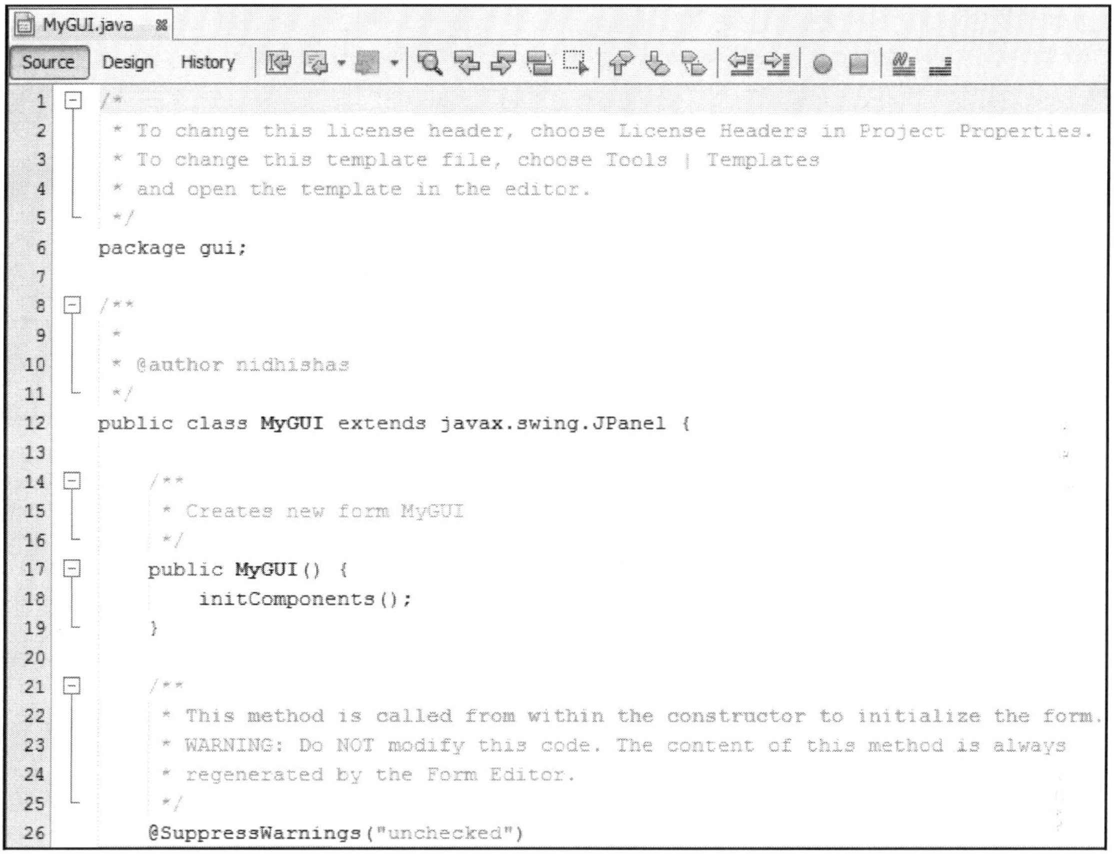

How palette works

We can see the Java code that comprises our file in the **Source** code tab; there's actually a whole lot of code in this file if we expand it out. It's all been generated for us by the NetBeans GUI editor called **Palette** as shown in the following screenshot. Changes we make to this Java file will affect our Design file and vice versa. From this Design file, we have access to a drag and drop editor, and we can also edit the properties of individual elements without having to jump into our Java code, that is, the Source file. Eventually, in pretty much any application we ever create, we're going to have to drop into our Java code to provide the backend programming functionality to the pieces we put into our editor; for now, let's just take a quick look at how the editor works.

I'd like to set up the framework for a password protection dialog. This isn't going to be too complicated, so we'll make the JFrame form a little smaller than it is right now. Then, take a look at some of the **Swing Controls** available; there's a whole lot of them. In fact, courtesy of NetBeans, we can use some other GUI extension systems as well:

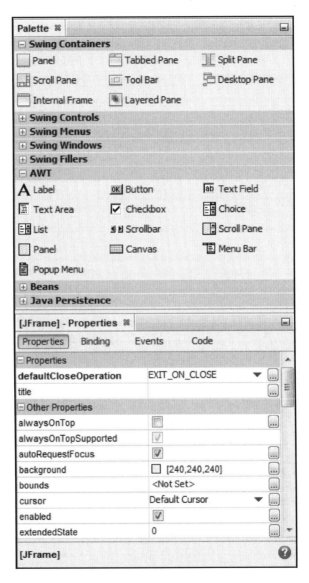

The following are the steps for setting up the framework for a password protection dialog:

1. Let's just stick with **Swing Controls** and stay pretty basic. **Label** is about as basic as you can get. Our password dialog is going to need some text:

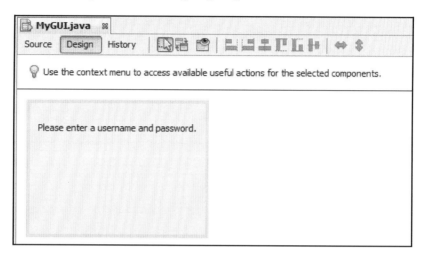

2. Now, a password dialog is also going to need some user interaction. We're going to need not only a password, but also a username for the user. To get the username, we will have to decide between a couple of options under **Swing Controls**:

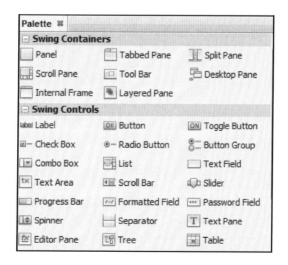

TextArea is a good one. It lets the user put text in a box, unlike **Label**, which only developers can edit. The user can click on the box and type some text into it. Unfortunately, this box is pretty big, and if we click on it and try to make it smaller, we'll get scroll bars to allow the user to bounce around its size.

We could modify the default sizes of this box when the scroll bars appear by changing any number of its properties that we can access from the editor. However, a much simpler solution would be to simply use **Text Field**, which doesn't have all of the multiline functionality of our box. Also, put **Label** next to **Text Field** and you'll notice that the graphical editor helps line things up. If we properly double-click on fields such as **Label**, we can edit their text right there:

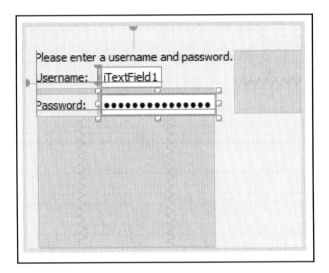

One of the cool things about modern GUIs is that there's some really specialized controls. One of these is **Password Field**. In many ways, it's going to act just like our **TextField** control, except that it's going to replace whatever text the user puts in there visually with dots so that someone looking over their shoulder will not be able to learn their password. If you fail to double-click on an editable element, it will bring you back to the source.

We're going to edit the two components – the text and password fields – that our user can place text in so that they don't appear to our user with their default values initially. We can double-click on the password field, or we can just edit the properties of our controls:

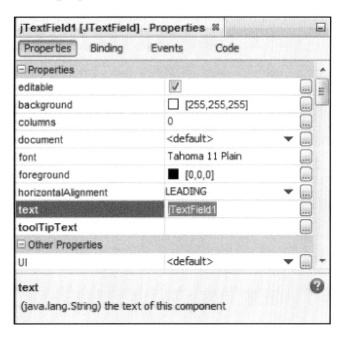

Here, the text value of our **Text Field** control can be modified to nothing at all to start off with, and we can do the same thing with our password. You'll notice that the text value of our password actually has text in it, but it is just displayed as a bunch of dots. However, programmers can access this value to validate the user's password. There's a whole lot of other options in the **Properties** tab: we can do things such as change the font and the foreground and background colors, give it borders, and all that.

When we run our program, you will see that it actually does exist and that the user can put values into these fields:

Of course, we haven't written any backend code to do anything useful with them yet, but the GUI itself is up and working. There's nothing magical happening here. If we jump into the source of this code and drop down to its main method, we'll see the code where the GUI is actually created and displayed to the user (see the following screenshot):

```
public static void main(String args[]) {
    /* Set the Nimbus look and feel */
    Look and feel setting code (optional)

    /* Create and display the form */
    java.awt.EventQueue.invokeLater(new Runnable() {
        public void run() {
            new MyGUI().setVisible(true);
        }
    });
}
```

The important thing to realize is when we access the elements within our source code, all of this methodology is also available to us through raw Java. That's all I really wanted to show you in this section, just the raw power and how quickly we set up a GUI window for the system using the NetBeans graphical editor.

Event handling

One of the best things about working in Java is how powerful its GUI extension libraries are and just how quickly we can get a program up and running that not only has functional code, but also has a slick, professional-looking user interface to back it up that would help anyone interact with our program. That's what we're going to do now: connect the design interface for basic username and password validation with some backend code that we're going to write which will actually check two text fields to see whether they're the ones we're looking for.

To start off, we have the basic GUI with a text field where someone can put a username and password, which will just show up as stars:

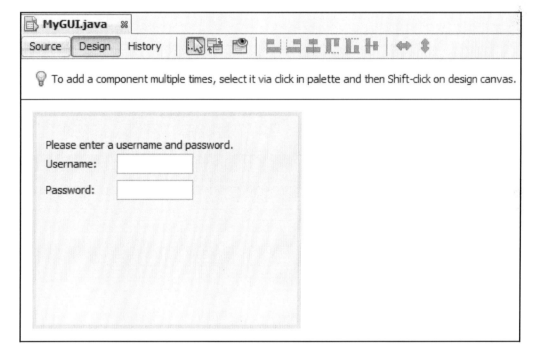

Adding a button

The source code for this GUI is so far completely autogenerated. We haven't touched it at all yet; it's just reflecting the design decisions we've made here. Before we can start writing backend code to do username and password validation, our user is going to need a way to tell us that they've put in a username and password and they'd like it to be validated. This seems like an apt job for the all-powerful button. So let's add a button to our GUI from the **Swing Controls** menu. We'll change its text to Submit in the **Properties** option, and the user will need to click on this button to submit their information. Now, when the button is clicked, we'd like it to perform some programming logic. We want to check the username and password fields for this section because we're just learning and doing things simply and easily; we'll just check them against some hardcoded text.

The question is how do we get from GUI to functional Java code? Generally, we're going to do this through the **event-driven** programming mode, where the interactions that our user has with the GUI determine what Java code is executed and what backend logic occurs. Another way to think of this is that we can set up pieces of our Java code, or methods, to listen for specific GUI-related events to occur and then execute when they do. You'll notice that our GUI components, or controls like our button, have a field under their properties called **Events**. These are all the things that could occur in relation to our control here. In theory, we could bind each one of these events to a method in our Java source code, and when a particular event occurs, either because of user interaction or other code we wrote, our related Java method would be called.

Adding functionality to our button

To let users click on our button field and perform some coded action, we're going to assign an event handler to our actionPerformed event. If we click on this field, we get an option already. Our GUI designer is suggesting we add a handler, namely jButton1ActionPerformed. That's an awful name for a method that's going to sit in our code; jBbutton1 is pretty nondescript. However, it has been chosen because it is the variable name assigned to jButton when it's created in the actual Java code:

```
// Variables declaration - do not modify
private javax.swing.JButton jButton1;
private javax.swing.JLabel jLabel1;
private javax.swing.JLabel jLabel2;
private javax.swing.JLabel jLabel3;
private javax.swing.JPasswordField jPasswordField1;
private javax.swing.JTextField jTextField1;
// End of variables declaration
```

If we scroll down in the source code, we'll see the actual declaration there. I'm sure we can change these settings, but NetBeans will let us know that we probably shouldn't modify this directly. This is because the designer is going to modify it too. So we'll just change the name of our button from the non-descriptive `jButton1` to `SubmitButton`:

```
// Variables declaration - do not modify
private javax.swing.JButton SubmitButton;
```

When we make this change, we'll see that NetBeans will update our source code and there's a `SubmitButton` object bouncing around. This is a variable that starts with a capital letter, so we'll make one more change in the **Events** section by changing it to `submitButton`.

Now the suggested action performed by NetBeans is `submitButtonActionPerformed`. When we head down to our source code, we'll see that an event would have been created and linked to `jButton` in a massive block of generated code that NetBeans has created to mimic our GUI, which we've been creating through their tools. If we search for our `submitButtonActionPerformed` method in the source code, we'll actually see it added to the generated code in the source code:

```
public void actionPerformed(java.awt.event.ActionEvent evt) {
    submitButtonActionPerformed(evt);
}
```

Our `submitButtonActionPerformed` method has been added as the final call of `ActionListener` placed in `submitButton`:

```
submitButton.addActionListener(new java.awt.event.ActionListener() {
    public void actionPerformed(java.awt.event.ActionEvent evt) {
        submitButtonActionPerformed(evt);
    }
});
```

`ActionListener`, of course, has one job and one job only and that's to see whether our button has been clicked. If clicked, it will call our `submitButtonActionPerformed` method. So, in this `submitButtonActionPerformed` method, we can put some good old functional Java code. For this, we need to do two things:

- Check the value of the password field
- Check the value of the username field

Only `ActionEvent` (as seen in the preceding code block) is passed into our `submitButtonActionPerformed` method. While there's a lot of interesting and useful methodologies attached to this event, the context of the action that caused our method to be called, it's not going to give us what we really need. What we really need is our password field and our text field, which fortunately are private members of our current class. The steps for validating the value of our text fields are as follows:

1. Start with the username, that is, `jTextField1`:

```
private void submitButtonActionPerformed
(java.awt.event.ActionEvent evt) {
    jTextField1
}
```

We should probably rename this when we get the chance, but we'll just roll with it for now because we only have one text field:

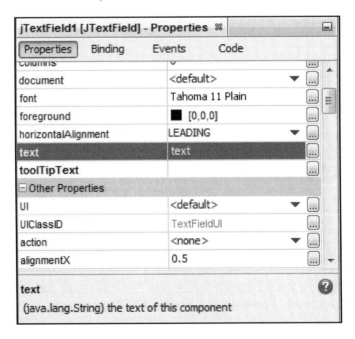

If you remember, in the editor under **Properties** tab, this text field had a **text** property. We got rid of the text in this because we didn't want our username text field to start with any text. We want it to be blank so that users would know they have to put their own information there.

2. Now, it stands to reason if that's the property exposed to us in the designer, there should be a related property exposed by the object itself, and there is, namely `getText()`:

```
private void submitButtonActionPerformed
(java.awt.event.ActionEvent evt) {
    jTextField1.getText()
}
```

3. When we call `getText`, of course, we return the text currently stored in our text field, and we'll make our super secret username the very "creative" word `username`.

This is a conditional statement, and we're going to want to make another conditional statement. We want to ask our program whether the text field and password field – which is going to expose a similar method, `getPassword` in this case – are both equal to the hardcoded string. Our secret password will be `java`. Note that `getPassword` actually returns a character array, not a string, so to keep things simple, let's just assign the password value to a string and then we're good to utilize it as a string. Put `if` in front of our conditional statement, within parentheses, and we're good to go:

```
private void submitButtonActionPerformed
(java.awt.event.ActionEvent evt) {
    String password = new
    String(jPasswordField1.getPassword());
    if (jTextField1.getText().equals("username")
    && password.equals("java"))
    {

    }
}
```

Now we need to give our user some indication whether or not they've succeeded in providing the proper username and password. OK, what to do if the user has successfully input a good username and a good password? Well, I think it would be cool if we showed a pop-up dialog here.

4. `JOptionPane` provides us with the `showMessageDialog` method, which is a pretty cool way to impart really important and immediate information to the user. It'll show a pop-up box, and it's pretty lightweight and easy to use. You may have to fix the imports on this one:

```
{
    JOptionPane.showMessageDialog(rootPane, password);
}
```

The only heavyweight information `MessageDialog` needs to create itself is a GUI component to attach itself to, to be its parent. We could acquire `button evt` through `ActionEvent`, but this doesn't make a lot of sense because the dialog is not tied just to the button; it's tied to the entirety of what this GUI is about, which is validating a username and password. So it'd be nice if we could tie the message dialog box to JFrame form itself, the GUI's top-level element, and in fact we can:

```
public class MyGUI extends javax.swing.JFrame {

    /**
     * Creates new form MyGUI
     */
    public MyGUI() {
        initComponents();
    }
```

5. If we scroll up a bit to our source code section to check exactly where we're writing code, we'll see that we're in a class, called `MyGUI`, that extends the `JFrame` class. This entire class is associated with the `JFrame` class we're working with. So, to pass `JFrame` as a variable to our `showMessageDialog` method, we simply use the `this` keyword. Now just type in a message to show the user upon password and username validation:

```
private void submitButtonActionPerformed
(java.awt.event.ActionEvent evt) {
    String password = new String(jPasswordField1.getPassword());
    if (jTextField1.getText().equals("username")
    && password.equals("java"))
    {
        JOptionPane.showMessageDialog(this, "Login Good!");
    }
}
```

Let's run our program and see what we've built. The dialogue box appears, which we've seen before and which we expect, and then perform the following steps:

1. Type in our valid username, that is, `username`.

2. Type in our valid password, that is `java`.

3. Then, hit the **Submit** button.

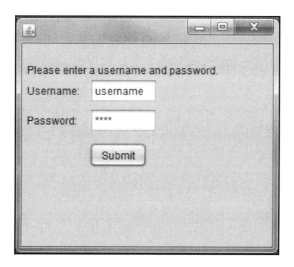

We get a dialog box that looks like the following screenshot. We can freely move this box in our JFrame instance:

Just to test things out, let's put in some gobbledygook. We get nothing no matter how many times we click on **Submit**. Also, a good username and no password also gets us nothing, pretty cool! We've only scratched the surface of what is possible with Java GUIs and, of course, Java itself.

Creating Java GUIs for our programs is easy and, in many cases, painless. Sometimes, the event handling model that GUIs force us to implement to some degree can even make creating our Java programs, which are heavily reliant on user interaction, easier than it would otherwise be.

The other important thing that I cannot stress enough is that even though the GUI designer is awesome, it's possible for us to create this exact same project by simply sitting down and writing the Java code in the **Source** code section.

I'm not saying we shouldn't use the GUI designer – especially because there's a lot of code and a lot of well-written code that's been generated for us by the GUI designer, which can save us a whole lot of time – but there's absolutely no magic happening here at all. This is all Java code making use of the `Swing` extension library.

Summary

In this chapter, we saw the basic functions of GUI in NetBeans. You learned how to create an application window with the `JFrame` class by setting its size, adding labels to it, and closing the application. Then, we dived into the topic of the GUI editor, palette. We saw a working palette and the components available in it. Lastly, you learned how to trigger events by adding a button and adding functionality to it.

In the next chapter, you'll learn about XML.

11
XML

Say we would like to store information that has a structure that is meaningful to our program. Also, we would like this information to be human-readable to some degree and sometimes even human-editable. To accomplish this, we very often turn to XML.

Java provides us with powerful tools for manipulating, reading, and writing XML raw text and files. However, as is the case with many powerful tools, there's a bit of a knowledge overhead for us to learn how to use them. In this chapter, we'll first look at how to use Java to load an XML file into a Java object. Next, we'll walk through how to parse XML data using Java. Finally, we'll see the Java code to write and modify XML data.

We'll cover the following topics in this chapter:

- Java code for reading XML data
- Parsing XML data
- Writing and modifying XML data

Reading XML data

In this section, we'll accomplish a very simple task to get ourselves started on the road to learning how Java interacts with XML. We'll use the XML information from the `cars.xml` file, provided in the code file of the book. This file should be stored in the current directory of our Java project, so when we run our Java program, it will be able to access `cars.xml` without any additional pathing required. We'll edit the following Java program to load the `cars.xml` file:

```
package loadinganxmlfile;

import java.io.*;
```

```java
import javax.xml.parsers.*;
import javax.xml.transform.*;
import javax.xml.transform.dom.*;
import javax.xml.transform.stream.*;
import org.w3c.dom.*;
import org.xml.sax.*;

public class LoadingAnXMLFile {
    public static void main(String[] args) {

        try {
            //Write code that can throw errors here
        }
        catch (ParserConfigurationException pce) {
            System.out.println(pce.getMessage());
        }
        catch (SAXException se) {
            System.out.println(se.getMessage());
        }
        catch (IOException ioe) {
            System.err.println(ioe.getMessage());
        }
    }
    private static void PrintXmlDocument(Document xml)
    {
        try{
            Transformer transformer =
             TransformerFactory.newInstance().newTransformer();
            StreamResult result = new StreamResult
             (new StringWriter());
            DOMSource source = new DOMSource(xml);
            transformer.transform(source, result);
            System.out.println(result.getWriter().toString());
        }
        catch(TransformerConfigurationException e)
        {
            System.err.println("XML Printing Failed");
        }
        catch(TransformerException e)
        {
            System.err.println("XML Printing Failed");
        }
    }
}
```

Before we get started, notice that there's a whole lot of imports necessary for this program. The `transform` classes we have imported are not necessary for anything we're going to write; I've written a function called `PrintXmlDocument()`, which will print our XML document to the console window if we successfully load it. If you're following along the code in this section, I'd recommend that you first import these `transform` classes from the start. Then, as you use additional functionality, go ahead and use NetBeans' **Fix Imports** functionality to see exactly from where the libraries, that the tools were utilizing, are coming from.

So let's get started. Our end goal here is to have an object of the `Document` class that contains the information in our `cars.xml` file. Once we have this `Document` object, all we would need to do to see the information in our console window is to call the `PrintXmlDocument()` function on the `Document` instance.

Unfortunately, creating this `Document` object is not as simple as saying the `Document dom = new Document();` statement. Rather, we need to create it in a structured and procedural manner that will properly preserve the parsable nature of our XML file. To do this, we'll make use of two additional classes: the `DocumentBuilder` and `DocumentBuilderFactory` classes.

The `DocumentBuilder` class, believe it or not, will take care of the responsibility of actually building the document for us. The `DocumentBuilder` class exists as a separate entity from the `Document` object so that we, as programmers, can logically separate the methodology we can perform on the document itself and the additional range of methodology needed to create that document in the first place. Similar to the `Document` class, we can't just instantiate the `DocumentBuilder` class. Instead, there's a third class we'll utilize to get `DocumentBuilder`, the `DocumentBuilderFactory` class. I have divided the code required to create a `Document` object, which stores our XML file, into three parts:

1. The `DocumentBuilderFactory` class contains a static method called `newInstance()`. Let's add the following method call to our first `try` block in the `main()` method. This will instantiate `DocumentBuilderFactory` for us to work from:

   ```
   DocumentBuilderFactory factory =
   DocumentBuilderFactory.newInstance();
   ```

2. Once we have `DocumentBuilderFactory`, we can acquire for ourselves a new `DocumentBuilder` object. To do this, we're going to call the factory's `newDocumentBuilder()` method. Let's add it to our try block:

   ```
   DocumentBuilder builder = factory.newDocumentBuilder();
   ```

3. Finally, we need to instruct `DocumentBuilder` to build us a `Document` object and that this object should mirror the structure of our `cars.xml` file. We'll simply instantiate our `Document` object with a value in our `try` block. We'll acquire this value from the `parse()` method of `builder`. One of this method's parameters is a string that references a filename. If we had a referenced file object in our Java program, we could also use that:

```
Document dom = builder.parse("cars.xml");
```

So now our `main()` method looks as follows:

```
public static void main(String[] args) {
    DocumentBuilderFactory factory =
    DocumentBuilderFactory.newInstance();
    try {
        // Write code that can throw errors here...
        DocumentBuilder builder =
        factory.newDocumentBuilder();
        Document dom = builder.parse("cars.xml");
        PrintXmlDocument(dom);
    }
    catch (ParserConfigurationException pce) {
        System.out.println(pce.getMessage());
    }
    catch (SAXException se) {
        System.out.println(se.getMessage());
    }
    catch (IOException ioe) {
        System.err.println(ioe.getMessage());
    }
}
```

Now it's time to check whether our code works. We acquired the `DocumentBuilderFactory` object using the static method of the `DocumentBuilderFactory` class, and this creates a brand new instance. With `DocumentBuilderFactory`, we created a new `DocumentBuilder` object, which will be able to intelligently parse our XML file. In parsing our XML file, the `DocumentBuilder` object understands the nature of the information contained within and is able to store it in our XML document or the `Document` object model element. When we run this program, we get the raw text view of the original XML document as output:

```
Output - LoadingAnXMLFile (run)  ✕

run:
<?xml version="1.0" encoding="UTF-8" standalone="no"?><cars>
        <owner name="Billy">
                <car vin="LJPCBLCX11000237">
                        <make>Ford</make>
                        <model>Fusion</model>
                        <year>2014</year>
                        <color>Blue</color>
                </car>
                <car vin="LGHIALCX89880011">
                        <make>Toyota</make>
                        <model>Tacoma</model>
                        <year>2013</year>
                        <color>Green</color>
                </car>
                <car vin="GJSIALSS22000567">
                        <make>Dodge</make>
```

Because there are so many steps to loading an XML file like this, I wanted to put it in its own section. This is so that down the road, when we, as programmers, learn about manipulating and reading valuable information from XML, we'll not be bogged down by all of the syntax we've seen here.

Parsing XML data

The `Document` class provides an easy way for us to store formatted information in an object. In the preceding section's program, we read in information from a `cars.xml` file into our Java `Document` object. Here's what the `cars.xml` file looks like:

```
<?xml version="1.0"?>
<cars>
    <owner name="Billy">
        <car vin="LJPCBLCX11000237">
            <make>Ford</make>
            <model>Fusion</model>
            <year>2014</year>
            <color>Blue</color>
        </car>
        <car vin="LGHIALCX89880011">
            <make>Toyota</make>
```

```
                <model>Tacoma</model>
                <year>2013</year>
                <color>Green</color>
        </car>
        <car vin="GJSIALSS22000567">
                <make>Dodge</make>
                <model>Charger</model>
                <year>2013</year>
                <color>Red</color>
        </car>
    </owner>
    <owner name="Jane">
        <car vin="LLOKAJSS55548563">
                <make>Nissan</make>
                <model>Altima</model>
                <year>2000</year>
                <color>Green</color>
        </car>
        <car vin="OOKINAFS98111001">
                <make>Dodge</make>
                <model>Challenger</model>
                <year>2013</year>
                <color>Red</color>
        </car>
    </owner>
</cars>
```

The root node of this file is the `cars` node and contained within this node are two `owner` nodes, namely Billy and Jane, each of which has a number of `car` nodes within them. The information stored within these `car` elements is mirrored by the information that can be stored by the preceding Java class we have.

Our goal in this section is to take the car information from `cars.xml` for only a specific owner-in this case, Jane-and store this information in our custom `Car` class so that we can utilize the `Car` class's `toString()` override to print all of Jane's cars to our console in a nicely formatted manner.

With the code we have already set up, our `Document` object `dom` mirrors the information stored in `cars.xml` in the same format, so we simply need to figure out how to ask this `Document` object this question: what cars does Jane own? In order to figure out how to write the code, you'd need to know a little bit about XML terminology. We're going to be dealing with the terms "element" and "node" throughout this section.

In XML, an **element** is an entity that has a start and end tag, and it also contains all of the information within it. When our `Document` object returns information, it will often return the information in terms of nodes. **Nodes** are the building blocks of XML documents, and we can almost think of them as an inheritance relationship, where all the elements are nodes, but not all nodes are elements. Nodes can be much simpler and smaller than an entire XML element.

Accessing Jane's XML element

This section will help us access the information about the cars owned by Jane, using the following code. I have divided the code to be added to our `main()` function in six parts:

1. So, in the pursuit of finding all the cars owned by Jane, let's see what functionality our XML document provides for us right off the bat. If we take a look at code completion to quickly scan through our list of methods, we can call `dom` from our `Document` instance. We're going to see the `getDocumentElement()` method return an element for us:

```
10   public class ReadingXML {
11       public static void main(String[] args) {
12           Document dom;
13           DocumentBuilderFactory factory = DocumentBuilderFactory.newInstance();
14           try {
15               DocumentBuilder docBuilder = factory.newDocumentBuilder();
16               dom = docBuilder.parse("cars.xml");
17
18               // Now, print out all of Jane's cars...
                 dom.getd
20           }          getDoctype()          DocumentType
         catch    getDocumentElement()      Element ) {
22           S   getDocumentURI()            String );
23           }   getDomConfig() DOMConfiguration
24       catch
25           S
26           }   org.w3c.dom.Document
27       catch  public Element getDocumentElement()
28           S
29           }   This is a convenience attribute that allows direct access to
30       }       the child node that is the document element of the document.
31   }
32
```

This is probably a good way to start. This method returns the top-level element in our XML; in this case, we're going to get the `cars` element, which contains all of the information that we're going to need. It also contains some information we don't need, such as Billy's cars, but we'll parse that out after we've accessed it. Once we've imported the right libraries, we can directly reference the concept of an XML element within our code using the `Element` class. We can create a new `Element` object and assign its value to the root element of our XML document:

```
Element doc = dom.getDocumentElement();
```

Of course, we need to go deeper. The root level of our XML document `cars` is not directly useful to us; we need the information contained within it. We only really want the information from one `owner` node (containing information about Jane's cars). But because of the way XML parsing works, it probably makes sense for us to first acquire both of these owner nodes and then find the one that we're really interested in.

To acquire both of these nodes, we can call a method on the root XML element we've just created and stored in `doc`. XML elements can contain other elements within them; in this case, our root element contains a number of `owner` elements. The `getElementsByTagName()` method allows us to collect a number of these inner elements. The tag name of an XML element is just what you would expect; it is the name we gave to that particular element of our XML. In this case, if we ask for all the elements with the tag name `owner` contained within our document's root element, we're going to further narrow down the amount of XML we're working with, getting closer to the small section we desire.

What's returned by the `getElementsByTagName()` method is not a single element though. There are two distinct elements in this section even at the highest level, two owners: `Billy` and `Jane`. So, the `getElementsByTagLineName()` method doesn't return a single element; instead, it returns a `NodeList` object, which is a collection of XML nodes:

```
NodeList ownersList = doc.getElementsByTagName("owner");
```

Now we're no longer dealing with our root node at all; we only have its contents. It's time for us to really narrow down our search. Our NodeList object contains multiple owners, but we only want an owner if the attribute name associated with that owner happens to be Jane. In order to find this particular element, if it exists, we're simply going to loop through NodeList, checking the attributes of each element it contains. Note that ownersList is not a traditional array. It's a NodeList object, its own kind of object. So, we can't use normal array syntax on it. Fortunately, it exposes methods to us that mimic normal array syntax. For example, the getLength() method will tell us how many objects are in ownersList:

```
for(int i = 0; i < ownersList.getLength(); i++)
{
}
```

2. Similarly, when we attempt to create a new Element object and assign that value to the currently looped-through portion of ownersList, we're not going to be able to use the normal syntax we would for an array. Once again though, ownersList provides us a method to do the same thing. The item() method provides, or asks for, an index as input.

> Note that ownersList is NodeList, but while elements are nodes, not all nodes are elements, so we need to make a decision here. We could check the nature of the objects that are returned by this function and assure ourselves that they are, in fact, XML elements. But to keep things moving, we're just going to assume that our XML was properly formatted, and we're simply going to let Java know that the node returned by the item() method is in fact an element; that is, it has a start tag and a closing tag and can contain other elements and nodes within it:

```
Element owner = (Element)ownersList.item(i);
```

Once we've successfully accessed an element from our list of owners, it's time to check and see whether this is the owner that we're looking for; therefore, we're going to need a conditional statement. XML elements expose to us the getAttribute() method, and the attribute that we're interested in is the name attribute. So, the following bit of code right here will ask the current owner, "What is the value of your name attribute?" If that value is equal to Jane, then we know we have accessed the right XML element.

Within Jane's XML element, now we only have a number of car elements. So, once again, it's time to create NodeList and populate it with these car elements. We now need to call the getElementByTagName() method on Jane, our current owner. If we were to use the top-level document to call this function, we would get all the car elements in the document, even Billy's:

```
if(owner.getAttribute("name").equals("Jane"))
{
    NodeList carsList =
    owner.getElementsByTagName("car");
```

3. This main() method is getting a little intense; this is how far I'm willing to go in one method. We're already a couple of levels deep in our code, and it's not exactly simple code we've been writing. I think it's time for us to parse out the next bit into its own method. Let's simply declare that we're going to have a PrintCars() method, and this function will take NodeList of the car elements to print the car nodes:

```
PrintCars(carsList);
```

Our main method now looks as follows:

```
public static void main(String[] args) {
    DocumentBuilderFactory factory =
    DocumentBuilderFactory.newInstance();
    try {
        DocumentBuilder docBuilder =
        factory.newDocumentBuilder();
        Document dom = docBuilder.parse("cars.xml");

        // Now, print out all of Jane's cars
        Element doc = dom.getDocumentElement();
        NodeList ownersList =
        doc.getElementsByTagName("owner");
        for(int i = 0; i < ownersList.getLength(); i++)
        {
            Element owner = (Element)ownersList.item(i);
            if(owner.getAttribute("name").equals("Jane"))
            {
                NodeList carsList =
                owner.getElementsByTagName("car");
                PrintCars(carsList);
            }
        }
    }
    catch (ParserConfigurationException pce) {
```

```
            System.out.println(pce.getMessage());
        }
        catch (SAXException se) {
            System.out.println(se.getMessage());
        }
        catch (IOException ioe) {
            System.err.println(ioe.getMessage());
        }
    }
}
```

Printing Jane's car details

Now, leaving our `main()` method, we'll define our new `PrintCars()` method. I have divided the definition of the `PrintCars()` function into eight parts:

1. Because we're in the entry class of our program and the `PrintCars()` method is being called by the static `main()` method, it should probably be a `static` function. All it's going to do is print to our console, so `void` is an appropriate return type. We already know it's going to take `NodeList` of cars as input:

    ```
    public static void PrintCars(NodeList cars)
    {
    }
    ```

2. Once we've entered this function, we know we have a list of `car` XML elements at our disposal. But in order to print each one out, we're going to have to loop through them. We've already looped through XML `NodeList` in our program already, so we're going to be using some very similar syntax. Let's take a look at what needs to change for this new code. Well, we're no longer looping through `ownersList`; we have a new `NodeList` object to loop through the `NodeList` of cars:

    ```
    for(int i = 0; i < cars.getLength(); i++)
    {
    }
    ```

3. We know that cars are still `Element` instances, so our casting a shortcut here is still appropriate, but we probably want to rename the variable we're using for each `car` we loop through to something like `carNode`. Each time we loop through a car, we're going to create a new `Car` object and store the information in that car's XML in this actual Java object:

    ```
    Element carNode = (Element)cars.item(i);
    ```

4. So, in addition to accessing the car XML, let's also declare a `Car` object and just instantiate it to be a new `Car` object:

```
Car carObj = new Car();
```

5. Now we're going to build up the values stored within `carObj` by reading them from `carNode`. If we jump back to the XML file quickly and take a look at the information stored in the `car` element, we'll see that it stores `make`, `model`, `year`, and `color` as XML nodes. The vehicle identification number `vin` is actually an attribute. Let's take a brief look at our `Car.java` class:

```
package readingxml;

public class Car {
    public String vin;
    public String make;
    public String model;
    public int year;
    public String color;
    public Car()
    {
    }
    @Override
    public String toString()
    {
        return String.format("%d %s %s %s, vin:%s", year,
        color, make, model, vin);
    }
}
```

Let's start with the easy pieces first; so, `make`, `model`, and `color` are all strings stored in the `Car` class and they all happen to be nodes within the `car` element.

Back to our `PrintCars()` function, we already know how to access nodes within an element. We're simply going to use `carNode` and the `getElementsByTagName()` function again. If we get all the elements with the tag name of `color`, we should get back a list that contains only a single element-the element we're interested in, which tells us the color of our car. Unfortunately, we do have a list here, so we can't manipulate that element directly until we pull it from the list. Once again though, we know how to do this. If we're confident that our XML is properly formatted, we know we'll achieve a list with exactly one item in it. Therefore, if we get the item at the 0th index of that list, that will be the XML element that we're looking for.

Color information stored in this XML element isn't an attribute though; it's inner text. So, we're going to take a look at what methods the XML element exposes and see whether there's an appropriate one to acquire the inner text. There is the `getTextContent()` function that will give us all of the inner text that's not actually part of the XML element tags. In this case, it's going to give us the color of our cars.

It's not enough just to acquire this information; we need to store it. Fortunately, all of the attributes of `carObj` are public, so we can freely assign them with values after we've created our `car` object. If these were private fields without setters, we'd probably have to do this information before constructing `carObj` and then passing them through to a constructor that it would hopefully have:

```
carObj.color =
carNode.getElementsByTagName("color").item(0).getTextContent();
```

We're going to do pretty much the exact same thing for `make` and `model`. The only thing we're going to have to change is the keyword we provide when looking for the elements:

```
carObj.make =
carNode.getElementsByTagName("make").item(0).getTextContent();
carObj.model =
carNode.getElementsByTagName("model").item(0).getTextContent();
```

6. Now, we can continue using the same general strategy for our car's `year`, but we should note that as far as `carObj` is concerned, `year` is an integer. As far as our XML element is concerned, `year`, just like anything else, is a `TextContent` string. Fortunately, converting a `string` into an `integer`, as long as it's well formed, which is an assumption that we'll make here, isn't too difficult. We're simply going to use the `Integer` class and call its `parseInt()` method. This will do its best to convert a string value into an integer. We'll assign it to the `year` field of `carObj`:

```
carObj.year =
Integer.parseInt(carNode.getElementsByTagName
("year").item(0).getTextContent());
```

7. This leaves only one more field for us. Note that `carObj` has a vehicle identification number field. This field is not actually an integer; vehicle identification numbers can contain letters, so this value is stored as a string. It's going to be a little different for us to get though because rather than being an inner element, it's actually an attribute of the `car` element itself. Once again, we know how to acquire an attribute from `carNode`; we're simply going to get the attribute with the name `vin` and assign it to `carObj`:

```
carObj.vin = carNode.getAttribute("vin");
```

8. With all of this done, our `carObj` object should be fully built with reasonable values in all of its members. Now it's time to use `carObj` for the reason it exists: to override the `toString()` function. For each car we loop through, let's call the `toString()` function of `carObj` and print that result to our console:

```
System.out.println(carObj.toString());
```

Our `PrintCars()` function will now look as follows:

```
public static void PrintCars(NodeList cars)
{
    for(int i = 0; i < cars.getLength(); i++)
    {
        Element carNode = (Element)cars.item(i);
        Car carObj = new Car();
        carObj.color =
         carNode.getElementsByTagName
         ("color").item(0).getTextContent();
        carObj.make =
         carNode.getElementsByTagName
         ("make").item(0).getTextContent();
        carObj.model = carNode.getElementsByTagName
         ("model").item(0).getTextContent();
        carObj.year =
         Integer.parseInt(carNode.getElementsByTagName
         ("year").item(0).getTextContent());
        carObj.vin = carNode.getAttribute("vin");
        System.out.println(carObj.toString());
    }
}
```

We should be good to compile our program. Now when we run it, hopefully it'll print out all of Jane's cars, making use of the overridden `toString()` method of `carObj`, to nicely format the output. When we run this program, we get two cars printed as output, and if we go to our XML and take a look at the cars assigned to Jane, we'll see that this information does indeed match the information stored in these cars:

```
Output - ReadingXML (run)  ✕
run:
2000 Green Nissan Altima, vin:LLOKAJSS55548563
2013 Red Dodge Challenger, vin:OOKINAFS98111001
BUILD SUCCESSFUL (total time: 0 seconds)
```

The XML and Java combination is really powerful. XML is human-readable. We can understand it and even make modifications to it as people, but it also contains really valuable information in terms of how it is structured. This is something that programming languages, such as Java, can understand as well. The program we've written here-while it does have its quirks and requires a certain amount of knowledge to write it-is much easier to write and far easier for a programmer to understand and maintain than a similar program from a raw text file.

Writing XML data

Being able to read XML information is all well and good, but for the language to be truly useful to us, our Java programs probably need to be able to write out XML information as well. The following program is a bare bones model of a program that both reads from and writes to the same XML file:

```java
package writingxml;

import java.io.*;
import javax.xml.parsers.*;
import javax.xml.transform.*;
import javax.xml.transform.dom.*;
import javax.xml.transform.stream.*;
import org.w3c.dom.*;
import org.xml.sax.*;

public class WritingXML {
    public static void main(String[] args) {
        File xmlFile = new File("cars.xml");
```

```
        Document dom = LoadXMLDocument(xmlFile);
        WriteXMLDocument(dom, xmlFile);
    }
    private static void WriteXMLDocument
      (Document doc, File destination)
    {
        try{
            // Write doc to destination file here...
        }
        catch(TransformerConfigurationException e)
        {
            System.err.println("XML writing failed.");
        }
        catch(TransformerException e)
        {
            System.err.println("XML writing failed.");
        }
    }
    private static Document LoadXMLDocument(File source)
    {
        try {
            DocumentBuilderFactory factory =
             DocumentBuilderFactory.newInstance();
            DocumentBuilder builder =
             factory.newDocumentBuilder();
            Document dom = builder.parse(source);
        }
        catch (ParserConfigurationException e) {
            System.err.println("XML loading failed.");
        }
        catch (SAXException e) {
            System.err.println("XML loading failed.");
        }
        catch (IOException e) {
            System.err.println("XML loading failed.");
        }
        return dom;
    }
}
```

Its `main()` method is extremely simple. It takes a file and then reads XML from that file storing it in an XML document's tree object. Then, this program calls `WriteXMLDocument()` to write the XML back to the same file. Currently, the method that reads in the XML has been implemented for us (`LoadXMLDocument()`); however, the method to write out the XML is not yet complete. Let's see what needs to happen for us to write XML information to a document. I have divided the code for the `WriteXMLDocument()` function into four parts.

Java code to write XML data

The following are the steps to be performed for writing XML data:

1. Because of the way an XML document is stored, we need to convert it into a different format before it's really feasible for us to print it out to a file in the same format in which we got the original XML. To do this, we're going to make use of an XML-specific class called `Transformer`. As with a number of the classes we deal with when dealing with XML in the document model, `Transformer` instances are best created using a factory. In this case, the factory is called `TransformerFactory`, and like many factories, it exposes the `newInstance()` method, allowing us to create one when we need it. To get our new `Transformer` object, which will allow us to convert our `Document` object into something streamable that we can send to a file, we're simply going to call the `newTransformer()` method of `TransformerFactory`:

   ```
   TransformerFactory tf = TransformerFactory.newInstance();
   Transformer transformer = tf.newTransformer();
   ```

2. Now, before `Transformer` can transform our XML document into something else, it's going to need to know what we would like it to convert our XML document's information into. This class is the `StreamResult` class; it's the target for the information stored within our current `Document` object. The stream is a raw binary information pump that can be sent to any number of targets. In this case, our target is going to be the destination file provided to the `StreamResult` constructor:

   ```
   StreamResult result = new StreamResult(destination);
   ```

3. Our `Transformer` object though is not automatically linked to our XML document, and it expects us to reference our XML document in a unique manner: as a `DOMSource` object. Notice that our `source` object (defined next) is being paired with the `result` object. The `Transformer` object, when we provide it both these objects, will know how to convert one to another. Now, to create our `DOMSource` object, we simply need to pass in our XML document:

   ```
   DOMSource source = new DOMSource(doc);
   ```

4. Finally, when all of that setup is complete, we can execute the functional piece of the code. Let's grab our `Transformer` object and ask it to transform our source, that is, the `DOMSource` object, to a streamable result targeted at our destination file:

```
transformer.transform(source, result);
```

The following becomes our `WriteXMLDocument()` function:

```
private static void WriteXMLDocument
(Document doc, File destination)
{
    try{
        // Write doc to destination file here
        TransformerFactory tf =
         TransformerFactory.newInstance();
        Transformer transformer = tf.newTransformer();
        StreamResult result = new StreamResult(destination);
        DOMSource source = new DOMSource(doc);
        transformer.transform(source, result);
    }
    catch(TransformerConfigurationException e)
    {
        System.err.println("XML writing failed.");
    }
    catch(TransformerException e)
    {
        System.err.println("XML writing failed.");
    }
}
```

When we run this program, we'll get some XML in our file, but you'll have to trust me when I say this: this is the same XML we had before, which is expected as we read in the XML first and then print it back as a result.

To really test whether our program is working, we're going to need to make some changes to our `Document` object within the Java code and then see whether we can print those changes out to this file. Let's change the names of the cars' owners. Let's transfer the deals of all the cars to an owner called Mike.

Modifying XML data

The power of the XML I/O system is that in between loading and writing our XML document, we can freely modify the `Document` object `dom` stored in memory. Also, the changes we make to the object in Java memory will then be written to our permanent XML file. So let's begin by making some changes:

1. We're going to use `getElementsByTagName()` to get all the `owner` elements in our XML document. This will return a `NodeList` object and we'll call it `owners`:

    ```
    NodeList owners = dom.getElementsByTagName("owner");
    ```

2. To convert the names of all of these owners to `Mike`, we're going to have to loop through this list. As a refresher, we can get the number of items in the list by calling the `getLength()` function of `owners`, that is, our `NodeList` object. To access the item that we're currently iterating through, we'll use the `item()` function of `owners` and pass in our iterating variable `i` to get the item at that index. Let's store this value in a variable so that we can use it easily; once again, we'll just assume that our XML is well formatted and inform Java that we are, in fact, dealing with a fully fledged XML element at this point.

    Next, XML elements expose a number of methods that allow us to modify them. One of these elements is the `setAttribute()` method, and that's what we'll be using here. Note that `setAttribute()` takes two strings as input. First, it wants to know what attribute we'd like to modify. We're going to be modifying the `name` attribute (it's the only attribute available to us here), and we're going to assign its value to `Mike`:

    ```java
    for(int i = 0; i < owners.getLength(); i++)
    {
        Element owner = (Element)owners.item(i);
        owner.setAttribute("name", "Mike");
    }
    ```

Now our `main()` method will look as follows:

```
public static void main(String[] args) {
    File xmlFile = new File("cars.xml");
    Document dom = LoadXMLDocument(xmlFile);
    NodeList owners = dom.getElementsByTagName("owner");
    for(int i = 0; i < owners.getLength(); i++)
    {
        Element owner = (Element)owners.item(i);
        owner.setAttribute("name", "Mike");
    }
    WriteXMLDocument(dom, xmlFile);
}
```

When we run our program and check our XML file, we'll see that `Mike` is now the owner of all these cars as shown in the following screenshot:

```
<?xml version="1.0" encoding="UTF-8" standalone="no"?><cars>
        <owner name="Mike">
                <car vin="LJPCBLCX11000237">
                        <make>Ford</make>
                        <model>Fusion</model>
                        <year>2014</year>
                        <color>Blue</color>
                </car>
                <car vin="LGHIALCX89880011">
                        <make>Toyota</make>
                        <model>Tacoma</model>
                        <year>2013</year>
                        <color>Green</color>
                </car>
                <car vin="GJSIALSS22000567">
                        <make>Dodge</make>
                        <model>Charger</model>
                        <year>2013</year>
                        <color>Red</color>
                </car>
        </owner>
        <owner name="Mike">
```

Now it might make sense to combine these two XML elements so that `Mike` is only a single owner, not split it into two. That's a little bit out of the scope for this section, but it's an interesting question and one I want to encourage you to reflect on and maybe take a shot at right now.

Summary

In this chapter, we saw the Java code to read an XML file into a `Document` object. We also saw how to parse XML data using Java. Finally, we saw how to write and modify XML data in Java.

Congratulations! You are now a Java programmer.

Index

Printed in Great Britain
by Amazon